HOW TO TEACH
PHILÖSOPHY
TO YOUR DOG

HOW TO TEACH PHILOSOPHY TO YOUR DOG

A QUIRKY INTRODUCTION TO THE BIG QUESTIONS IN PHILOSOPHY

Anthony McGowan

ONEWORLD

A Oneworld Book

First published by Oneworld Publications in the United Kingdom,
Republic of Ireland and Australia, 2019

Hardback ISBN 978-1-78607-674-8
Paperback ISBN 978-1-78607-795-0
eISBN 978-1-78607-675-5

Typeset by Fakenham Prepress Solutions, Fakenham, Norfolk, NR21 8NL
Printed and bound in Great Britain by Clays Ltd, Elcograf S.p.A.

Oneworld Publications
10 Bloomsbury Street
London WC1B 3SR
England

MIX
Paper from
responsible sources
FSC® C018072

To Monty, of course, who has brought
so much love into our family.

Contents

Therefore the brutes are incapable alike of purpose and dissimulation; they reserve nothing. In this respect the dog stands to the man in the same relation as a glass goblet to a metal one, and this helps greatly to endear the dog so much to us, for it affords us great pleasure to see all those inclinations and emotions which we so often conceal displayed simply and openly in him.

Arthur Schopenhauer, *The World as Will and Idea*, Volume II, Chapter V, translated by R.B. Haldane and J. Kemp

Outside of a dog, a book is a man's best friend. Inside of a dog, it's too dark to read.

Attributed to Groucho Marx

Author's Note

How to Teach Philosophy to Your Dog is intended as a welcoming introduction to the world of philosophy. As with walking the dog, there are always different routes you can take in this sort of enterprise, varying in the direction, the distance, and even the purpose. Is it exercise, entertainment, or merely a quickie to get your business over and done with as efficiently as possible? Some introductions to philosophy simply start at the beginning, with the speculations of the earliest Greek thinkers in the sixth century BCE, and gradually work their way through the ages, until we reach whatever the 'now' is for that author. Others are more biographical, sugaring the pill with anecdotes about the eccentricities and oddities of the philosophers. More recently, it has become popular to take a purely thematic approach, breaking the subject down into questions or themes, with an emphasis on topics that are still 'hot'.

These different approaches reflect the fact that philosophy has an oddly hybrid nature – it's less of a purebred Afghan, and more of a labradoodle. English literature is a subject that essentially consists of its history. Chaucer and Shakespeare and Austen and George Eliot are not read for their historical interest, but because their writings are still living works of art. Furthermore, their greatness lies not in some ideas that could be abstracted and summarized, but in the language: the words and sentences and paragraphs and longer, deeper, musical movements of the texts.

Mathematics and physics, on the other hand, are subjects that can be taught without ever mentioning the backstory. To calculate the area of a circle, you don't need to know that pi was first roughly computed by the Ancient Egyptians and Babylonians, and then brought to seven decimal places by Chinese mathematicians in the first millennium CE: you just need a pocket calculator. And Newton's laws of motion have a meaning and importance that have nothing to do with the words in which he expressed them. Aristotelian physics, with its abhorrence of the void, its straightforwardly wrong conception of motion and its ingrained cosmology, with the Earth at the centre of a static universe frozen into a series of concentric crystalline spheres, is of no use whatsoever to a modern scientist, other than to make her feel superior.

Philosophy spans both these worlds. It's certainly possible to discuss the ideas of Plato, Aristotle and Wittgenstein without ever quoting them. In this sense, they are like Newton. However, the problems of philosophy tend not to get solved. They are news that stays news. Professional philosophers today still engage with Aristotle and Descartes, still argue with Locke and Bentham, in a way that no scientist would think to dispute with Archimedes or Copernicus. And so the *history* of philosophy never goes away, never becomes irrelevant.

It's also a fascinating story in its own right. And so, in this book I have tried to capture that crossbred *labradoodleness* of philosophy. The form I have adopted tips a hat to the history of the subject. It is structured as a series of walks, which connects to Aristotle's practice of teaching while on the move – a habit that gave the name *Peripatetic*, from the Greek word meaning to walk about, to his school. And on these strolls my dog Monty and I, in the dialectical tradition of Socrates, discuss the central problems in philosophy, taking the broad subject divisions of the field as our guide.

After the introduction, the first three walks are about ethics and moral philosophy. We then have a couple of minor side-strolls, one dealing with the concept of free will, and another on logic. Next, there are three walks in which we discuss metaphysics, those knotty questions around the nature of reality and existence. After that we stroll our way through three walks on epistemology, or the theory of knowledge. Four walks, really, as there's also a discussion of the philosophy of science. Finally, there's a chapter on the meaning of life, which also briefly examines some of the proofs for the existence of God.

Although this broad structure is thematic, within each subject we look at what the great philosophers have had to say about it. My hope is that this will both help the reader to understand the problem, and also to give a real sense of the history and development of thought.

I should say that this is a very partial history of ideas, in that I have concentrated on the Western philosophical tradition. This is not because of a parochial disdain for Islamic or Chinese or Indian philosophy, but simply because these are vast and complex fields in which I have no expertise, and it would have been insulting to add snippets, merely to make this work seem more diverse. Each of the great non-Western traditions deserves a Monty of its own...

Finally, this is not one of those introductions to philosophy that gives the reader bullet points to help revision. It is arranged as a series of walks, and just as on a walk, there are times when we wander off the path, beat around for a while in the under-growth, disturb a rabbit, feed the ducks. There is the occasional dead end. And sometimes, you have to walk beside a busy road, or through a field of stubble, before you get to the good bits, that lovely clearing in the woods, or the stream with the kingfisher.

Prodogue

I have a dog, a scruffy Maltese terrier, called Monty. I say 'have' not to suggest ownership, particularly, but more in the way you'd say I have dandruff or a cold. Monty looks like a failed cloud that has fallen to earth and rolled around in the muck for a while. He has inscrutable black eyes, a black nose and a nicotine-stained moustache gained from sticking his snout into aromatically enticing nooks and crannies, both biological and geological.

When it comes to intelligence, Maltese terriers are generally described as 'middling': slower-witted by far than highly strung poodles and chess-playing collies, but a notch or two up from the bewildered boxer, staring in bafflement at a tennis ball in the hope it comes back to life, or stoner Afghans, intellectually exhausted by the effort of not swallowing their own tongues. Monty has no tricks, and he doesn't *come*, or even *sit* reliably; although he will wait passively for you to approach him if the world has nothing more interesting to offer. His greatest triumph came when he won Best Boy Dog at the Cricklewood, or, rather, 'Cricklewoof', dog show. A rabbit was runner-up. Third prize went to a teddy bear.

Although I've been a little harsh on his intellectual accomplishments, Monty has a sort of earnest, quizzical look to him, as if he's methodically striving to understand some secret code, or seriously pondering the hidden meaning of the universe. I think of him as a sort of Dogter Watson – no, don't worry, this isn't going to be one of those books full of awful puns, there will be no more. If he's Watson, does this make me Sherlock? Alas, I fear that Monty and I are like one of those double acts made up of two straight men – we are both Watsons, both of us huffing and puffing our way to a truth that more agile minds might reach with greater speed, if not accuracy.

So, I find Monty a useful companion as I wander here and there, trying to make sense of the world, applying, where I can, the philosophy I've picked up over years of academic study and private reading. We chat things through. Bounce ideas off each other. I've come to be able to guess his thoughts. Articulate them, even.

The following chapters present some of our philosophical conversations, undertaken on our walks across the streets and parks and graveyards of north London (and occasionally a little further afield). They are intended to form an accessible introduction to the great questions in philosophy – you know the ones, the usual suspects. What is the right thing to do? Does free will exist? What is the ultimate nature of reality? How do we know anything? Is there a God? Why do I always try to put the USB stick in the socket the wrong way round first time?

It's a book intended for people rather than dogs, and deals with human problems, rather than the worming schedules and faecal-disposal strategies that take up so much of our canine-oriented energy. But there is, nevertheless, a doggy flavour… I kept an eye out for the appearances of humanity's best friend in the classics of philosophy. And it turned out that there were more of them than I expected. A bit like wigs. I should probably explain.

Back in the early 1990s I was going out with a girl who had a curious obsession with men in wigs. I don't mean in a kinky way – she didn't like me to don a judge's horsehair and flail around with a gavel, pronouncing her guilty of wearing a negligee without due care and attention. No, it was simply that she liked to spot them, like a birdwatcher ticking off a goldcrest or chiffchaff. She'd nudge me in the pub or on the tube, and whisper, 'Syrup,' and I'd have to try to locate the wig-wearer. (Syrup, by the way, is Cockney rhyming slang: syrup of fig – wig.) Back in those days, hair replacement technologies were still in their infancy – weaves and transplants and follicle regeneration unguents hadn't achieved their current state of sophistication; and even then, the classic three-strand comb-over was no longer an acceptable option, so there were more wigs around to observe.

After the alert from my girlfriend, I'd scan the room or the train carriage. In the early days of our relationship, other than the obvious and terrible wigs – the ones looking like a slumbering beaver, or those with a rigid consistency like fibreglass or overbeaten cream or melted plastic – I'd usually entirely fail to spot the target. But, gradually, I learned to pick up the clues: the unnatural darkness contrasting with greying eyebrows; a follicular density undermined by the puckered visage below; a glossy iridescence reflecting the neon of the streetlights.

Before our relationship, I'd never noticed a wig, never *seen* one. It was a detail, a granularity, that my world did not contain. Ludwig Wittgenstein – a philosopher we'll meet again in these pages – writes at length in *Philosophical Investigations* of the process by which we learn the meaning of a word. Rather than there being a simple linear relationship between an object and its name, we acquire the meaning of a word by seeing how it is used, by learning the rules governing its utterance, and the *form of life* – the rich matrix of cultural procedures and traditions – in which it is embedded. Knowledge is behaviour, a thing we *do*, rather than a thing we *have*. And so I had to learn to perceive the wigs, by following the lead of my master, and soon a whole new aspect of the world became distinct to me. I began to see them everywhere, and together we rejoiced in this shared element, like porpoises breaching in the surf. And even after she'd gone, although the joy of shared discovery was past, I still found myself picking out a wig in a crowd, the rich, dense, chocolatey mass above the melancholy face, and I'd murmur 'syrup' to myself, wistfully…

As with the wigs, I'd never really *seen* the dogs trotting through the pages of Western philosophy until I started actively to look for them. And then suddenly they were everywhere, sometimes skulking in the textual margins, as if they knew they were in trouble for some gastric mishap or act of store-cupboard larceny, and other times hiding in plain sight.

Given humanity's long and intimate association with dogs, it is not surprising that they have insinuated themselves into so many aspects of our intellectual culture, our myths, our stories, as well as our philosophical investigations. Archaeologists have found it tricky to tie down the precise moment when dogs were first domesticated, although the best guesses tend to cluster around thirty to forty thousand years ago. It seems likely that wolves began hanging around the encampments of our ancestors, and that over tens of thousands of years something like the modern dog began to peel away from the wolf, a process driven by a combination of natural selection and selective breeding.

By fifteen thousand years ago, well before we'd discovered farming, humans and dogs were entwined in life, and death.

The very first unequivocal evidence of humans and dogs living together comes from three Palaeolithic skeletons found in a quarry in Germany: a man, a woman and a little dog, all buried together. The dog had suffered from distemper, and could only have survived as long as it did if it had been looked after by the people. Too weak and feeble to be of any use on a hunt, it must have had some other function in the lives of the group it lived and died among. It was a pet...

Inching our way forward through time, we find dogs generally revered and respected in most human cultures. In pre-Columbian America, dogs were regarded by the Mayans and Aztecs as benign guides and guardians, leading the dead to the spirit world. The Egyptians may have been better known for their fondness for cats, but dogs were also often mummified and entombed with their owners. And one of the very first animals whose name has come down to us was a graceful hunting dog called Abuwtiyuw (no, I've no idea how to pronounce it, either), who thrived sometime in the Sixth Dynasty (2345–2181 BCE).

A little closer in time and place to the roots of the Western philosophical tradition, the Persian Zoroastrians were much taken with both the sagacity and moral rectitude of dogs. In a curious echo of the Mayans, Persian dogs guarded the bridge over which the dead sauntered to paradise. But they were also key combatants in the endless war of light against darkness, fighting for the wise Ahura Mazda against the insects, slugs, rats, lizards, frogs and, I'm afraid, cats that served the dark lord, Angra Mainyu. That curious way that dogs have of standing stock-still and staring silently into the middle distance was explained by the fact that they can see evil spirits invisible to us. To mistreat such a powerful ally in the good fight must incur terrible punishments, in this life and the next. The murder of a dog could only be atoned for by a demanding list of penances, including the killing of ten thousand cats. So, yes, the Zoroastrians were definitely dog people...

Inching still closer to the origins of philosophy, the heroic age of Greece gives us Odysseus' faithful hound, Argos, who waited for twenty years for his master to return from his travels. Once glorious in the chase, but now lying on a dunghill, starved and beaten, he alone of all those left behind on Ithaca recognizes Odysseus. He is repaid with a tear from the hero and, happy at last, expires. On the other hand, the ultimate post-mortem shame for any Homeric hero was to be stripped of his armour on the battlefield and left naked for the dogs to eat.

So far, we have history, myth and legend, but our first fully philosophical dog has to wait until Plato's *Republic*. In the *Republic*, Plato attempts, among many other things, to define justice and to set out the criteria for a perfect society. A key component of the ideal government is the class of Guardians, philosopher-soldiers who lead and protect the state. What qualities would we look for in these Guardians? They must be friendly and benevolent towards the citizens of the city, but harsh and aggressive to their enemies. And where might these qualities, which constitute true wisdom, be found? Why, in the household dog, who instinctively knows good from evil, friend from foe, who licks the hand of his master's drinking buddies, even when he knows nothing else about them, and savages the unwelcome intruder.

> And surely this instinct of the dog is very charming;
> your dog is a true philosopher.
>
> Why?

Why, because he distinguishes the face of a friend and of an enemy only by the criterion of knowing and not knowing. And must not an animal be a lover of learning who determines what he likes and dislikes by the test of knowledge and ignorance?

Most assuredly.

And is not the love of learning the love of wisdom, which is philosophy?

Not a bad way for our philosophical dog to make its entrance bow-wow. Plato's view of dogs wasn't always quite so laudatory, and he was capable of hurling the insult 'Dog!' at those with whom he disagreed. This leads us on nicely to the most famous dogs in philosophy. Today, 'cynic' – a word that derives from the Greek term for 'dog-like' – has come to mean (in the words of the *Oxford English Dictionary*): 'One who shows a disposition to disbelieve in the sincerity or goodness of human motives and actions, and is wont to express this by sneers and sarcasms; a sneering fault-finder'.

It's not an attractive picture: the thin-lipped misanthrope, mocking good intentions, forever pulling away the mask of virtue to reveal the hypocrite behind. We can certainly find elements of this modern sense in the original Cynics, a straggling group of thinkers who emerged just as Plato was undertaking his very different philosophical project. The Cynics lived simply, disdaining all the trappings of wealth and worldly success, dressing in rags, sleeping rough, railing against the greed and materialism of the affluent. No convention was sacrosanct; no moral or religious tradition left unmocked. But Cynicism was, above all, a creed devoted to achieving a virtuous life, and the Cynic's critique was a necessary, if destructive, first step to enlightenment.

Where do the dogs come in? There are a couple of different stories explaining the origins of the name. It may simply have been that the very first Cynic, Antisthenes, taught at a gymnasium called 'the place of the white dog'. However, I prefer the story that Plato, annoyed by the constant goading and gulling he got from the greatest of the Cynics, Antisthenes' pupil, Diogenes of Sinope, spat out, 'You're a dog!' This delighted Diogenes, who revelled in the role. When another member of the elite threw bones at him and repeated the slur, Diogenes raised a leg and pissed on him. In truth, Diogenes does seem to have been a bit of an oaf, notorious for eating noisily during lectures and for ostentatiously breaking wind mid-conversation, always either picking his teeth or picking a fight. Everyone's worst nightmare in the quiet carriage… And he could be a little too pleased with himself. The only time Plato got the better of him was when Diogenes wiped his filthy feet over Plato's favourite rug. 'I trample upon Plato's vainglory,' he said. Plato's riposte was, 'How much pride you show, Diogenes, by seeming not to be proud.'

The main reason the 'dog-like' tag seems to have stuck was because the Cynics, like dogs, were notorious for their lack of shame in the expression of their bodily functions. Diogenes would urinate and defecate in the streets. His pupil, Crates of Thebes, took things to the next stage, copulating with his wife Hipparchia in public view. I suppose there's a reason why this activity is still known as dogging.

Crates and Hipparchia lived into decent old age, camping in the doorways and porticos of Athens, but their master,

Diogenes, lived yet longer, into his nineties according to some accounts. And at the end, the dogs return. There are different versions of his death – one is that he simply held his breath for several days (that'll usually do the trick). A more prosaic demise has him eating a raw ox foot, and perishing from food poisoning. But yet another version is more apt for the Cynic. Diogenes was dividing up an octopus for his own dogs when one bit him. The bite festered, and so he died. A variation sees the dog infecting him with rabies.

Diogenes was not, in fact, the first philosopher to suffer death by dog. One of the earliest, Heraclitus, came to a particularly unpleasant end. Heraclitus was an aristocrat with a loathing for the common people, convinced that the truths he told could only be understood by a select few. The top people, he said, are prepared to give up everything for immortal glory, while the masses gorge themselves mindlessly, like cattle. His fate therefore seems, if not quite deserved, then somehow fitting. Suffering from dropsy, he self-medicated by smearing himself in cow excrement, which he believed would draw off the excessive moisture. In this condition he was discovered by a pack of dogs, which, unable to recognize him as human, ate him.

The next couple of thousand years of philosophy were relatively under-dogged, at a time when, ironically, philosophy was, under the dominion of Plato's great pupil Aristotle, rather *dog*-matic. But when, post-Renaissance, philosophy wakes from its slumbers, the dogs come back.

A dog makes a solitary appearance in one of the greatest – and most difficult – works of Western metaphysics, Immanuel Kant's *Critique of Pure Reason*. We'll encounter Kant several more times in the perambulations that follow, but for now it is enough to know that, in the *Critique*, Kant attempts both to criticize and heal one of the abiding divisions in the history of philosophy: between those on the one side who believe that knowledge must come from pure thought, and on the other those who claim that we can know only what reaches the mind through the senses. In explaining how this gap between ideas and sensory experience can be closed, he uses the example of a dog.

> The concept of a dog signifies a rule according to which my imagination can trace, delineate, or draw a general outline, figure, or shape of a four-footed animal without being restricted to any single and particular shape supplied by experience.

Without the concept of a *dog*, says Kant, the various sensory perceptions – ears, fur, lolling tongue, cocked leg – would be lost in the background noise. The idea *dog* is solid enough to force unity onto those various bits of the world in front of us, forming them into our familiar friend and companion. But the term remains vague enough for us to include the annoying little Chihuahua, and the imperious Great Dane.

We have already mentioned Wittgenstein, and the way he locates the meaning of a word in a network of linguistic and social practices. Communication involves taking part in an interlocked series of 'language games', and our knowledge of these different language games is what makes communication possible. In probing the limits of what it is to *mean*, Wittgenstein returns again and again to a rather puzzled dog, who seems to be trying quite hard to be human. But lacking the necessary abilities to comprehend the appropriate language games, our dog can feel neither hope for the future, nor fear at what it might bring. And a dog cannot lie.

> Lying is a language-game that needs to be learned like
> any other one… Why can't a dog simulate pain? Is he
> too honest? Could one teach a dog to simulate pain?
> Perhaps it is possible to teach him to howl on particu-
> lar occasions as if he were in pain, even when he is not.
> But the surroundings which are necessary for this
> behaviour to be real simulation are missing.

I think that Wittgenstein is quite right in saying that it would be
impossible for a dog to simulate pain. But surely not even a philosopher would claim that a dog cannot *feel* pain? My last example
of a philosophical dog is an upsetting, but also an instructive
one.

We're going to go back to the seventeenth century, and the
work of René Descartes. Descartes has become notorious
among animal lovers for his view that all non-human animals
were merely 'natural automata': soulless mechanical devices
incapable of thinking, or feeling emotion, or, indeed, pain.

Two anecdotes often repeated about Descartes point to the
consequences of such a theory. One day while walking with his
friends, the philosopher saw a pregnant dog. First, he tickled
her ears, and fussed over the animal. Then, before the horrified
gaze of his companions, he kicked her in the stomach. He
calmed the distress of the appalled observers by explaining that
the dog's howls were merely the grinding of the gears, reassur-
ing them that animals could feel no pain, and that they should
reserve their pity for suffering humanity.

The other, more horrific anecdote concerns his wife's lapdog.
Fired by his reading of William Harvey's discovery of the
circulation of the blood, and determined to observe it for himself, our philosopher waits until his wife and daughter are out

on an errand. He picks up the little dog – a papillon, with those big ears, like a butterfly's wings – carries the dog down into his basement, and there performs a ghastly vivisection.

How do Mme Descartes and the little girl react when they find the corpse? History does not record.

History does not record because there was no Mme Descartes. No daughter. The philosopher remained unmarried. The story is a myth, rising on the thermals generated by the moronic inferno of the internet. Something very like the horror here described did, in fact, occur, some two hundred years later. The perpetrator was the celebrated nineteenth-century anatomist Claude Bernard (1813–78), a heartless slicer of living, conscious, unanaesthetized dogs (and rabbits). He didn't much care for his wife, and he truly did vivisect her little dog. Understandably outraged, she left him, and set up an organization to campaign against animal cruelty. The story seems to have become attached to Descartes because of his views on animals as automata.

And the episode involving the pregnant dog? If it happened at all, the guilty man was a later French philosopher, Nicolas Malebranche (1638–1715). Once again, Descartes' reputation meant that such stories gravitated to him.

But enough, now, of dogs in philosophy, let's get some philosophy into our dog!

Walk 1

Good Dog, Bad Dog

On this first walk, Monty and I begin to discuss ethics, or that branch of philosophy that addresses questions of moral right and wrong. Why is it that moral issues are so hard to resolve? Does morality just come down to whim, or power? In this section we look at some unsatisfactory ethical theories, which are nevertheless helpful in working out what a good moral theory needs to do.

Philosophy may not always be fun; but it should at least strive to be useful. It will help you to decide between good and bad arguments wherever you encounter them, whether on social media or in the pub. It will help to clarify what you think about the great issues of the day. It may empower you to become a better person, someone who reflects on the right course of action, and the proper goals for life. It will lead you to spend quiet hours pondering the big questions: Why are we here? What is the

13

ultimate nature of reality? How do I know that the light really goes off when I close the fridge door?

One of the many good reasons for studying philosophy, however, isn't that it will enable you to triumph in any domestic dispute. In fact, I'd go as far as to say that you should never use a philosophical sleight of hand when your partner is annoyed at you. Never wield Hume's fork, or Ockham's razor, unless you want to be faced with the Spouse's frying pan. No, domestic arguments won with the aid of philosophy are always Pyrrhic – the cost of the victory far outweighs any benefit in terms of, for example, having the dishwasher stacked in a logical and efficient manner, or not having to sit through *Sleepless in Seattle* for the fifteenth time.

There are also many good reasons for owning a dog, and one of these is that it provides an excuse for when you need to escape from your flat following just such a Pyrrhic victory. Dogs, after all, need walking, even philosophically inclined Maltese terriers with little legs and no great love of the outdoors.

'Which mood are you in, Monty?' I asked as the old lift clattered down from our flat. 'Graveyard or the Heath?'

Monty shrugged, as if our route were a source of indifference to him. He could do a lot of work with a shrug. A Monty shrug could express many different moods, judgements, ideas, even arguments. A Monty shrug could suggest agreement or disagreement; it could convey wry amusement or angry condemnation; it could find fault with your logic or endorse your reasoning. This one said, *Pee on a grave, pee on a tree? I'm neutral. You decide.*

'The graveyard's closer, but Hampstead Heath is less…'
Morbid?

I nodded. 'The Heath it is.'

The Heath is a twenty-minute walk away, through the streets where the oligarchs and hedge-fund managers live. Unlike most of London's open spaces, the Heath feels unplanned, unmanicured, un… predictable. One moment you're in suburbia, the next, wilderness. OK, not quite wilderness, but you can go whole minutes without seeing or hearing another human being. And perhaps that transition isn't quite as dramatic as I made it sound. The Heath and the streets interpenetrate each other in a space that is neither town nor country. This brings to mind a paradox or puzzle that exercised the mind of one of the earliest Stoic philosophers, Chrysippus (c.279–c.206 BCE).

The Stoics were one of the philosophical schools that flourished in Athens in the third century BCE. They went on to conquer Rome, to the point that one of the greatest Stoic philosophers was the Emperor Marcus Aurelius. We'll talk more about the Stoics later on, but for now, a key part of their vision was that each philosopher should aspire to be the infallible sage, a figure who fully understood the connectedness of the physical world, who saw the necessity in all things, and who could answer any conceivable question.

Such as, how many grains of sand make a pile? (This is known as the sorites paradox – *sorites* being the Greek word for 'heap'.)

Clearly, we all know a pile of sand when we see one, and we also know that three grains don't equal a pile. So there must be a point at which adding an extra grain turns the *not-pile* into a *pile*. But how can one single grain make such a difference? The same problem applies to balding men. The full head of hair gradually thins, until the man is undeniably bald. But when does he become bald? Again, a single hair must mark the transition, and yet how can *bald* and *not-bald* be distinguished by so fine a… hair?

And at school, a version of the sorites paradox formed an introduction for me to the world of speculation. A big rough kid would come up to you in the playground, grab you and demand an answer to the question: 'Would you snog Hilda for a quid?'

Hilda was the ancient, irascible, snaggle-toothed dinner lady who ladled reconstituted dried mash and a brown meat slurry onto your school tray.

'No!' would come your answer.

'So, what would you snog Hilda for, then?'

'Nothing!'

'Hah, you'd snog Hilda for nothing!' And soon the whole schoolyard would be singing out the fact that not only would I snog Hilda for nothing, but that I loved her and wanted to marry her.

Well, that isn't quite the paradox. The paradox would come later when you'd think through the question. Would I snog Hilda for, say, ten million pounds? I probably would, yes. So, for some figure between one pound and ten million, I would agree to snog Hilda. And that means at the threshold, one pound would make the difference between snogging and not snogging Hilda. So, in effect, you would always snog Hilda for one pound.

We'll come back to Hilda, or rather, Chrysippus and his pile in due course.

But, anyway, we passed through the interzone, and were undeniably snogging Hilda, which is to say we reached the Heath. It's especially beautiful at this time of year, as the leaves burn on the ancient oak and ash, and you crunch over acorns and beech mast and sweet chestnut shells.

I prepared to unleash Monty. Then I groaned as I saw what was approaching. It was a pug, or perhaps a French bulldog – I can't tell apart any of the multitude of dogs that look as if they've run into a patio door, with their goggle eyes and guppy mouths. Monty hates a pug. I've never worked out if this is an aesthetic, a moral or a political objection, but as soon as he sees one, he shoots to the end of his lead, and strains at his harness, like a husky pulling at an overladen sled. I sometimes used to pretend at moments like this that Monty, who has the muscle mass of a heavy sneeze, was dragging me helpless through the streets.

So Monty went into his ravening-wolf impression, and the pug had a go back, the dogs knowing they weren't likely to get into an actual rumble, as they were both still on their leads. It's the sort of confrontation that between men is sometimes referred to as 'handbags', a thing of sham and shadow, rather than real malevolence.

'Bad dog,' I snapped at Monty, giving his lead an ineffectual tug. And then, cringingly to the owner, 'I'm so sorry.' He was a neatly dressed man, who took little steps that precisely matched his pug's gait. 'He never actually draws blood or anything – it's just for show.'

The man said nothing, and stepped on, his nose in the air.

'I wish you wouldn't do that,' I hissed at Monty.

He looked at me innocently, as if I'd interrupted him as he reflected on the beauty of a butterfly or rose.

It's a dog thing. It's what we do.

'Not all dogs.'

Sure, maybe you get a few that are scared or bribed. But underneath, we all want to. Anyway, pugs…

When this pug was safely out of range I unhooked Monty's lead. He trotted off down the path that wound through the trees, sniffing and peeing. And then he froze, like a kid playing grandma's footsteps. In a second or two I saw why. It was the huge black Rottweiler that we'd encountered once or twice before on the Heath. It was the size of a small horse. Even though it had never shown any obvious signs of aggression, it struck fear into Monty's cowardly soul. And, if I'm honest, into mine. Monty made a couple of feints in its direction, growling and barking. The Rottweiler put up with it for a minute or so, and gave one sonorous woof, which sent Monty scampering back to me through the undergrowth. He jumped up, scrabbling at my knees with his front paws.

Carry carry carry carry carry.

'But you're all muddy!'

But his desperation was such that I picked him up anyway.

The Rottweiler ambled harmlessly away, like some benign Palaeolithic herbivore. Perhaps if he'd seen Monty as more of a threat he'd have raised himself from his martial slumbers and eaten him. I put Monty down and he snarled and barked at his retreating enemy.

I could have taken him. That dude was in serious trouble.

'Yeah, he might have choked on you.'

Monty shrugged.

'We need to talk about this.'

About what?

'Doggy behaviour. What makes you a good dog or a bad dog. Actually, not so much dogs, more people.'

Great, another walk ruined.

'Humour me.'

Fine, then, but I'm going to run around for a bit first. See how many wees I can do in two minutes, sniff up everything to be sniffed, find some leftover Kentucky Fried Chicken bones you can try to pull out of my mouth, that sort of thing, OK?

I wandered up to a higher spot on the Heath. There was a bench, where on one side you could gaze across to the glass towers of the City, glinting with a sinister frigidity in the morning sunlight, and on the other the trees rolled on as if we were in the middle of some ancient and eternal forest, evergreens showing as pools of darkness amid the golds and yellows. And this spot had the advantage of being off the beaten track. Talking to your dog about philosophy can be perceived as a little strange, so I'd found it was best to do it where we wouldn't be overheard.

Monty came back and flopped down at my feet. He only had little legs and this walk was about at the limit of his range.

'OK, let's have that talk about right and wrong.'

You mean why sometimes you say to me 'good dog', and sometimes you say 'bad dog'? Well, I've got a theory. You say 'good dog' when you like what I do, and you say 'bad dog' when you don't like it, and that's all there is to it.

I smiled, and stroked Monty.

'Good dog. You've actually put your paw on the heart of the problem. There's even a name for the theory you've just outlined. It's called *emotivism*. Emotivists claim that whenever we make a moral judgement, whenever we say that an act is right or wrong, or moral or immoral, all we're really saying, indeed all we can ever possibly say, is that we approve of it. That it makes us feel fuzzy and warm inside. It's the same sort of judgement we'd be making when we eat a good pie, and say, "That's delicious!" Or, it's like a dog wagging its tail when its master says "walkies".'

Monty wagged his tail, reflexively, when he heard 'walkies'.

'And if emotivism is true, if moral judgements ultimately do come down to *I like this* or *I don't like this*, then there are certain consequences. It suddenly becomes very difficult for our moral judgements to have any kind of force, or any influence on the world.'

Monty gave me a quizzical look.

'If a person says that they like spinach, and you don't like spinach, there's not much more either of you can say or do. There's no way of rationally arguing for or against spinach. A full list of the nutrients contained in the leaves won't help. I say *boo*, you say *hurrah*. You can shrug and smile and walk away, or you can fight it out. But there's no place for evidence, reason, logic. And so any hope of making real moral judgements that might carry enough weight to change what we do, disappears.'

Monty gave me one of his expressive shrugs. This was very much a *so what* shrug.

'And if we take away our ability to argue rationally about moral issues, then something else will rush in to fill the vacuum.'

Such as?

'Well, anyone who now thinks about morality does so in the shadow of Friedrich Nietzsche (1844–1900). Nietzsche argued with great force and panache that morality is always a matter of power, a way of asserting your will. What is right is what those in charge, or those who want to be in charge, say to preserve or enhance their own position in society. Nietzsche's main target was Christianity. He hated Christianity not as other critics have done, for its pomp and hypocrisy, but for what we might think of as its best features: its advocacy of mercy, meekness, turning the other cheek, blessed are the peacemakers, all that stuff. He regarded Christianity as a slave religion, as the attempt by the weak and feeble to wrest power from the strong, i.e. those who should naturally be in control. To achieve this, the slaves employ the only weapons at their command: whinging, mithering, complaining. He suggests a history, or, as he puts it, a *genealogy*, of morality. In the heroic age of Homer, morality was a matter of *good* and *bad*. The *good* was what marked out the life of the aristocratic hero: happiness achieved through victory in battle, through sexual conquest, feasting, wealth. The *bad* was the miserable lot of the slave: weakness, poverty, helplessness. Christianity replaced the fine and noble good–bad dichotomy with the wretched distinction between good and evil, where goodness represents piety, and evil those same aristocratic virtues, now overthrown and marking out the possessor for damnation.

So morality – all that talk about gentleness and cheek-turning – was a weapon forged by cowards and weaklings to combat the natural aristocracy of the bold and strong. This takes us to a place beyond the emotivist position that morality is just whatever happens to make us feel all warm and fuzzy inside; it is now a malign force, a way of interfering with the naturally ordained order of the universe, a hierarchy with glorious Supermen at the top, and cringing slaves at the bottom.'

So not a huge Nietzsche fan, then?

'Nietzsche is the greatest philosopher of the past two hundred years. Great in that he forces you to think, challenges everything you assumed to be true. And he writes like an angel, which is more than you can say for most philosophers. No one else has managed to combine his grandeur and power with such clarity. He wants us to live not *ethically*, i.e. by the pettifogging rules, the injunctions, fasts and prohibitions of Christianity, but bravely, beautifully, creatively. The way, in other words, that great men (and, yes, he means *men*) have always lived. His seductions are almost irresistible. But we have to resist them, unless we really want to live in a world where the powerful can do as they wish, where might really does equal right, and it is not just that the strong are able to crush the weak, but it is their *duty* to do so. And, well, there's a reason that if serial killers ever read anything, it's always Nietzsche... He's the philosopher for those who feel that their true greatness has not been recognized by society, for those who think they should create their own morality, and that other people exist just to gratify their will to power.

It's become unfashionable to link Nietzsche to the horrors of Nazism, but the fact is that much of the ideology of Nazism is in Nietzsche: the right of the strong to crush the weak, the idea that some people are naturally superior to others – a Master race, indeed; that war is a good and natural thing; that non-white races are inferior. It's true that Nietzsche wasn't a narrow German nationalist, and that he wasn't especially anti-Semitic by the standards of his times, but the rest is there, hiding in plain sight.

But the fact that he has been used, posthumously, to bolster evil cannot help us to escape the profound and terrible questions Nietzsche asks. Where is the moral law that prevents the Superman from doing as he pleases? What law either of reason or of nature forbids me from achieving what I want, from reaching the greatness within me, by trampling over you?'

Er, you know you're ranting a bit?

'What? Oh. That's Nietzsche for you.'

Don't look now, but there are people...

Monty was right. A man and a woman and some scampering children were approaching, the kids swiping at thistle heads with sticks, the harassed parents looking like they needed a break from their recreation.

When caught talking to your dog, all you can do is carry on, but in a more conventional style, so I 'good-boyed' Monty a bit, and tickled his jowls, like any sane, normal dog-owner. I noticed while I was doing this that Monty had a bit of a shiver on.

'OK, fella, let's go home.'

Back amid the trees, I continued.

'So that's our challenge. Can we find a rational basis for morality, showing that we're not just dogs wagging our tails, or weaklings trying to chain the strong so that we can usurp their rightful place at the top of the pile?'

And can we?

'It's going to take more than one walk. But let's spend the rest of this one restating the problems as clearly as we can. Then we can look at the solutions that have been proposed by philosophers over the past couple of thousand years. Then we'll see if any of them can withstand a rigorous philosophical kicking.

First the problem. And it is a problem. If we want to reject Nietzsche and the tail-waggers, and argue that there are universal truths about right and wrong, or at least that morality has a solid rational basis, then there are serious issues that we need to address.

First is the fact that it's fairly obvious that there is precious little agreement about moral issues. No sane person would dispute that the internal angles of a triangle add up to 180 degrees, or that humans evolved from more primitive apes, or that the Earth orbits around the sun. That is because these things are reasonable, well-established facts. But with moral issues, we find that our society is riddled with disputes that turn on ethical matters. Some of them are personal, some with a wider political flavour. Can I lie if telling the truth will hurt someone's feelings? Should I give a proportion of my income to charity? Is a man who regards women and non-white ethnic groups as inferior a fit person to hold high political office? Can we take money from people in taxation to pay for things they don't care about? Is personal freedom more important than physical wellbeing? Is it right to build a railway line through someone's garden against their will, if it serves the public good? Should we invade countries the governments of which offend against certain "civilized values"? What are those civilized values? Should we feel obliged to welcome refugees from other countries? If so, on what grounds? Is it OK to kill and eat animals? If it's OK to eat them, what moral obligations do we owe to animals? Does a woman have an absolute right to choose to have an abortion? Are there crimes for which the penalty should be death? If we decide to blow up a terrorist using a drone, how many innocent children is it acceptable to kill at the same time? Or let's say you have a ... pet, who might need some very expensive medical treatment. Can you justify spending that money, when you could use it to save or improve human lives?'

Er, well, if I were allowed to express an opinion on that last one, I'd say a definite woof.

I gave Monty a chin stroke and a quick belly tickle.

'What's interesting, and also frustrating, about these arguments is that they seem interminable. We can't google the answer, as moral disagreements seldom ultimately come down to matters of fact. If morality is rational and objective, then why can't we agree?'

Er, objective ... ?

'Oh, sorry. Let's get a few semi-technical terms out of the way. *Subjective* and *objective* are going to rear their heads a lot in these walks. If I say that something is subjective, or subjectively true, it means that it is true from the point of view of a particular person, the subject. You're a subject, I'm a subject. I'm cold. Dogfood smells terrible. I love cheesecake. You're making a statement about your own feelings or perceptions. On the other hand, if you claim that something is objectively true, it means it has a reality independent of the views of any person

24

or even group of people. The air temperature is eleven degrees Celsius. We are four kilometres from home. The Earth orbits the sun. The square on the hypotenuse of a right-angled tri-angle is equal to the sum of the squares of the other two sides. These are objective facts. Their truth or falsehood isn't decided by how I feel about them. Got that?'

I think so. Subjective is just what I think, objective is true or false whatever I think…?

'Close enough. While we're at it, we may as well slip in another term: *relativism*. Relativism is the idea that there is no simple *universal* truth, that any statement needs to be preceded by the qualification *for me*. Relativism may be limited to certain areas, for example the idea that all motion is relative, or that beauty is in the eye of the beholder; but often relativists take a more general view, and hold that all *truths* are relative, and dependent not on universal laws or principles, but on the sub-jective feelings and perceptions of individual people living at particular times and places.'

So, are subjectivism and relativism the same thing?

'Not quite, though clearly there's an overlap. I think that most of us would accept that many judgements are subjective, and they're usually clear enough. I might have a subjective view of, I don't know, say, beer, that I find it refreshing and cheering, and it helps to numb the pain of existence; but then I might also accept certain objective, non-relative things about it, for example that taken to excess it will rot my brain and liver. But, in general, you have a division, with subjective and relative and local on one side, and objective and universal on the other. And morality is right in the middle of this battlefield.

Returning to those endless moral debates, the fact that we can't seem to reach an agreement is often because the two different sides to the dispute have fundamentally opposed conceptions of morality. Not just opposed, but incompatible. The word philosophers use for this is *incommensurable*.'

Er, a bit of consideration for your audience … ?

'It's like a dog show, and the categories have got mixed up, so you're trying to judge a Pekinese and a Great Dane and a Dalmatian.'

Thank you.

'Or as if two people are trying to decide on what's the best biscuit, and one is using, say, how well the biscuit stands up to dunking as their criterion for judging, and the other is using how much chocolate it has coating it. So, of course they'll never agree. One person might say (or at least think), I can lie to my husband about kissing Ken from accounts at the Christmas party, as telling him about it would cause unnecessary anguish; her friend will say, no, it's never OK to tell a lie, ever, whatever the consequences. One person will say taxes should go up to fund health care; another will ask, by what right do you take my hard-earned money?

So, within our own society, there is no general agreement on what counts as right and wrong. And where there are disagreements, there doesn't appear to be any conclusive way of resolving them.

It might be worth pointing out here that modern Western society is not typical in this respect. Most people in Ancient Rome or medieval Europe would not have found it quite such a struggle to establish common moral ground. Most earlier civilizations had a functioning system of ethics founded on a common religious outlook, or an unquestioning belief in the laws of the state, or a shared system of cultural norms, taboos and injunctions.'

But that's not us?

'Nope. The modern world has lost its monolithic moral outlook. It may not be the case that we are literally free to choose whatever morality we like – the state will certainly intervene if we decide that, like the Ancient Zoroastrians, fire is to be worshipped in all its forms, and so burning your next door neighbour's tool shed counts as a religious obligation – and traditional moral thinking certainly still has a gravitational pull, but we nevertheless have a uniquely wide range of moral viewpoints from which to choose.'

And this all means what exactly?

'You could argue that this variety, indeed chaos, is highly suggestive that morality can never be grounded in anything more than the changing habits and customs of people. One of the very first philosophers, Archelaus, who lived in the fifth century BCE, put this succinctly, when he said, "Things are just or ignoble not by nature, but by convention."'

Monty had gone on ahead a little, but now he turned and waited for me, either nervous about lurking Rottweilers, or anxious to discover if there was a way out of the maze laid by the Nietzscheans, the tail-waggers and the relativists.

But there's an answer to this, right?

'*An* answer? It's best not to prejudge these things. Philosophy is all about the search, the enquiry. And it's a bit like when you go up into the attic to look for that old picture frame, or the trainers you knew would eventually acquire retro-status. You might never find the frame or the trainers, but you'll uncover all kinds of other cool stuff up there: a broken tennis racket, Grandma's dentures, a dot-matrix printer, an Etch A Sketch …'

You're not really making your point, you know …

'Fine. Let's start out by making sure we know what the problem is. Dogs fight. Say, over a bone. It belongs to one dog, and another one wants it.'

It happens…

'And the stronger one wins.'

Usually.

'And he gets the bone.'

Or she. That dachshund at number forty-seven may have the eyes of a temptress, but she fights dirty.

'And it's OK, is it, for the strongest to get the bone?'

That's the way it is, with dogs…

'For us, too, sometimes. And it has a, well, pedigree. We find it argued forcefully in Plato's *Republic*. Bit of background. Plato (428/427–348/347 BCE) expounded his philosophy in a series of dramatic dialogues, thirty-eight of them, which pretty well established what it is we mean when we use the word 'philosophy'. It's almost impossible not to go back to Plato when you're discussing philosophy. It's been said that all of philosophy is a set of footnotes to Plato, and it is certainly the case that almost all of the key philosophical questions that puzzle us to this day, and which we'll be chewing over on our walks, were first clearly framed in his dialogues. But the fact that, two and a half thousand years later, we are still puzzled, still chewing, strongly suggests that his answers are seldom as fruitful as his questions. The dialogues are not just major works of philosophy, but also great works of literature. Most of them feature Plato's teacher, Socrates, as a main character. (In all of these walks, whenever I say "Socrates", I usually mean Plato. Socrates himself never wrote anything down, so we have no real idea what his own philosophy was, other than the way it is presented by Plato.)

In the earlier dialogues, Socrates usually encounters some person who thinks he knows the meaning of a concept – often a virtue, such as courage or piety or beauty. From then on, the discussions tend to follow a similar pattern. Socrates, who always claims that his own wisdom consists only in knowing how little he knows, will question the other characters, showing that what they believe about the subject under enquiry is absurd or self-contradictory. The dialogues end on a note of puzzlement or frustration, summed up by the Greek word *aporia*, meaning an impasse. The characters leave the scene having had their certainties removed, but nothing put in their place.

These early dialogues are usually taken to be fairly accurate depictions of the historical Socrates, who finally irritated the Athenian state so much that they put him to death.'

Harsh!

'Yes, well, it's often thought to be one of the great crimes committed by the state against an individual, but those were difficult times. Athens had just been beaten in a terrible war. The war was followed by a revolution that installed a brutal dictatorship – the so-called Thirty Tyrants. Socrates himself was politically neutral, but many of his friends sided with the Tyrants, and one of his old pupils, Critias, was their leader. So when the tyranny was overthrown, and democracy installed again, Socrates was potentially in trouble, as someone tainted by his friendships. But his way was to carry on questioning, goading, annoying, and eventually the regime decided to shut him up. They put him on trial on charges of corrupting the youth of the city, and impiety, and in due course he was found guilty. Even then Socrates could have got away with a slapped wrist. The legal system in Ancient Athens had an interesting quirk. After a guilty verdict, the prosecution and the defence could both propose a punishment, with the jury deciding which was fairer. If Socrates had proposed anything sensible – banishment, perhaps, or a hefty fine – he could have walked away.'

But…

'But he proposed that he be given free meals at public expense as a reward for helping to educate the citizenry.'

Oh dear.

'And so the prosecution's sentence, death by poisoning, was chosen. But I was saying about the dialogues. The early ones follow Socrates as he interrogates the heck out of anyone who claims to possess knowledge, and you never find out what Socrates – or Plato – actually thinks about anything, other than that everyone else is wrong about everything. But then we get to the later dialogues, where most scholars think that Plato leaves the historical Socrates behind, and presents us with his own views. The greatest of these dialogues is the *Republic.*'

And this is where he says that the strong dog should always get the bone? Doesn't sound very just.

'Remember, Plato was writing dramatic dialogues. He puts various opinions in the mouths of the characters in the dialogues, and then exposes their inadequacy. The *Republic* begins with a discussion of the meaning of justice, or "doing the right thing". Socrates has already dealt with a few different ideas of what justice might be. Is it telling the truth? Paying your debts? Helping your friends and harming your enemies? Socrates finds holes in them all. A character called Thrasymachus has been listening to Socrates with increasing impatience, and finally he can't help but jam his oar in. *Justice is nothing but what benefits the strongest,* he splutters. *Whoever is in power enacts laws to their own advantage. In a state ruled by the rich, the laws are for the benefit of the rich. If the poor grab control, then the laws favour the poor.*

Justice is power. Having power means you control justice. That's all there can ever be to it – anything else is pretence and make-believe. Sound familiar?'

Nietzsche?

'Just so.'

But your guy, Plato, you said he was the best … He had an answer to this Thrasywhatsit guy?

'All in good time. Let's add more fuel to the fire, first. In another of the dialogues, the *Gorgias*, the issue at stake is the relationship between power, justice and happiness. One character, Polus, asserts that power always brings happiness. Socrates counters that a person can only be happy if they are virtuous, and that the tyrant who uses his power to obtain what he wants must be miserable. The misery is compounded if the wrongdoer is never brought to justice. Being punished for your crimes is good, says Socrates, in the way that being proved wrong in your argument is good, as it means you have moved closer to the truth. Punishment should bring the same satisfaction that you get from being able to repay a debt. And so the tyrant who throws his enemy in the dungeon is less fortunate than the prisoner.'

Hang on, so I should enjoy it when you shout at me for innocently eating a sausage that I had no idea you wanted, and for accidentally making pretty patterns on your carpet when I come in out of the rain? That's just crazy talk.

'Firstly, me saying in a slightly raised voice, *Hey, Monty, what's happened to my dinner?* hardly makes me a tyrant …'

I'm a very sensitive dog, and sometimes you are quite loud …

'And secondly, your view is very much shared by another of the characters, Callicles, who now makes his intervention. Callicles is incensed by the idea that the prisoner, tortured and

31

abused, is happier than the tyrant. On the contrary, he fumes, freedom is happiness, and the tyrant who does what he wants, however violent or depraved, is by definition the freest and happiest of men. The law of nature, as opposed to the artificial laws of convention, dictates that the strong should rule, and that whatever they do is true justice. Anyone with sufficient energy and courage can and should shake off these shackles, and trample our fake laws – "formulas and spells and charms" he calls them – into the mud.'

Gulp. And Socrates answers… ?

'In this dialogue his answer is again that such a tyrant cannot be happy. His desires will be limitless, and therefore impossible to satisfy. He's a leaky jar that can never be filled up. And perhaps it's true. How many tyrants have died happily in their beds, a smile of contentment and satisfaction on their lips? Think of Hitler raging in his bunker, Mussolini shot and strung up on the gallows, Stalin smothered by his terrified underlings while lying helpless from a stroke.

But trying to refute the idea that evil will always bring unhappiness seems rather weak. For a start, it's always going to be open to counterexamples, those cases where criminals have got away with their villainy, and lived happily ever afterwards on their ill-gotten gains. But also, individual happiness seems oddly unsatisfactory as the ultimate measure of virtue. It is pleasant to think that being good will make us happy, but do we want to conflate the two – to say that goodness *is* happiness? Or even if we keep them separate, should the fact it makes us happy be the only reason to do good? What if I'm constitutionally incapable of happiness – does that mean I should never behave morally? What if small acts of wickedness genuinely make me happy – should I then indulge my tastes? And it's an answer that Plato is himself dissatisfied with. He has a more profound idea of the good, which we'll soon encounter.'

We were nearing the edge of the Heath, and it was time to slip Monty's lead back on.

'OK,' I said, 'we've spent this entire walk in setting up the problem, and we haven't reached a decent answer yet. We've seen that emotivists want to dismiss all moral judgements as tail-wagging. We've seen how positively Nietzsche restates the case first found negatively presented in Plato, that all moral judgements are either meaningless conventions or power-grabs by those not equipped by nature to do battle with the noble weapons of tooth and claw.

Any ethical theory needs to address these points. But I want to give one more example of the sort of thing a solid ethical theory needs to be able to resist. We're going to go back thirty years or so before Plato wrote the *Republic*.

Athens was in the middle of that war with Sparta, a war that was to go on for fifty years, with a few uneasy periods of relative peace. And most of the other states nearby had to pick a side. It was the sort of war that was quite hard to stay out of.

One island – Melos – tried to stay neutral. They had ancient ties to Sparta, but Athens had the strongest navy, and the Melians knew that as an island they were vulnerable. So, they tiptoed around, trying not to get noticed. But the Athenians didn't trust them. The island was strategically important, and they thought the Melians' old kinship with the Spartans would tell in the end. And the war was beginning to turn against the Athenians, so maybe they were getting a little desperate. Finally, they decided to send an expedition to the island, and demand that the Melians join their alliance against the Spartans and contribute to the Athenian war chest.

The Spartans were the greatest warriors in the Ancient world, but they weren't, er, very nice. They had a whole class – the helots – who they basically kept as slaves. If any helot showed signs of intelligence or initiative or courage, they killed him or her. They had nothing much in the way of art or literature. Their whole civilization was about turning Spartan boys into efficient killing machines. And they weren't just tough, they were cunning, too. They thought anything was fair in war – you could lie or cheat if it helped you get the victory.

In contrast, the Athenians had it all: art, architecture, literature, democratic politics and, of course, philosophy. Most people hearing the story of the war between the Athenians and the Spartans would have the Athenians down as the good guys. But here they are, on Melos, besieging the main town. Negotiating, as they say, from a position of strength. And they don't try to dress it up in fancy language. It's not because you've done something wrong, or because we've earned this, they say, it's just that we're stronger than you, and so the only rational course of action for you is to do what we want: surrender, join our alliance and pay tribute. If you resist, we will destroy you. Why? Because we can.

The Melians, being proud and stubborn, didn't cave in, but argued it out with the Athenians. They made several perfectly reasonable points. We're no threat to you. If you crush us, other neutral states will realize that you're a bunch of dangerous maniacs, and so they'll side with the Spartans against you. And, sure, we're outnumbered, but we're tough and brave, and war by its nature is unpredictable, so we might just beat you. And our kinsmen the Spartans might come and help us, and then you'll be sorry. So we may as well try our luck, rather than give in, and live in shame.

But for each of these arguments the Athenians have a rebuttal. If there's one thing that might get the neutral states to side with Sparta, it's a sign of Athenian weakness. The Spartans might be the kinsmen of the Melians, but they are above all a practical people, and never put themselves at risk for anyone else. Even if the vicissitudes of war mean that there is always a tiny chance that things may go well for you, the most likely outcome is disaster for Melos. So the choice is clear: bend the knee and live, or take the ludicrously optimistic path of resistance, and face almost certain annihilation. Notice anything about the Athenians' arguments?'

Not really about right and wrong, are they. Just about power.

'And for the most part the Melians reply in the same language. Except for once, when they say that the gods would punish the Athenians for acting *unjustly*. It's still about bad consequences for the Athenians, but at least hints at some wider idea of justice. And the Athenians' reply is—'

Let me guess – that justice just comes down to who has the biggest stick?

'Good dog! Yeah, they say that the gods don't interfere with the natural way of things, and the natural way of things is for the strong to dominate the weak. And now it looks like we've reached this point where it seems that justice equals being able to get your own way. That might *is* right.

So there we have it. Our challenge is to convince the Athenians not to attack, to fend off the tail-waggers and Nietzscheans.'

Monty looked at me, a half frown on his little face. Maltese terriers are prone to dark stains flowing from their tear ducts, which always give Monty a thoughtful air, as though frowning his way through a deep thought.

And if we can't?

'Then we'll still have learned something. Sometimes we advance by learning our limitations. Sometimes to find out what we are, what we have, you have to shade out, not colour in.'

Halfway back down the hill home, I saw that Monty was limping.

'Want a lift?' I said. I'd noticed for a while that he'd been a bit less sprightly than usual. He used to leap on to our bed in the morning, but these days he put his front paws up, and waited to be hoisted the rest of the way.

OK, but put me down before we get back to our street. Don't want that dachshund to see me…

So I picked him up, muddy as he was, and carried him until we reached the top of our street, so he could strut the rest of the way. Then, when we were almost home, he stopped dead and looked up at me.

I nearly forgot. Those Melian guys… what happened?

'Oh, yeah. They didn't agree to the Athenians' terms. The Athenians besieged them. Eventually they captured the town.'

And then?

'And then they killed all the men, and sold the women and children into slavery.'

Oh.

'You asked.'

I asked.

Plato, Aristotle and the Good Life

On this second walk, Monty and I discuss the ethical theories of Plato and Aristotle, along with other Ancient philosophies that focus on the idea of happiness and the nature of the good life. We also examine the idea that morality is a special kind of *sense* or *feeling* possessed by people.

'Heath or graveyard?'

Graveyard. But you promise not to be morbid, and start composing your epitaphs again?

'It's just a bit of fun. A hobby. A chap needs a hobby.'

Our local graveyard really is quite beautiful. Some parts are well manicured and as neat and regular as a couplet by Alexander Pope. Other areas have gone wild and, should my domestic situation deteriorate drastically, I've had vague fantasies of living there in a shelter made from bent willow boughs, and sleeping on a bed of bracken, with Monty for warmth and a bottle of methylated spirits for company. We don't have many major celebrities, but we do have the inventor of mouthwash, Joseph Lister, buried under a plain granite slab. And it's true, I spend a lot of time in there composing my own epitaphs, and imagining them neatly carved on my own plain slab.

Beneath this stone

There lies poor Tone;

Once flesh, now bone,

He died alone.

No, not morbid at all.

There was a bench at the far side of the graveyard, nestled among hawthorn and elder scrub. Blackbirds and chaffinches sang in the thickets, and, if I was lucky, a green woodpecker would fly heavily down (they always look as though they've just eaten a pie and had a skinful of ale) and start probing for ants in the grass. It was a good place to philosophize. Or it was once Monty had gone on a quick rampage, scampering along the rows of graves in pursuit of whatever it was that had left the scent: fox or tramp. Finally, he came back and scrambled wetly onto my lap.

'That hip of yours feeling better?'

Just the odd twinge. Anyway, where were we? he said, stifling a yawn.

'Late night?'

That was a yawn of excitement. It's a dog thing. Maybe you can give me the bullet point version.

'Sure.

1. There is little agreement about moral values, which vary greatly between individuals, and over time and space.
2. Some say that this is evidence that morality boils down to power, or custom, or whim, all of which change.
3. So our challenge is to see if we can find an objective basis for making judgements about right and wrong, a way of saying that you're a good dog or a bad dog in the same way I could say that you're a triangle or a square.
4. And with any luck we'd be able to persuade the Athenians not to kill and enslave the Melians…'

Got it, thanks.

'There have been many attempts to give an objective basis for morality, but you can divide them fairly neatly into, let me see, five different strands of ethical thinking.'

Worth listing them for me?

'OK, but it won't make much sense before we go into the details. First, we have the extreme moral realism of Plato – realism in this sense just means that he believes that the Good, for example, is a thing that really exists as a separate, objective entity. Second, we have the idea that humans possess a moral sense, akin to our sense of vision or smell. Third, we have Aristotelian virtue ethics, and other ethical systems based on the idea of living a good life. Fourth, we have deontological ethics, or ethics as a form of rule-following, particularly focusing on Immanuel Kant. And finally, we have utilitarianism, or ethics based on maximizing happiness. Got that?'

I think so. Sorta. As you say, at the moment it's just words. But a quick question about some of those words. You sometimes say 'moral' and you sometimes say 'ethical'. Are they the same thing?

'Good dog – now you're thinking like a philosopher. It's very important to make sure that we're using words in a consistent way, and that their meanings are made clear. Up until now I've been using the terms a bit randomly, to mean, broadly, *concerned with how to tell right from wrong*. However, usually, *ethics* means the code of behaviour that exists in a particular setting or organization – so you'd talk about *business ethics*, meaning the sorts of behaviour deemed acceptable in that context. But it would also include the code that exists in a whole society. *Morals* usually means the set of principles by which a person lives their life. But there's a slight woolliness in the distinction, so let's just assume that when I use either I'm using them in that sense of *issues to do with deciding right and wrong*.'

Check.

'So, these five strands... I'm going to begin with what I take to be a couple of duds – ways of thinking about ethics that don't really help us at all. Then we'll look at the good ones, and we'll find out if any foot fits the golden slipper.'

It's a plan!

'I'm going to begin again with Plato. Although, as I said, he's the most revered of all philosophers, and pretty well invented the subject, controversially I'm a little of the opinion that he gets almost everything wrong.'

Eh?

'We've already seen that Plato has, in some dialogues, associated virtue with happiness. But what he means is that virtue will result in happiness, and vice in unhappiness. He's not saying that they are the same thing. So what then is virtue for Plato? To answer this fully we'll need to look into Plato's metaphysics—'

His what?

'... and particularly his ontology—'

His who?

'OK, I really am going to talk much more about those things later on, but for now, metaphysics and ontology are the parts of philosophy that deal with the ultimate nature of reality.'

Okaaaaaay...

'Plato is the supreme objectivist in ethics. He believes that Virtue or Goodness are *real things*, types of entities he terms *Forms*, existing in a special, transcendent realm with other similar concepts such as Beauty, Justice, Equality and Courage.

Plato's theory of Forms is one of the most famous, but also difficult, of all philosophical theories, but for now think of the Forms as the Ideal, the perfect, timeless template for things that are copied crudely in the world around us.'

Struggling a bit, if I'm honest.

'You will do, it's hard. But it'll become clearer. Just stick with me. The reason why the poor citizens in the early dialogues were so bamboozled, unable to satisfy Socrates' question "What is X?", was that they did not know the true nature of Goodness, etc., but only saw the various confusing examples before them, poor reflections of the true Good. Plato believes that if a person knows what is right, he or she will always do it. Wickedness comes only from ignorance. And so the path to virtue is through knowledge. And that knowledge is knowledge of the Forms.

So, an act is good if it resembles or *partakes in* the Form of the Good. On another walk we're going to examine the problems with Plato's theory of Forms at considerable length, but for now it's enough to point out that it is very difficult to show plausibly how we can come to know the Form of the Good, given that we do not have direct access to the transcendent realm where the Forms dwell. But even if we could, somehow, discover this objective Good, there is the question of the relationship between the Form of the Good and any individual act of goodness. How does a huge blob of perfect goodness somewhere in this transcendental realm, a place beyond perception, help me to decide if I should put a pound into this busker's hat, or grab the hat and run laughing to the nearest pub?'

Don't look at me, I'm just a small blob of imperfect dog.

'Plato's answer is that it all becomes clear as soon as we come to know the Form of the Good. The Platonic system sets up a triangular structure for any moral judgement. There is the Form of the Good, there is the act in the world and there is the moral judgement. We look at the act, check it against the Form and make our ruling. Simple.'

Sounds reasonable.

'But there is a serious problem here for Plato. The great eighteenth-century Scottish philosopher David Hume had a profoundly troubling insight into the language of ethics. He saw that there were two very different types of statement involved in moral claims. There are *is* statements, and there are *ought* statements. *Is* statements tell you about matters of fact, things that exist in the world. *Ought* statements make moral judgements, or tell you what ought to be the case. Hume points out that there is no logical way of getting from one to the other.'

Huh?

'Hume says that whenever he reads other philosophers or moral thinkers, he finds that they will use the language of *is* and *is not*, and then they'll suddenly move on to the language of *ought* and *ought not*, without ever explaining or justifying that transition.

Now let's assume that it is a statement of fact that the Form of the Good exists; but how can we go from this *descriptive* statement to the *prescriptive* statement that you should behave in a certain way? There is, it appears, simply no compelling reason to make the leap between them. Do you follow?'

I think so. You have this Form of the Good thingy, and then you have some people doing stuff. And you want to use the Form Thing to show that what the people are doing is right or wrong. But why should the Form Thing, even if it exists, be a reason for you to say that what the people are doing is right or wrong? Is that it?

'Roughly. Or woofly.'

But then isn't this a big deal for all these theories about right and wrong? Don't you always have this gap between the is *and the* ought?

'Excellent point. And you're right. Hume's exposure of the gap between the *is* and the *ought*, between statements of fact and assertions of value, is a problem for any objectivist theory of ethics, and its shadow looms over this whole discussion. In fact, most of the moral theories we'll be examining are designed to overcome that gap. Hume's own solution was that the *is/ought* gap can never be bridged using logic or rationality. What happens is that custom and habit simply lead us to connect certain facts (stealing the busker's hat) and the moral judgement (Stop, thief!). However, Plato needs more than that. He wants to establish a *necessary connection* between the existence of the Form of the Good, and the moral demand that we imitate it.

A more fundamental problem is that the very existence of the transcendental Forms is highly contentious – and we'll be contending that most vigorously on a later walk!

Before moving on to some of the other ethical systems, I should point out that Plato's most detailed working-out of how we should live doesn't actually explicitly entail the theory of Forms. In the *Republic*, Plato describes his ideal society, which in its organization replicates the structure of the human soul. For Plato the soul is made up of three parts, *spirit*, *appetite* and *reason*. Spirit is the fount of courage, as well as anger. Appetite, unsurprisingly, is the source of lust and hunger. Reason is the boss, the charioteer harnessing and guiding the energies of the other two.

In the state, there are also three classes: the rulers – those Guardians we met right at the beginning, who are like faithful dogs, looking after the inhabitants of the house and seeing off intruders—'

They sound like fine fellows!

'You may come to reconsider that... Then we have the soldiers (or Auxiliaries) and, finally, the workers. The Guardians, who correspond to reason in the soul, would be trained from childhood in wisdom, a wisdom that would enable them to know and understand the Forms, and govern the state in accordance with them, bringing human life into a harmony with the underlying beauty and perfection of the universe.'

What could be better?

'In the state, as in the soul, justice comes from each part or class performing its own proper function, without interfering with the others. The job of the Guardians is to rule, the Auxiliaries to fight and the workers to work. It is a rigid regime, embodying Plato's own distrust of democracy and the disorder he believed it brought.

One of the more modern-sounding and attractive aspects of Plato's state is the relative equality it affords to women. Women could be Guardians, and Plato explicitly argues that they are just as capable as men of attaining the required wisdom and knowledge. The children of the Guardians were to be brought up collectively, preventing favouritism or family ties from interfering with the correct governance of the state. And for the same reason the Guardians would be prevented from owning any property. Famously, Plato banned most art, music and literature from his perfect city. Art, being a copy of a copy, takes us further away from reality; music, other than certain military marches, corrupts. Literature lies…

And talking of lying, perhaps the most sinister aspect of the system is the concept of the Noble Lie, or pious fiction, depending on which translation you read. To dissuade the workers from thinking that they might be worth something more than toiling all day for their betters, Plato suggests that they be told something he admits is untrue – that each class is formed from a different type of metal, the workers from iron and brass, the Auxiliaries from silver and the Guardians from (of course!) gold. The only defence for this dishonesty is that it promotes social cohesion and patriotism.'

You're not really selling it, you know.

'I know. We've got a state with an elite ruling over the masses with force and lies; a place with little art, and not much pleasure. Its closest real-world embodiment was Sparta, democratic Athens' old enemy. Unsurprisingly, Plato's ideal state doesn't have many advocates today. He was included by Karl Popper – who we'll meet on a later walk, when we discuss the philosophy of science – among the enemies of what he calls the *open society*. But there are ways to offer at least a partial defence. Most of us agree that expertise is important in all sorts of areas. Plato himself uses the example of the captain of a ship. Given a choice between sailing with a captain who had trained for years, acquiring all the skills necessary to navigate safely, and someone who just said, "Yeah, I reckon I'll give that a go" without acquiring any of the skills needed, then you'd walk up the gangplank with the guy who'd earned his Captain's hat, wouldn't you? The same would apply to brain surgeons or bridge builders. Is it really so strange, then, to expect the most important job of all – leading the state – to be in the hands of experts?

Plato yearned for stability and order – unsurprising, given the chaos his home state suffered for most of his life. Democracy for him signalled havoc. The other systems of government, based on a single ruler (kingship, or tyranny) or on a group distinguished only by their wealth (oligarchy) or inherited privilege (aristocracy), seem worse, if anything.

But it's no good. Plato's Forms are a failure when it comes to finding a workable moral theory, and his state, despite being based on ethical principles, the search for virtue and truth, feels like an anticipation of the totalitarian regimes of the twentieth century.'

So that's Plato kicked into touch. What's next?

Don't worry, Plato will be back! Our second attempt to build a solid foundation for ethics has some things in common with the objectivism of Plato. It begins with that intuition that many of us have that we just know what is right and what is wrong. *I feel it in my guts*, you might say, about some action that you know to be wrong. If pressed about where this might come from, you find yourself repeating *I just know it*, perhaps accompanying the statement with a frown, or a hand laid on your breast.

This conviction that each human has an unfailing moral sense, akin to our other natural faculties, was first set out by philosophers in the seventeenth and eighteenth centuries, such as Anthony Ashley-Cooper, 3rd Earl of Shaftesbury (1671–1713) and Francis Hutcheson (1694–1746). It might be given a religious emphasis – that knowledge of good and evil is planted in us by a benign God – or it could be given a more humanist spin

– we are by our natures benign and kindly creatures. If sometimes this light of goodness is dimmed, that is because of the corruptions of so-called civilization.'

I'm liking this one, so far. It's nice to think that you lot might just know what's right.

'One version of this conception of morality (and humanity) was put forward by Jean-Jacques Rousseau (1712–78). For Rousseau, humans naturally have just two moral sentiments. The first is a perfectly rational sense of self-preservation, which he terms *amour de soi*. The second is a horror at suffering experienced by others, which he calls *pitié* (compassion). The process of civilization takes away our ancient freedom, and replaces it with all the familiar vices of the modern world and corrupts *amour de soi* to *amour propre* – the very different self-love of "modern" man, a self-love driven by envy, and the desire for power and wealth.

The most recent version of the idea that we have an in-built moral sense was put forward in the twentieth century by G.E. Moore (1873–1958). Moore argues that good is a simple entity, a thing we recognize instinctively without having to define it. Indeed, we can't define it, other than by pointing at it. We simply *grasp* the good when we see it (or feel it), as an intuition. In this way it is like a colour. You don't need a complex theory to explain *red* – anyone with normal colour vision can see it. (Of course there is a scientific definition of red, having to do with light waves at a certain frequency, but that is never what we mean when we say "The car is red".) So, in the same way, we *see* the good. Or perhaps a better comparison is taste. The good is like a sweet taste; the bad like a sour one.

There's an initial plausibility to this view, and it was very popular among artists and intellectuals (though not many philosophers) in the first half of the twentieth century. Indeed the emotivist argument outlined on the last walk was originally devised to counter it.'

Really? I don't quite get that.

'The G.E. Moore line was that as long as your moral sense is working correctly, the judgements it makes will have an objective *rightness*, in the way someone with normal colour vision will be right in saying an apple is green and the sky blue. The emotivist agrees that it's a feeling that you may well have, but says it does not correspond to any objective truth. It's purely like your preference for tea over coffee.'

OK, with you.

'So we must enquire a little more closely into what these good things are that Moore claims we perceive so readily. It is not really very surprising that Moore and his friends regarded as *good* those things that happened to be most in fashion in their group, the Bloomsbury set. They valued friendship, love, art, nature. They disapproved of laws or rules that interfered with the enjoyment of their particular pleasures.'

Sounds OK. So what's wrong with it, then?

'We can pick away at each of the various strands of Moore's version of the moral sense theory. The first, that the good is indefinable, rather begs the question. (Remembering that if the good *is* definable, then our intellects can pick it out, without the need for the moral sense.) There have been endless attempts to define the good. We'll come across many more of them as we go on. Moore's response to any definition is to say, "Oh, that's just not what the good *really* is. These are things that may be *associated* with the good, but the good is something else, this other thing that I can see, and you, dear boy, appear not to be able to see." Moore's theory therefore replaces argument with assertion:

we are not given reasons for the statement that the good is a simple, obvious quality, like colour. We're just told that if we don't see it, it's down to a lack of intelligence or education, like someone not getting opera or the ballet.

But a more fundamental challenge to both types of moral sense argument (I'm lumping together here Moore's objectivism and the earlier views about morality being a capacity within us) is presented by those who simply dispute the benign conception of humanity and society it presents.'

What, you're going to tell me that people aren't naturally good? Pardon me if I don't faint with the shock.

'Plenty of philosophers have found humans to be anything but benign. Thomas Hobbes (1588–1679) famously saw life in a state of nature as being a war of all against all, with human existence being nasty, brutish and short, and no hint of a moral sense in the heart of the ignoble savage. Hence his belief that we need a strong, undivided sovereign to keep the peace. In *The Fable of the Bees* (1714) Bernard Mandeville (1670–1733) shows us a vision of humanity driven by selfishness and greed. He even turns the old clichés about the innocence and naturalness of children on their head. Yes, he says, we can find humanity in its purest form in the hearts of children ... and it is a ruthless, selfish thing, egotistical, craving, gorging, violent. The irony is that Mandeville sees these things not as humankind's ruin, but its salvation. Society needs the selfishness, violence and ambition of people to function. Without thieves, the lawyers would be out of business, and without the lawyers, sundry other trades would disappear, throwing thousands into destitution. The vain and lecherous libertine employs tailors, cooks, hairdressers and others to pander to his depravities. The commercial success of a society is driven by the greed and selfishness of the individuals who make it up. All of these private vices add up to a public benefit.

So, the inner-sense school of ethics fails because it looks too much like a simple justification for certain preconceptions, rather than an objective basis for making ethical choices. Its view of humanity is naïve and simplistic. Another criticism is that relying on some inner sense of right and wrong or on a simple perception leaves no place at all for reason. For many philosophers, morality, in order to count as morality at all, *has* to be a rational process, something arrived at using the highest human faculties, not some matter of appetites or perceptions. This is a view we'll soon see brilliantly argued by Kant.

However, before Kant, we're going to go back again to the Classical world, and the ethics of Plato's great pupil, Aristotle (384–322 BCE).'

Is Aristotle one of the, er, dog-friendly philosophers?

'If you mean is he easy to read and understand, sadly, he can be a bit dry and technical. That's because almost everything we have by him – and it's quite a lot – has come down to us in the form of his lecture notes. So, unlike Plato, we don't have polished works of art, but bare outlines, which he would have elaborated on and illustrated during his lectures. But he's one of the philosophers still very much alive and kicking, ideas-wise.'

OK. I'm all ears.

'Aristotle's thinking is representative of a number of other ethical systems in the Ancient world, all based around the idea of living a good life. And by a *good* life, Aristotle means a *happy* one. The Greek term used by Aristotle when discussing the good life is *eudaimonia*, which is famously hard to capture in translation. It means in some sense happiness, as we use the term, but is rather wider than that. Eudaimonia includes the idea not only of being happy, but of living well, of fulfilling your promise, of flourishing. So it has a material element, as well as a psychological component. The happy tramp, contented on his park bench, would not, for Aristotle, be enjoying eudaimonia. And nor is eudaimonia limited to your own direct experience. Harm to your reputation after your death would have an impact on your eudaimonia, as would misfortunes occurring to your family.

I sometimes think the English term that comes closest is *doing well*, in the way that we'd reply "he's doing well" when asked about our child, off at university or starting a new job. Doing well, meaning that, yes, he's happy, but also things are progressing acceptably in a material way, and that he hasn't been arrested yet for dancing naked in the street with a traffic cone on his head.

Aristotle argues that the aim of ethics is to help us to achieve eudaimonia, that expanded type of happiness. An approach to ethics such as Aristotle's is called *teleological*, coming from the Greek words *telos*, meaning goal or end, and *logos* meaning (in this case) a reason. We perform good acts not for their own sake, but in order to achieve something else.'

So like when I sit and come and whatnot, just to get a treat?

'Exactly. That's teleological behaviour. As I said, Aristotle's was not the only Ancient ethical system geared towards attaining eudaimonia. Two of the Ancient world's most profound and subtle philosophies also had that goal in mind. The Epicureans, named after their founder, Epicurus (341–270 BCE), thought that happiness came from pleasure, and so they have been caricatured as indulgent hedonists, seekers after the easy gratification of physical delights. There certainly were such philosophers in Ancient Greece – one group, the Cyrenaics (not to be confused with the Cynics), really did think that the only thing that mattered in life were the pleasures of the flesh. The Cyrenaic school was founded by Aristippus (c.435–356 BCE), a follower of Socrates and a contemporary of Plato. The hedonism of the Cyrenaics stemmed from their belief that the only things that really exist are physical sensations. It follows that the only thing that matters is physical pleasure, and the only way to experience it is *now*. Grab every sensual experience you can, gorge yourself, booze, love. Don't put it off. Tomorrow is an illusion. There is just now, and *this* sensation. Eat, drink and be merry, for tomorrow you die.'

What's not to like?

'The Epicureans were influenced by the Cyrenaics, but were profoundly different. Happiness may come from pleasure, but pleasure itself is a complex business, and certainly not best achieved by the reckless indulgence of our basest instincts. For Epicurus pleasure was the only good, but he defined pleasure not as a positive quality, but as the absence of pain. The goal of life is not to cram in as many hedonistic delights as possible, but to reduce stress and discomfort. The pleasures he advocated were quiet reflection, friendship, conversation and the practice of philosophy itself – a long way from the orgiastic feasting of the Cyrenaics.'

Don't knock it till you've tried it.

'Yeah, well, I guess the dog way is the path of the Cyrenaics – how many times have I had to rescue you from death by chicken bone?'

One time! Maybe twice. Three at the most.

'Whatever, not a good way to go. Epicurus actually believed that the greatest source of discomfort to any person was the terror of death and the punishment that might well follow. And so he was one of the first thinkers to argue that death should not be feared, because there is no afterlife, and so nothing left of us that could be punished. Only pain is to be feared, and death brings an end to pain. (Epicurus' defusing of the death bomb was one of his many subtle attacks on Plato, who had warned evil-doers that terrible and fitting punishments awaited them beyond the grave...)'

Can I just say that I'm not a hundred per cent convinced by that line?

'Go on...'

I like dinner. It gives me a lot of pleasure. What I'm afraid of isn't choking on a bone and then going to a place where the dinners are horrible, or where some nasty version of you shows me a nice sausage and then eats it himself. What I want is to carry on eating dinners here forever. The thought of no more dinners makes me sad.

'You make a good point, little dog. What Epicurus would answer was that the future version of you can't be unhappy or in pain or hungry, because the future version of you doesn't exist. And so it makes no sense for you to worry about what you'll be feeling then, because there won't be a you to feel. But I see that that isn't really an answer to your argument. Your argument is that your life is pleasurable, and it is irrational not to want that pleasure to go on for as long as possible. But I guess that Epicurus would come back and say that there might be a point when old age and illness mean that you aren't enjoying your life any more, and in that situation, you shouldn't fear what is to come.'

OK, can we change the subject?

'The Epicureans' main rivals at the time were the Stoics, who also taught that death should not be feared.'

I thought we were changing the subject.

'Relax, that was just a stepping stone. Perhaps more than any other Ancient philosophy, Stoic ethics was bound up with their view of the nature of the universe. For the Stoics, the universe is an orderly, benign system, in which every event is determined by a divine law, or rational principle. This divine law, which could also simply be seen as God, formed the material universe from fire, and continued to shape its development and destiny. As the spirit that determines every event that happens is good, then everything that happens must be good. All apparent evil is an illusion, and the illusion disappears as our understanding of the universe deepens.'

Really? So every time you step on an upturned plug or Lego block, that's really a good thing? You'd never know from the howling.

'They obviously didn't have electric plugs or Lego back then. Chrysippus (who we left pondering those grains of sand...) argued that every seeming evil is necessary for the existence of a corresponding good. There can be no courage without cowardice, no pleasure without pain. The same senses that scream out in agony when I step on a plug rejoice in the pleasure of stroking you. When seen in this light, the evil becomes necessary, and melds into the greater good. The philosopher's task is to understand nature, and that understanding will bring peace, even in the face of terrible suffering. The Stoic goal is to face death and disease and other calamities with calmness; a calmness made possible, not just by courage, but by the knowledge that everything, ultimately, is going to be OK. Such was eudaimonia for the Stoic.'

Do we like the Stoics?

'That's a tough one, and I think their usefulness depends on your situation. If things truly are hopeless, and you're in a position that cannot be remedied, then I think the Stoic mindset is exemplary. One always imagines a just man, wrongly accused and imprisoned. Each day he is tortured and tormented by his guards. The Stoic says, *I will endure. This is the way the world is. Viewed under the aspect of eternity, my sufferings are trivial, and in any case they are part of a plan that if I only understood it, I would see is for the best.* And more than one Stoic got the chance to put their faith to the test. Seneca the Younger, implicated in a plot to kill Nero that in reality he had nothing to do with, was ordered to commit suicide. He calmly opened his veins and then dictated his last letters and a will as he lay in the bath.'

Respect.

'On the other hand, Stoicism tends towards conservatism and the placid acceptance of whatever state of affairs you find yourself in. There are times when accepting fate is a type of moral cowardice.'

And how do you know which is which?

'It's our human duty to make these choices. But we can probably take the best of Stoicism, and say that if you can change it, change it, and if you can't, then put up with it.'

Sounds like a plan. What happened to Aristotle?

'Oh, sorry, we wandered a bit. Aristotle's analysis of eudaimonia begins with the obvious truth that human beings desire all kinds of goods. We want food, and pleasant company, and the esteem of our community, and good health. However, Aristotle says that all of these things are the means to an end: they are intended to achieve some other goal, some higher or ultimate good. This ultimate good must meet three criteria: it must be desirable for itself; it shouldn't be desired to enable you to achieve some other good; and the other goods that we desire should be desired in order to achieve it.'

An example … ?

'Take wealth. Wealth is a good, but generally it is a good because it enables you to obtain other goods, not simply for itself. Just sitting on a pile of banknotes would be crazy, wouldn't it?'

I guess.

'So, what can this ultimate good be, the thing to which all the other goods are directed?'

Buying a softer bed?

'Hah, very funny. Aristotle thinks that there is only one candidate, just one good we desire for itself: happiness. You don't want to be happy to achieve something else. On the contrary, all those other goods are simply a way to help you become happy. He barely even feels the need to justify this: he thinks it's simply obvious that we all want to be happy, bearing in mind, of course, that we are talking about the extended sense of happiness.

So, Aristotle has established happiness/eudaimonia as the ultimate good. But that doesn't quite tell us what happiness means, for humans, and without knowing that, our quest will be blind. To zone in on this, Aristotle next enquires into what the purpose or function of a *person* is. What are we good *for*? What are we best *at*? He compares us to other living things. We have many qualities and abilities in common with animals and even plants. All living things grow and reproduce and move and perceive. Or, as Aristotle puts it, our souls have *nutritive, locomotive* and *perceptive* capabilities. However, humans are unique in also possessing a *rational* part of our soul. This, then, is our function, our one unique distinguishing quality: we can use reason to control and direct our activities. Therefore the good life for us must involve our reason. Reason can help us select those qualities that help us to live the highest life a human is capable of. These qualities are the virtues.

Here we get to the meat of Aristotle's thinking on moral philosophy, and the part of his theory that has been most influential. Aristotle stands at the beginning of the tradition of so-called *virtue ethics*. The virtues are those moral guidelines or qualities that the good person must follow in order to achieve eudaimonia, defined as living the highest, most rational life that a person is capable of. For the Stoics, the virtues that were most prized were those that helped the ideal sage meet with the pains of experience: courage, fortitude, resolution. But Aristotle's idea of happiness requires other qualities.'

Which are…?

'What Aristotle did was to examine various areas of conduct, or types of feeling, and show how the way people behave could go wrong either by displaying an excess of a quality, or an insufficiency. And right smack in between those extremes we find what he termed the *golden mean* – the sweet spot, which is virtue.'

Er, examples might help here…

'Of course. In a battle, there are those who show an excess of fear and a tendency to run away. That is the vice of cowardice. But there are also those who are excessively confident, who rush into fatal situations without any regard to the chances of success. That is the vice of rashness. But between the two, we find the mean of courage. The courageous man will be aware of, but undaunted by, danger, and will perform his duty. He will not be without fear, but will face it with calmness and resolution. Aristotle has a whole table of virtues, showing the excess, the deficiency and the mean. With regard to physical pleasures (which few Ancient Greeks ignored), we have the extremes of licentiousness and insensibility – one displayed by a person enslaved by his desires, the other the fault of someone blind to the authentic pleasures of the flesh. In the middle, we have the person who is temperate, who does not overindulge, but is moderate in his enjoyments of food and drink and the other bodily delights. (Interestingly, Aristotle says that the person deficient in this quality is so rare as to not even have a name. The Greeks were evidently a fun-loving people. We, of course, do have such a name: Puritan.) Turning to what Aristotle calls self-expression, we have braggarts on one side, who always exaggerate their accomplishments, and those who deliberately understate on the other, ironically self-deprecating. Aristotle takes this to be another form of vanity, and he has a little dig at Socrates, who was always claiming to know nothing. And then there is, at the mean, the sincere and truthful person.

Not all the virtues examined by Aristotle are particularly exalted. As we've seen, the Greeks liked to talk. On one side we have the buffoon, who descends to vulgarity to get a laugh. On the other side there is the sour-faced bore, who takes offence at everything and ruins everyone's fun. And between them our witty person, who entertains all without straying from good taste. Aristotle imagines all these qualities existing on a continuum, and most people will find themselves on it at some point. Knowing the mean enables you to strive towards the ideal.'

This all sounds quite good. I like this formula. You get big ugly dogs, and little runty dogs, and perfect me-sized dogs in the middle.

'Aristotle's way of identifying what counts as a virtue has a lot going for it. In most situations we can see that there are excessive extremes and a sensible middle path. Generosity manifests itself not simply in reacting against meanness, but by steering clear of vulgar and excessive recklessness.

It's possible that we could find some virtues that don't quite seem to work in this way. Is honesty really the mid-point between lying and telling too much truth? But for many of them, Aristotle's scheme is persuasive. And it's worth pointing out that Aristotle himself said that ethics and politics were not sciences, offering the same sort of secure truth that geometry or (he claimed) metaphysics could deliver, but "soft" sciences, in which we can only hope to get somewhere near the truth.

And how do we acquire the virtues? Education education education. We become virtuous, says Aristotle, by practising virtue. If we inculcate the young with good habits, they will become second nature. Much like training a, er, dog.'

Woof.

'Aristotle's vision for achieving the good life – that we all aim for a version of eudaimonia, that our rationality is bound up with happiness and that we achieve the best life through exercising the virtues – is an attractive package, and has been hugely influential. The Ancient philosophers gradually focused on the virtues of wisdom (or prudence), courage, temperance and justice, and these then were handed on to Christianity as the cardinal virtues. But some early Christians felt that these pre-Christian qualities needed to be supplemented, and so the four became seven, each virtue balancing a corresponding vice: chastity/lust; temperance/gluttony; charity/greed; diligence/sloth; patience/wrath; kindness/envy; humility/pride. And rather than Aristotle's worldly happiness, the goal was to share in eternal happiness with God. What Aristotle's ethical system does is to ground the way we ought to live in an idea of the kind of creatures we are, social and rational, and find a way for us to live together.'

And now the downside?

'The way that the virtues could be adapted, changing with the needs of the evolving culture, is both a strength and a weakness. True, it means that the ethical code can stay relevant, but it also means that the virtues simply look like a list of the things that are valued by whatever society you happen to be in. If we asked Aristotle why courage is a good thing in itself, his answer would be that it and the other virtues he describes are simply what we, as rational, social beings, need to live well in the typical Greek city state. There is no deeper grounding than that. So, if Nazi Germany, or the Soviet Union under Stalin, requires different qualities for living well, Aristotle can offer no critique.

Another problem with the virtues is that it's possible to think of situations in which we might well not see them as virtuous. Is courage in pursuit of an evil end still a virtue?'

I hear you. You get brave bad dogs.

'However, the main criticism that I can see is that in some ways Aristotle's ethics aren't ethical at all, in the sense that we usually understand the term. For Aristotle, and the other Classical eudaemonists, it is your *own* happiness that is your central concern. The happiness of others simply isn't your business. Living ethically is the psychological version of going to the gym or eating well: you're looking after yourself. Even though the virtues are social in nature, the justification is always egotistical: this is the best thing for *me*. This is how *I* should live to get the most out of *my* life.'

I noticed that Monty was shivering a little.

'Talking of ethics, I'm thinking it's a little unkind to keep you out in this damp. Anyway, I'm peckish. You?'

I wouldn't say no to a biscuit.

So we walked back through the old monuments to the dead who were loved, or feared, or just rich enough to be commemorated in marble. There were angels, and there were draped urns, and there were ziggurats, as though an exiled Babylonian potentate had washed up in West Hampstead.

Walk 3

Dare to Know: Kant and the Utilitarians

On this walk, Monty and I complete our ethical chat. Much of this section is taken up with Kant's moral philosophy, which tries to find universal rules of conduct that any rational person must obey. We then discuss the utilitarians, who regarded happiness as the only true measure of good. We conclude by seeing if any of the moral systems we've looked at can resolve the moral dilemmas we all face.

The next day I felt that we needed to go somewhere fresh to finish off our ethics conversation, but I liked the idea of continuing our graveyard theme, death always helping to focus the mind on what sort of a life you've been leading. So we walked up the hill to Hampstead Village, and the lovely church of St John's. The churchyard is a tiny piece of wilderness in the heart of the city, elegantly overgrown and dotted with ancient graves, many too worn to read. The painter John Constable is here, and 'Clock' Harrison, of *Longitude* fame. Or has that fame already wound down? Harrison designed a clock accurate enough to enable mariners to establish their longitude, and robust enough to survive the rigours of a long voyage. He is credited with saving the lives of thousands of sailors. Did that make Harrison's life a virtuous one? It's possible that without his device the British Empire, dependent as it was on mastery of the seas, would not have been so successful for so long. Do we lay two hundred years of colonial oppression at the feet of the clock-maker? How far does our personal responsibility go? Is it my intentions, or the consequences of my actions, that count?

I don't know; you tell me.

'Oh, sorry, I hadn't realized we'd started. Was I talking aloud?'

Don't worry, it's just you and me.

There was a particular bench I always sat on. It was springy and supple, and the time-smoothed strakes of ash moulded comfortingly to my back. The bench was on a raised bank, and it gave me a view over the graveyard wall, and across the gardens and roofs of Hampstead. I pulled Monty up beside me, and let him nuzzle under my coat. The coat was a Bulgarian army-surplus issue, and made me look like one of the more interesting varieties of tramp, the survivor of a forgotten Balkan war, per-haps, or a destitute former goth-band bass guitarist.

'You ready?'

Hit me. Maybe a quick recap, first?

'Sure. As we've seen, with the exception of Plato, most of the Ancients looked to found morality on some concept of living a "good" life, which generally meant a way of living happily or well in the world. The Cynics enjoined us to live simply, casting off the empty luxury of modern life; the Epicureans nudged us towards a life of pleasure, but advised us to maximize the pleasure not through excess, but through moderation, calmness, friendship and reflection. Aristotle's good life was one in which we devote ourselves to philosophical contemplation, if we can, and otherwise live a life guided by rationality, embodied in the practice of the virtues. Plato's ethics had a more objective basis, in that being good involved acting in accordance with the Form of the Good. What this might mean in practice is indicated by the *Republic*: justice is each person fulfilling his or her appropriate role in a state ruled by philosophers, in which individual rights are subservient to the good of the whole. But there is also a strong suggestion that this life is also a good one in the same sense as the others: it provides the best chance of living happily and well.

However, for one great philosopher – possibly the greatest – none of these ways of thinking about ethics was adequate. Immanuel Kant (1724–1804) belongs to a completely different strand of philosophical ethics to the eudaemonists. For Kant, acting morally, doing the right thing, for the right reasons, always means acting in accordance with some rule. Ethics based on rule-following is usually called *deontological ethics*. The word comes from *deon*, the Greek for obligation or duty, and it isn't directly connected to "ontological" or "ontology", the philosophical investigation of being or existence. You don't really need to remember the word "deontological", other than to make you sound clever.

Kant has a reputation for being dry and difficult. It's a reputation he's earned: his greatest works are astoundingly challenging, expressing the most complex ideas in the most convoluted and technical language. It's easy to see his life as being correspondingly dry and, if not difficult, then dull. He lived his life entirely in the town of Konigsberg, in Eastern Prussia. Not quite the backwater it has sometimes been portrayed as, but not exactly the beating heart of the intellectual universe. Prussia was a closely monitored and regimented society, with both a fundamentalist church and highly militarized state encroaching into almost every aspect of life.

Externally, Kant seemed well suited to such a state. He was utterly chaste and correct in his behaviour (at least after he settled into middle age – there are stories of moderate high jinks and a mild dalliance or two as a young man). He never married, wore plain clothes, which over the course of his long life changed in hue only in that the light brown of his giddy youth became the dark brown of his maturity. He was famous for the regularity of his habits. There's one familiar story about Kant's afternoon stroll being so predictable that the local folk would set their watches by it. Though this always made me wonder about how Kant knew that his own watch was telling the right time. I imagined that he'd send his boy down into town to enquire – perhaps of the self-same burghers who set their watches by Kant's stroll…'

Focus! I'm still waiting to find out how we can save the Melians…

'Sorry! And yet, despite all this external conformity, Kant was also a revolutionary and inspiring intellectual, a genuine radical in every sense of the word. Over the course of the eighteenth century, the writers and philosophers of what came to be known as the Enlightenment had begun to challenge the intellectual, social and political status quo. The Enlightenment is in many ways an elusive and shifting concept, the term encompassing proto-Romantics such as Rousseau, and cold rationalists like La Mettrie, who believed that man was a machine. But everywhere they challenged, goaded and satirized the existing order. Their rallying cry was *écrasez l'infâme* – slay the infamous, the infamous being variously the established churches, the aristocracy, the monarchs. Kant is the culmination of Enlightenment thinking about the nature of man and the world. He believed that people should throw off the shackles that had restricted both their freedom and their reason – the political shackles of a repressive society and the intellectual shackles of traditional thought, religious and secular. His own slogan – he wasn't really a slaying kind of person – was *dare to know* – accept the challenge to stand on your own feet, thinking for yourself, exercising the two defining characteristics of humanity: freedom and rationality.'

I noticed that Monty was looking at me strangely. He almost appeared a little embarrassed.

'Oh, er, yes, I can get carried away with Kant. It's a bit silly and immature to have favourite philosophers, but if I had one, it would be him. We'll talk about his revolutionary contributions to epistemology and metaphysics later, but today it's his ethics.

But Kant's is not the only ethics to be based on the notion of following a rule. So I'll first make a couple of general points about the concept. One key idea is that you don't follow the rules because they suit you, or because you like the results or consequences of following the rules, or because they give you a warm feeling inside. You follow the rules *because they are the rules*. In fact, the less you want to follow them and the more you have to sweat to force yourself to obey, the more moral it is to follow them.'

Huh?

'Think it through – if you wanted to do it anyway, you wouldn't need a rule. And if you followed the rule because the consequences were appealing to you, then you'd have acted as you did not for the sake of the rule, but for the consequences.'

Monty gave me one of his faintly baffled looks.

Some examples might help. What sort of rules are we talking about? And, er, where do they come from?

'That's two good questions. One answer – the first – is that they come from God. Almost every religion has them. In fact, you could say in one sense that that's what religion is: the series of rules that you follow.'

You're talking about the ten thingies, aren't you?

'That's not a bad place to start. Take maybe the most famous one—'

Thou shalt not covet thy neighbour's ass?

'Funny. No, *Thou shalt not kill*. There it is in all its glory and simplicity. It doesn't say thou shalt not kill unless it brings you some benefit. Or thou shalt not kill unless you can prevent some greater harm by killing. Killing is wrong. End of story. Why is it wrong? Because the rule says so.'

Brilliant. I haven't killed anyone. Therefore I'm a good dog.

'You're forgetting the other nine. Can I just mention *Thou shalt not steal*?'

At this Monty looked suitably embarrassed.

She shouldn't have left that cheesecake on the coffee table when she went out of the room.

'Remember how the rules work? It's not OK to steal just because someone leaves their cheesecake unguarded.'

Hmmmm… OK, these rules, you're supposed to follow them – why?

'You could try to argue that following these rules – the Ten Commandments, for example – leads to a better society for everyone. A society in which people (or dogs) go around randomly killing each other isn't going to be a happy one, is it? But, as I said, that's a different sort of argument to the rule-following one. It's a kind of argument we'll come to later, one based on consequences (it is a version of what is called rule utilitarianism). The rule-following argument doesn't look to those sorts of defences. It's not about the consequences – it's about the rule.

Another one would be *don't lie*. You might think of all kinds of situations in which it might seem right to lie – if a small lie stops a greater harm, for example. But the rule is *don't lie*, so it's never morally acceptable to lie.

Deontological ethics has various good things going for it. Well, one big thing, really. Simplicity. You know where you are with a rule. With all the other ethical systems we've looked at, the moral agent has to do real work. Work that lasts a lifetime. To begin to comprehend Plato's Forms takes years of education and study. Aristotelian virtues also take years of inculcation to become good habits. Understanding nature fully is almost impossibly hard for the Stoic sage. Even the life of pleasure envisaged by the Epicurean involves the careful consideration of which actions will lead to the greatest ease, the least discombobulation. But following a rule? Anyone can do that. And billions do – if we assume that much of the world's population takes its ethical stance from religion.'

Well, that's nice and straightforward. I get that. Are we done?

'You know very well that there's a but.'

Sure I do.

'The obvious question to ask about the rules is how they originate. Where do the rules come from?'

God, you said…

'So what might go wrong with that?'

Monty shrugged. *God's not really my, er, field.*

'Well, first, some people believe in God, and some don't, and if your morality depends on there being one, that's a whole load of people who get a free pass from having to be good.'

I see that. If you say don't steal the cheesecake, and I say why, and you say because God says so, and I don't believe in God, then I can steal the cheesecake.

'Nail. On. Head. And there's another sort of problem – one our guy Plato pointed out way back. Let's take our *Thou shalt not kill* rule. Is it wrong to kill because God gave us the commandment, or did God give us the commandment because it's wrong to kill?'

Huh?

'Not sure how I can make it any simpler. So I'll just say it again. The rule against killing – is it a rule just because God says it's a rule? Would anything God commands be the *right* thing, whatever it was? If the commandment had been *Thou shalt kill*, would that then be the right thing to do?'

That's nuts! Why would God say that?

'God can say anything.'

Well, I don't like it. God – if there is one – wouldn't tell us to do bad things… would he?

'Some gods might. Plenty of gods seemed to enjoy the odd human sacrifice… The God of the Old Testament wasn't above a bit of that himself. But, no, you've struck on the heart of the matter. We recoil from the idea that these rules are arbitrary – that they simply reflect the whims of God. We want to believe that they somehow embody a greater principle…'

You mean that God chose them because they are right, not that they are right because he chose them?

'Exactly. And you see the next stage of the argument?'

Oh, if God chose them because they were right, it means that the rightness – the rules – must have existed separately from God. He just put into words something that was already there. Something, er, greater than him?

'Not sure we can say greater, but certainly something independent. So, you see, we've managed to cancel God out from the equation. For now. Another way to look at this argument is to think about the different ways in which, for example, Christianity has been used and interpreted over the years. There is enough material in the Old and New Testaments to justify any number of moral stances. If someone offends you, do you pluck out their eye, or turn the other cheek?

This range of interpretations is not just historical, but contemporary. Fire and brimstone American evangelicals who want to send gay people to hell for all eternity, and sweet liberal Anglicans, both give their sermons on a Sunday morning. Both would say that they are following the word of God, but each side selects what they want from the Bible. I've done it myself. The story of the woman taken in adultery always gets me. The scribes and Pharisees come for Jesus. They've got a woman who has committed adultery. The sentence in the law is clear: she must be stoned. Jesus is known for his reverence for the law, but also for his mercy. It's a trap – either he upholds the law, proving that he is a good Jew, and abandons his principles, or he sticks by his principles, and shows that he is a bad Jew. His solution, with the crowd looking on, is wonderful. He writes first in the dust with his finger. We're not told what. I suspect he's doodling, trying to come up with the right answer. Finally he hits on it. If anyone here hasn't sinned, let him cast the first stone. The mob, reduced to silence, disperses. Go away, and sin no more, says Jesus to the woman.'

Nice story. And your point… ?

'Oh, yeah, sorry, my point was that I chose that story out of the many possible stories in the Bible, because it appeals to my pre-existing moral framework. But I'm basically just supporting

Plato's critique of the view that something is right because God or the Bible says it is so.'

Hmmph. So is that the end of the idea that morality is all about following rules?

'No. Like I said, philosophy is a very long conversation… The question now is can you save the rule-based approach to ethics without having God there to back you up? And that takes us neatly back to Kant.'

Ta-dah!

'Kant tried to find some rules that would apply to any human being, any time, anywhere, and which didn't need God. Not because he was irreligious, or anti-God. He was brought up as a devout Lutheran, and although there's a big debate about the extent to which God plays any role in his philosophy, what he writes is not incompatible with a religious view of the world. But his ruling principle is reason. Morality is doomed, Kant believes, unless it can be grounded in universal reason, in rational principles that can be grasped by the intellect.

Kant begins his great project by summing up and dismissing all previous ethical systems, whether based on following some internal feeling, or simply following custom, or on the supposed practical benefits of being good. In all these cases, behaving morally is *contingent*: it's a way of achieving something else, or an almost accidental by-product of some other process. But this isn't good enough for Kant. He wanted to find a way of establishing that lying, for example, is *always* wrong, whatever the circumstances.

As well as universal, Kant says that reason demands that the law be simple. Real life is complicated, and human beings have endless wants, desires and needs that can get in the way, and confuse our understanding of the right way to behave. But if morality really can be founded on reason, the way that mathematics is, then we can ignore or cut away those complications, and see the truth standing clear. (There's an interesting contrast here with Aristotle, who, as I've said, regarded ethics and politics as imperfect sciences, unlike metaphysics and mathematics. He thought the best we could do with ethical principles was to get it almost right, feeling our way towards the truth in the murky light of evening, rather than seeing it in the crystalline clarity of midday.) So that's what we're looking for, a single universal principle that tells us what to do. Or what not to do.'

Big ask.

'He began, as I said, by assuming that human beings really are rational, and able, by clear thought and careful pondering, to work out the universal moral laws. He thinks we really can find this *categorical imperative*—'

The what now?

'Don't panic! A categorical imperative just means a rule you *have* to follow, not in any particular situation, but in every case. It's distinguished from a *hypothetical imperative* of which there are countless, and which is a rule you follow in order to achieve something else.'

Oh, a bit like the lesser goods that Aristotle talked about? The ones that help you get to the ultimate good.

'Excellent, yes! If we set ourselves a goal (an end) – say, getting that box of treats from the cupboard – this compels us in practice to follow certain actions or means, which will help us achieve that end. These acts are hypothetical imperatives – imperatives because if we would achieve the end, we must do them; hypothetical, because these means only pertain to that specific aim. Sometimes it will be right to do these things, and other times not. But what Kant wants is an imperative that is not a means to a specific end, but one that is *right all the time*. The categorical imperative is obeyed as a duty, and not merely to achieve some advantage or some other goal.'

I still don't quite get it.

'What sort of rule could be followed in every ethical situation? *Do the right thing* just begs the question. *Do what God says* has already been shown to be circular, or insane. *Act according to the virtues* has been shown to merely conform to the existing norms of society. *Seek eudaimonia* is more about personal happiness and fulfilment than helping you to make difficult moral decisions.

Right, drumroll, the categorical imperative says *Act always in such a way that your action could become a universal rule.*'

OK… and this means?

'So, let's say you think that it must be acceptable to steal the cheesecake, because, frankly, it's her third slice, and nobody needs that much cheesecake, and she probably doesn't really want it anyway, and they've forgotten to feed me tonight so I'm starving and could easily die.'

Yeah?

'Then Kant would say, before you steal the cheesecake, ask: would it be right to universalize that action? To say, in effect, that it's always OK to steal cheesecake? If it isn't, then don't do it.'

That actually sounds quite clever. But there's something not quite… I don't know, I'm only a dog, but doesn't it need something more? Like, er, why?

'No, that's a good point. Why should we make this our one moral principle? How is it better than any other way of thinking about morality? Let's go back to Kant's faith in reason. If we assume that humans strive to act *rationally*, then you can correct someone's behaviour by pointing out that they are behaving *irrationally*. One of the ways in which you can convince a person that they are acting irrationally is if you can show that their actions or statements are self-contradictory, in other words that the effects of doing something undermine the reasons for doing it. If someone says that they want to lose weight, yet eat a cheesecake on their own in front of the telly every night, you could probably convince them that their actions are self-contradictory.'

Good luck with that one!

'Kant argues that a moral *maxim* (that's just his name for a moral rule, a thing you do because you think it's right) must not entail contradiction. If it does, it will obviously fail to convince a rational subject. We can see how it applies to cheesecake, but how to apply it to ethics?

The example he gives is breaking a contract. If you agree to a contract and then break it, the categorical imperative asks that you imagine a world in which it was a law of nature that all contracts were broken. In that world, nobody would ever enter into a contract, and the whole institution of contracts would collapse. So, your goal – to benefit by breaking your contract – would end in failure. Or take lying. Lying is only a useful strategy in a world in which most people tell the truth. If everyone always lied, there'd be no point in you lying, as you wouldn't be believed.

So, the categorical imperative says check what you do against this principle: what would happen if everyone did it?

There is an intuitive feeling of rightness to this principle of universalizability. We've all heard the exclamation (as children, probably), *What would happen if we all did that?* And perhaps we feel its weight.'

Well, I'm quite impressed. But I presume you're about to pick holes in it?

'To begin with, I should say that Kant's ethical system still has many adherents. But his view certainly isn't invulnerable to criticism. One attack says that the Kantian formula is *empty*, in that it doesn't actually have any ethical content. All we have is a rule that says what would happen if I universalized *this* (whatever *this* is). Why can't I have as my maxim *Always tell the truth, unless you're Anthony McGowan*? I'd be quite happy to have that law universalized.'

And Kant would say...?

'One answer is to do with the definition of a maxim. Kant says a maxim has to be a general rule, with wide applicability, and the *Do x except for Anthony McGowan* doesn't fit that. He would also say that he has made an assumption that we are talking about a community of people who have what he calls a *good will*, a desire to do the right thing. Indeed, Kant has assumed that our rationality means that we must want to find the best maxims to live by. Nobody with a desire to do the right thing would build in that kind of exception. If you really are a psychopath who derives pleasure from torturing and killing puppies, it's difficult to see what any set of morals, as opposed to a tightly fitting straitjacket, could do to keep you in check. Nevertheless, plenty of philosophers have enjoyed themselves looking for examples that would undermine Kant's system.

I always suspect that there's another critique – the so-called Yossarian defence, from *Catch-22* by Joseph Heller. In the novel, our hero, a bombardier on an American aircraft in the Second World War, is quite correctly terrified of dying. He contemplates faking mental illness, in order to get out of flying a dangerous mission. "But what would happen if everyone did that?" asks a superior officer. "Well, if everyone did it, I'd be insane not to," Yossarian replies, or words to that effect.'

Hah.

'However, once again, the idea that we are in a community of "good-willed" people might rule that out. More importantly, Kant has another formulation of the categorical imperative that works alongside the first.'

Hang on, there are two categorical imperatives? I thought there was only supposed to be one?

'Kant says they're both aspects of the same thing. The second formula is rather beautiful. *Always treat other people, not as the means to an end, but as an end in themselves.* It's fine to treat an axe as a means to an end. Or a horse. Or a cheesecake. But humans are uniquely different. Our possession of rationality means that we must never be treated as an instrument, as a means to something else. Even without the rest of the Kantian moral scheme, this is a damn fine principle to try to live by. Don't use other people as a way of achieving your own pleasure or benefit; don't see others as rungs on a ladder you're climbing. If you use this together with the first version of the categorical imperative, and assume that you have a community of people who genuinely want to live ethically, then we have a very powerful system.'

So, we have a winner?

'We have a contender… But let's stress it a bit, first, to see how it stands up. Remember, for Kant what makes his system an ethical one is that when we find a maxim that can be universalized, we follow it, no matter what our inclinations, or what the consequences are. So, let's say we decide that our maxim is *Help old ladies across the road.* I apply the test of the categorical imperative, and yes, I'm delighted to assert that we should all always help old ladies across the road. Now imagine two people. One, let's call him Tony, loves helping old ladies. He takes delight in escorting Doris, aged ninety-two (gets a bit confused about where she is sometimes, but can still do the Sudoku puzzle in the paper), across the road.

Now imagine his nemesis, Toby. Toby hates old ladies. He thinks they smell funny. Perhaps one was mean to him when he was a kid, giving him a boiled sweet, and then telling him that she'd already sucked it for five minutes, thereby ruining his enjoyment of boiled sweets forever—'

Hang on, was that you…?

'That's not the… But even though Toby hates old ladies, he's decided that *Help old ladies across the road* is a rule fully in accordance with the categorical imperative and so, grudgingly, his soul crying out in misery and torment, he helps Mavis (eighty-seven, but still with all her marbles) across the road to the chemist to collect her angina prescription. So there are two people: Kind Tony and Mean Toby. Now, according to Kant's ethics, only one of the two is performing an ethical act: Toby.'

Huh?

'You can work this out. For Kant, being good means following the rule out of duty. Things you enjoy doing can't be ethical – or they can't be the test of what is ethical. Because what if you like doing bad things? Toby would like to throw stones at ducks, rather than help old ladies. Kant gives you no points for enjoying being good.

For some, this is enough to discredit Kant's system. It seems to go against our fundamental view about what it means to be a good or bad person. If you can't distinguish between Kind Tony and Mean Toby, what's the point? And there's an even more awkward side to this. Remembering the second formulation, could we see Tony's insistent walking of old ladies across the road as falling foul of the injunction not to use other people as a means to an end? Isn't he using them for his own pleasure, just as much as a sadist might pull the wings off flies for his delight?

On the first point, I think that this is actually one of the *strengths* of the categorical imperative. There is a special kind of virtue in resisting your impulses to do wrong for the sake of an ideal that you've signed up for. And who is it that needs ethical guidance the most? Exactly those who find the allure of wickedness strong.

But there are other criticisms that cut deeper. Recalling that the categorical imperative must be obeyed without any exceptions, whenever a student of philosophy comes across the concept, their first thought is to concoct a situation in which it would be insane to obey the categorical imperative. And they almost always come up with a mad axe murderer, who knocks on their door, asking for the whereabouts of their intended victim. The categorical imperative informs us that we must never lie, and yet who could in conscience reveal the hiding place of the little doggy the murderer has come for?'

Hey!

'Just making sure you're still awake. The amazing thing is that Kant anticipated this, right down to the weapon.'

And the doggy?

'No, not the dog. A person. And his answer stays true to his rule. He says you must not lie to the axeman.'

Nuts!

'His reasoning also helps to explain why he thought you cannot base a moral system on looking at the consequences of your actions. The trouble with consequences is that they are, by definition, in the future, and the future is unpredictable. You might lie to the axeman, telling him that your dog or friend isn't at home, when you know he is. But, seeing the axeman at the door, the friend might already have slipped out the back. And now the axeman encounters him in the street... For Kant you can never be held morally responsible for the consequences of telling the truth. Though you are responsible for the bad consequences of a lie. And there's always the option, not in any way forbidden by Kant, of simply refusing to answer the axeman's question, or of slamming the door in his face and calling the police.

Of course, this is a slightly unlikely situation. Most of us will live out our lives without having to face that kind of dilemma. Far more common are the times when we lie because it's convenient to us, or perhaps to avoid some mild embarrassment. In fact, often we might think that we are lying for the most benign of reasons – yes, you look lovely tonight, no, your bum doesn't look big in that, the sprout and mung bean lasagne was delicious. Here Kant is unequivocal. Do not lie. If lying were ubiquitous, then your flattery would be seen through. It probably is anyway. We can always think of reasons to lie, but these are too often self-serving, even when not obviously to our benefit. Telling the truth can take courage. The categorical imperative gives backbone to that courage.

But one problem continues to nag at me. There are times when it seems that we can apply the method, and it genuinely seems to help us plan the right course through life. But other times it leaves us with too much work to do. This is related to the "emptiness" of the formula – we have to apply the content ourselves. Sometimes it is clear. Don't drive through a red traffic light – if we all did that, chaos would ensue, and rather than helping you get home a little earlier, you'll never get home at all. But what about the more subtle and complex moral issues? How does it help us to decide, for example, whether or not it is

OK to kill and eat other animals? So, if you want to eat a bacon sandwich, you make it a universal maxim – *It is morally correct to eat animals*. It is difficult to see how any moral clarity has been added here. A meat-eater will raise her burger in salute. A vegan will shake his goatee. How can the categorical imperative help? We have simply restated our problem.

And the precise way in which you frame your maxim can have a dramatic effect. Let's consider the death penalty. Imagine our axeman has found his victim, killed him, been apprehended, tried and found guilty. Your maxim might be *Never kill another human being*, which would obviously rule out killing someone in any circumstances, including as a sentence for murder. Or your maxim might be *Only take another life after a correct judicial process has found them guilty of murder*. It seems both would pass Kant's test, but they deliver opposite outcomes. Although, it's possible that the *Never use another person as a means to an end* might come to the murderer's aid. It wouldn't be permissible to kill someone in order to achieve the end of making the world a safer place, or of satisfying the victim's demand for vengeance…

(In fact, Kant argued in favour of the death penalty. His argument is that in order to ensure our freedom, human beings must set up a strong state, incorporating a rational system of justice. Without it the rights that ensure our freedom cannot be guaranteed. And that system of justice must operate with a system of punishments that counterbalance the wrong-doing. Kant saw that humans flourish within a society that allows them to become fully human, fully themselves. And so, this in turn means that in a sense the criminal commits an offence against himself. The punishment should make that theoretical offence against himself into a real one. The murderer must die.)

79

But the biggest flaw, I think, is trying to work out the exact ontological status of the universalizing principle.'

Whoa! Ontological status? What the heck is that?

'Whoops, sorry. I know we mentioned it earlier on, but we haven't done ontological properly yet, have we? In this context it just means what kind of *thing* is it? What sort of reality does it possess? Specifically, does the universalizing principle mean anything in a situation in which you doing or not doing something makes no difference to the real world? If I dump my rubbish by the side of the road, that genuinely does make it more likely that other people will do the same, and so the categorical imperative has real bite. But back to that motorist contemplating running the red light. It's in the early hours of the morning. She's been working a late shift, and is desperate to get back in time to give the middle-of-the-night feed to her small baby. There are no other cars on the road. If she runs the red light, no one will know. Other drivers will not suddenly start running red lights. Kant whispers in her ear, *But if everyone did this…* and her reply is, *But they won't!* In that situation, if you knew for a fact that your minor rule infringement would not start a catastrophic collapse in law and order, must you still obey?'

I know what I'd do. If I could drive.

'Yeah, me too. That means we're bad Kantians.

The last moral system we're going to look at is one that, in the circumstances I've outlined, would say unequivocally, *Yes, run the light. It's for the best.*

It's a view that says human beings (and little dogs) are hedonists, which is to say that for us happiness is the same thing as pleasure. We crave happiness, and so are driven by the desire for pleasure, and the urge to avoid pain. Everything we do in life is governed by the irresistible pull of one, and repulsion of the other. And pleasure is the only rational basis for deciding what is morally right and morally wrong. Indeed, when we say that something is right, we mean nothing more than that it delivers or promotes or causes pleasure, and when we say something is wrong, it means that we think it will deprive us of pleasure, or actively cause pain.'

At last, something that makes sense!

'This view is called utilitarianism, and was formulated by Jeremy Bentham (1748–1832), and further developed by John Stuart Mill (1806–73). For the utilitarian, to act ethically means always consider first the consequences – measured purely in terms of pleasure and pain – of our individual actions. If I give a pound to this beggar, will it increase the overall amount of happiness in the world? If so, I must dig into my pocket and hand over the cash. Will this new train track provide more happiness (by facilitating easier and better transport) than it causes displeasure (by disturbing the peace of those forced to listen to trains hurtling past at the bottom of their garden)? If so, we must build that railway line.

And that, really, is utilitarianism in a nutshell. Of all the moral theories we've discussed, it's probably the easiest to grasp. And, well, cards on the table time, although I praised Kant in the last section, I'm very drawn to utilitarianism. It offers us an objective test for any action. Does this act increase or diminish the happiness of the world? If it increases the happiness, do it. If it increases the amount of pain, do something else.'

I'm still liking the sound of this. Who could possibly object to any of that?

'It all seems very straightforward, but problems begin to emerge as soon as you start poking it. One of these is that finding the correct moral path might well involve comparing different pleasures (and pains). How can you possibly compare the pleasure/pain of the commuters and blighted homeowners in the example of the railway? And what about comparing a good meal to a night at the opera? Or a football match to the ballet? (It might be objected that these aren't really the province of morality, but as soon as you equate good and bad with pleasure and pain, then anything that promotes happiness is within the remit of morality.)

One tack, taken by Mill, was to argue that there is a hierarchy of pleasures, with intellectual and moral pursuits at the top, and the coarser entertainments of the masses at the bottom. This is based on a distinction he makes between true *happiness* and mere *contentment*. He says that it "is better to be a human being dissatisfied than a pig satisfied; better to be Socrates dissatisfied than a fool satisfied. And if the fool, or the pig, are of a different opinion, it is because they only know their own side of the question". So it would always be better to build a library than a football stadium. However, this is so clearly Mill's own cultural prejudices speaking that it really hasn't caught on much, and most modern utilitarians are content to let people decide on their own pleasures.

Mill's teacher, Bentham, thought that you cannot have a hierarchy of pleasures based on the cultural or intellectual esteem they receive. There is simply pleasure and pain, not higher and lower pleasures. However, he does offer a way to assess the amount of pleasure, to help you decide which course of action to take. Bentham was enthralled by science, and was convinced he could apply scientific methods to the measurement of happiness. He called this the *felicific calculus*. For each pleasure, you can allocate marks for Intensity (how strong is the pleasure?); Duration (how long does it last?); Certainty (how likely is it that the pleasure will occur?); Propinquity (how soon will the pleasure occur?); Fecundity (will more pleasure follow on its heels?); Purity (how sure can you be that the pleasure won't be followed by pain?); and Extent (how many people will the pleasure affect?). You get a little notebook, you tot up the scores, and bingo, you know what to do.'

You, er, don't really believe all that, do you?

'It's quite easy to satirize the cruder kind of utilitarianism – Dickens did a pretty good job of it in *Hard Times*. And there are other more difficult objections. Kant was opposed to utilitarianism before it had the name. As we've seen, he argued that we can't base a system of morality on consequences because consequences cannot be fully known. And he thought that pleasure can never be a reliable guide to what we ought to do. Would you base a system of morality on something as irrational and uncontrollable as sexual desire, or hunger? He thinks that rather than basing your ethics on these pleasures, your ethics should help you control them.

But the real objection to utilitarianism is that in assessing the overall amount of happiness produced by an action, it does not treat people as separate individuals, each with their own unique world view, experiences, rights and desires, but lumps them fatally together. If the only aim of ethics is to produce the maximum amount of good, it doesn't matter who gets the good, or who might suffer in the process. If we discover through careful research that public executions effectively deter murderers, and that, say, one execution will result in two people who would otherwise have been killed being saved, then utilitarian duty demands that someone be executed. And if there isn't a suitable murderer available on Death Row, then we must pick someone up from the streets, and execute them.

And although this seems quite absurd to us, many of the most terrible crimes of humanity have been based precisely on this sort of crude utilitarian thinking, which finds it acceptable to kill and enslave in order to improve the lot of others. The SS officer who rounds up and kills French villagers to deter attacks by the Resistance acts on precisely this principle. Even non-totalitarian governments have made life and death decisions based on utilitarian grounds. For years, the United States has found it acceptable to kill innocent civilians, including children, in drone attacks in order to assassinate members of terrorist organizations.'

Those seem like quite big problems.

'They are, but utilitarianism can answer them, up to a point. A totalitarian regime that sacrifices innocents is clearly not a happy place to be, and so utilitarianism demands that we don't go there. It is perfectly possible to say that, overall, we will be happier if we give individuals rights that prevent them being sacrificed. As long as we say that our aim is to produce the greatest happiness, then such a defence of human rights is within the scope of utilitarianism. This idea that we should entrench certain basic principles in a utilitarian framework has been called *rule utilitarianism*, distinguishing it from *act utilitarianism*. Act utilitarianism focuses exclusively on the particular act and its consequences. Rule utilitarianism takes a step back, and says that maximizing pleasure involves us all obeying certain rules, and even if occasionally breaking that rule would lead to a spike in happiness, we should follow the rule to secure the greater, long-term good.

Returning to our mother, desperate to get home, confronted with a late-night red light, the act utilitarian would say, *Run it*: there are no bad consequences from, on this occasion, going through. The rule utilitarian would say, *Stop*. The rule that we stop at red lights is so valuable in securing long-term utility that we just have to obey it. In the same way, rule utilitarians would say that the rule *Do not harm people simply to secure a greater good* in fact results in exactly that greater good.

Mill argues that many of the preceding ethical systems are disguised versions of utilitarianism. What is Kant's categorical imperative other than a rule that asks us to imagine the consequences of our acts, even as it says they are not relevant? Jesus was a utilitarian, for Mill: the Christian ethic of love, peace and charity being a good guide for maximizing happiness. And it doesn't take too much work to turn Aristotle's egotistical and individual eudaimonia into a prescription for general happiness.

Another complication of utilitarianism is the question of whose happiness counts. It is usually resolved by saying that the basic unit for considering happiness is the person. The question then becomes, what counts as a *person*? Is it only humans? Or do animals count? If animals, then all animals, or only those passing a certain threshold of intelligence? And with humans, is it all humans? Do we extend it to the unborn?

Although these problems are knotty, they don't seem to be insoluble. They are details to be worked out, if we decide that happiness truly is the guide to morality.'

I'm confused. All these systems, all these ideas. What should we do? Which is the right way? How can we save the Melians?

'We came in, didn't we, by describing the state of moral confusion that we see in contemporary debates. We saw that as a problem that we should try to solve. Could the history of ethics offer us a single theory that could unite us all, give us that feeling of security in our moral judgements that we crave? But the more I think about it, the more it strikes me that this confusion, rather than being a problem, is actually a strength.'

Huh?

'If we think about the types of thing that come under the description of ethics or morals, we find a dizzying variety. There are the small deceptions that are part of almost every human relationship; there are more brutal betrayals of friendship and love; there are criminal offences, in turn split into those we find hardly worth bothering about (parking offences), and those we find utterly repellent (murder, rape). There are government decisions, which have huge impacts on the lives of citizens, decisions about spending money on health care or weapons, decisions about who to bomb with those weapons. Some of these ethical issues impact on other people, others might have no purchase on the world at all, beyond our own soul.

Would it not then be a little odd if *one* ethical rule, or one *set* of rules, were applicable to all these situations? And of course, there have been times in history when a single ethic has been imposed on the people – fundamentalist Christian, or Stalinist, or Fascist or Islamist, and it hasn't, on the whole, gone well. So perhaps our patchwork of moral feelings somehow fits reality, in an ad hoc, make-do kind of way.

Even within our legal system there are contradictions. A crime needs both a criminal intention (*mens rea*) and a criminal act (*actus reus*), aligning it in some ways with a Kantian perspective; but a civil offence requires only the demonstration of the act, which has a utilitarian ring to it. Yet the character of a defendant – the extent to which he embodies certain virtues or vices – may well have an impact on how he is sentenced, which brings us closer to Aristotle.

We're encountering here for the first time something that is going to come up again and again in our walks. It's the fact that we have certain intellectual faculties and abilities, and also certain analytic tools – principally, language – which we use to try to make sense of the world. And it sort of works. We get through the day without walking over cliffs or, usually, offending our neighbours to the point they go looking for the axe in their basement. But this cannot change the fact that there are two quite separate things: reality on the one side, made up not only of the grand complexities of the physical world, but also the even more intricate, thorny and obscure convolutions of other minds; and on the other our attempts to model, comprehend and analyse that world. Our model is a good one, but it cannot capture everything. The fine grains of reality run through our fingers as we try to grasp it.

On an earlier walk we talked about the distinction between objective and subjective realities. The objective is the realm of absolute, unconditional truth, whereas the subjective concerns those matters that depend on the limited perspective of an individual. David Hume developed a moral philosophy that aimed at a middle way between these extremes, a position later called *intersubjectivity*. He argued that humans have an innate capacity for empathy (he used the term *sympathy*, but he meant the ability to experience the pleasures and pains felt by others). With this limited capacity as a starting point, we acquire the rules and norms of the particular culture in which we are nurtured. The names *good* and *evil*, Hume tells us, become associated with the feelings we experience when we see certain types of behaviour – those smiled or frowned upon by our particular society.

Good and evil cannot be found, Hume argues, in the events themselves, but belong to the emotions we feel in certain situations. But because of the social nature of humans, and the way we are brought up with shared beliefs and customs, and because of that innate ability to empathize, within that culture there will be a common response to the same moral stimuli, making judgements to a degree common within that culture, thus *intersubjective*. This takes it away from the simple emotivism we discussed previously. The emotion is given a meaning because of its social context and shared nature.

This approach explains how, despite the many differences we've discussed, there is much agreement on moral issues within a culture. It also accounts for the distance between the ethical frameworks of remote cultures, which lack a common language of morals. We and the Aztecs would look on each other with equal repugnance. Yet there may well be enough in common between all cultures to provide a few shared elements in the grammar of ethics. When humans live together, there will always be some rules that apply, certain norms without which we simply couldn't exist as a collective. Keeping your word, repaying a debt...'

Loving your dog.

'Loving your dog. But because of the variety of human experiences even within a culture, and the complexity of what it means to make a moral decision, this common cultural response will never be all-embracing. It will fray and break.

What we crave is a moral approach that will be like a broad-spectrum antibiotic, killing all germs, curing all ills. But as in medicine, so with ethics, there are too many pathogens, too many ways of being ill, for one drug to zap them all. Therefore we have this superabundance of ethical approaches – all of which have flaws, and all of which capture some aspects of what it means to be moral. Government policy should (and sometimes even does) look to benefit the majority of the population. The rule that we shouldn't lie is a good one to follow, even if it sometimes gets you into hot water. The mother probably should run that red light (assuming it can be done safely); we really should admire the Classical virtues of courage, temperance, magnanimity and modesty; and perhaps those Christian ones of faith, hope and charity. Because ultimately the concepts of good and evil are fuzzy. And fuzziness is something we'll return to…

And perhaps there's one final subtlety to this. When we judge morality, there are two possible things we could be examining. We could be looking at the act, or we could be looking at the person. It's possible that we could decide the person was innocent, but the act terrible, such as an awful unforeseen disaster that happens because of an accidental mistake; and it's possible we could judge a person to be appalling, even though his act might have good consequences.'

I sense a quirky example coming.

'Imagine a would-be serial killer, up on the top of a high building. He has a rifle, and takes pot shots at the people in the street below. But he's a terrible shot, and all his bullets miss. Except for one, which just flicks a mole on the neck of a middle-aged woman. The bullet magically shoots away the mole, without causing serious injury to the woman. Now it transpires that the mole was on the verge of becoming cancerous. Without the lucky bullet, the woman would have died from malignant melanoma.'

This is kind of silly.

'Yeah, I know, but sometimes an extreme example helps to clarify the point. So here we would unambiguously describe the man as bad, and equally agree that the outcome was good. Utilitarianism smiles on the consequence; Kant frowns on the shooter. My point is to emphasize again that we might need different ethical standpoints to capture the full complexity of the moral universe.'

That's great. And the Melians…?

'Ah, the Melians. Nietzsche would cheer on the Athenians. The fact that the Melians lost the battle meant that they were inferior, and the law of the Superman says that he can do as he pleases with the vanquished. I think that Plato's conception of justice would have led him to argue that the Melians should not be destroyed. The *Republic* imagines the ideal state going to war in only two circumstances: to ensure its own survival against aggression, and to spread justice through the world. Aristotle's ethics doesn't hold out much hope for the Melians, unless the virtue of moderation might restrain the Athenians' violence. But Aristotle was the tutor of Alexander the Great, whose gift was not for moderation… I can't see anything in Aristotle's conception of eudaimonia that would cause the Athenians to spare their foes, though he did think that Greeks should stop fighting among themselves, and unite against the barbarians.

The act utilitarians would say that the Athenians should strictly apply the felicific calculus. Will this atrocity result in a greater amount of happiness? And the Athenians must, of course, not count only their own happiness, but that of all affected by it. It's possible that if the evil of the Spartans winning the Peloponnesian War was so great that it overbalanced the evil committed against the Melians, then the massacre would be right. That's the sort of calculation that the Allied powers took in bombing German cities in the Second World War. The evil of killing women and children "bought" the good of defeating Hitler. However, on balance I don't think an objective assessment of the consequences would permit the Athenians their massacre. Rule utilitarianism would be clearer about rejecting the action. It's objectively a happier world for us all, in the long run, if we moderate and control this sort of behaviour.

Kant would be clearest of all. You cannot kill and enslave the Melians. It is impossible to make a categorical imperative of: *If anyone gets in the way of your plan to win a war, you may kill and enslave them.* That would be to invite the same fate to be inflicted on you. And, it so occurred that a few years later, this is precisely what happened to the Athenians. A disastrous campaign against the Sicilian city of Syracuse ended with the utter defeat of the Athenians. Most of the army was killed. Those who survived were worked slowly to death in the mines, lamenting only that they had been denied a swift end to their suffering. And then the Spartans won the war.'

So it was all for nothing?

'Yeah.'

Karma.

'Karma. Let's go home.'

Walk 4

Other Minds and Free Will

On this walk, I first ponder the question of other minds, i.e. how we can be sure that other people are not simply androids, but have mental processes and experiences like our own? And then Monty and I discuss the problem of free will: are people free to make choices – moral or otherwise – or are all our thoughts and actions determined by things beyond our control?

The next day I decided on a whim to go for a walk with Monty along the Thames, from Richmond to Strawberry Hill. It meant taking the train to Richmond, but Monty likes public transport, and seldom disgraces himself. He sat on my knee in the crowded carriage as I read, his nose nestled into the cleft between the two halves of the book, and it must have looked a little as if he were reading it, too. I glanced up, hoping that someone might be enjoying this little scene, and that we could exchange smiles of an 'isn't he cute' variety, but the other passengers were too involved in their phones, jabbing or swiping at the screens, smiling at some WhatsApped witticism, or YouTube video of a panda sneezing.

It's at times like this, when everyone seems enclosed in their own world, that I find myself pondering the so-called *problem of other minds*. It – the question of whether other people have minds like mine – is one of the few that doesn't go back to the Greeks. No one before J.S. Mill in the nineteenth century seems to have worried about it. But sitting there watching the people around me on the train it was hard not to wonder how the commonplace assumption that other people think and feel and experience the world the same as oneself can be proven. I cannot experience your pain or your joy. I can't feel your sensations as you scratch your head or wriggle your toes in your too-tight shoes. Does your happiness feel like my happiness, your sadness like my sadness?

Of course, genuinely not believing that others have minds like ours is a sign of madness: people with schizophrenia and other personality disorders are often convinced that those around them have been replaced by soulless replicants or automata. Sane people believe in the identity of human consciousness, that the differences between us are simply variations within a theme. But belief is not the same thing as knowledge. Can we know that we are the same, or at least acquire the same certainty about the mental workings of our fellow humans that anatomists have of the physical body?

There are two subtly different sides to the problem. The first is, how can I know what's in your head? What would count as evidence or proof? The other is more conceptual. To really know if we were the same, I'd have to think another person's thoughts, and feel their feelings, and how is that possible? My thoughts and feelings cannot ever somehow include or encapsulate yours. Such a thing is literally inconceivable outside the realm of science fiction.

I'm going to have to say straight away that philosophy hasn't got any kind of answer to this second formulation of the problem. And its answers to the first aren't entirely satisfactory, either. But at least with the first question there are attempts at an answer, even if they are as solid and robust as dry meringues ...

Philosophers have put forward three different answers to the problem of other minds. The first is the argument from analogy. I know that *I* have *this* sort of mind. I feel and think and intend and itch and ache. Other people are like me in so many external ways that I can clearly see. So, they must, surely, be like me on the inside, too, mustn't they?

This is what most of us instinctively think. It's a form of inductive reasoning. Induction is the process by which we attempt to form general laws from particular instances. You find a certain number of cases in which X is followed by Y, and then you make the inductive leap of saying that all Xs will be followed by Ys. I note that in my own case I have certain processes and experiences, and so I form the general rule that all people must experience these same things in the same way.

Leaving aside the various problems with inductive reasoning (we'll examine those at length on a later walk), there is a major flaw with the argument from analogy. Usually, with induction, the idea is that you gather evidence from many cases, form a general law, and then use that to predict a future case. But with the problem of other minds, the argument from analogy almost reverses that process. We have only one example from which to make our generalization. We then apply it to all of the several billion humans on the planet. Despite being superficially attractive, and universally employed, it's a threadbare argument.

The second argument sounds similar, but is in fact quite distinct. It's an argument by inference, not analogy. Rather than simply assuming that, because I have a mind of this sort, other people must have one, it is based on observing the behaviour of others, and from that forming the best hypothesis we can to explain it. If we see a vehicle on wheels moving down the street, we would assume that it was powered by an engine, rather than magic, or cunningly concealed horses. We see people behaving in various ways, walking, talking, loving, hating. If we now try to account for this behaviour, there are various possibilities. They could, as already mentioned, be life-like robots, with no consciousness like mine. They could be computer simulations. There could be some other, as yet unknown, mechanism guiding and driving them. But the most rational explanation is that they have a mind and a consciousness. That simply fits the facts we observe better than any other explanation.

The trouble here is that, at best, we merely arrive at the conclusion that the most likely explanation for the behaviour of other people is that they have minds more or less like our own. It then relies on the argument from analogy to take us the rest of the way, to assuming that the real texture of their experience is the same as ours. And we've already seen the problem with that.

The third 'solution' is the most simple and seductive (to me, anyway). It suggests that mental states aren't hidden at all. The stuff happening in your mind is written on the body. To itch is to scratch. To think is to look thoughtful. To be happy is to smile. In a sense, it shatters the mind/body dichotomy. Rather than there being two things, the mind and the body, there is one thing: a unitary thinking organism. This view presupposes our life as social beings who have evolved to read each other.

Consciousness isn't some private chamber in our minds, but an open arena that we share.

Linked to this argument is the idea that language is only possible if our minds operate in the same way. Language is always communal, depending on a shared understanding of the world. Words represent ideas; communication is a fact: all kinds of things happen, demonstrably, because accurate information or instructions are conveyed. As Wittgenstein said, if a lion could speak, we wouldn't understand it. That's because the lion's mental and social world is so different from ours. But people speak, and are understood.

Of course, there are also problems with this view. We can deceive and be deceived, we can misunderstand the physical symptoms of thought. We can think without displaying any emotion or other signs. There is no art to find the mind's construction in the face.

Yet the exceptions presuppose a rule. Deception is only possible because usually we are not deceived.

Many will say that outlandish ideas about other minds – the automata hypothesis, etc. – can be readily put to bed by a little time spent in an autopsy room. A few minutes with a deftly wielded circular saw will show that every skull we encounter has a brain inside it, and a quick probe with the scalpel will reveal that they all have a similar structure, with no hidden circuitry or alien implants. Such an investigation would satisfy most sceptics, although it falls short of actual proof. Could the technology be disguised as organic material? Is the whole thing a dream or fantasy I'm having? How do I know that my cross-sample of brains is representative? Perhaps the hundredth skull would reveal the microchips? And, even if I excavated the skulls of every other human being, and finally sat upon a monstrous mound of the dead, how would I know that my own skull contained a gelatinous organ like these? Might I, in fact, be the one with the bleeping circuitry?

Where does this leave us with the problem of other minds? As so often, philosophy helps us to understand the problem, without giving us a wholly satisfactory answer. I think that we can infer enough, and with sufficient strength, to carry on treating those around us as if we were the same, even if I can never truly know if your pain is like my pain, your bliss like my bliss.

And in another walk we'll look at what it is to know, and what it is to doubt…

I felt Monty shift on my lap, and then he jumped down. I looked about me. The carriage was empty, and the train slumbering at its terminus. A cleaner was making her way towards us with a huge bag of rubbish.

'Sorry, boy,' I said. 'Must have drifted off.'

From Richmond, the walk takes about an hour each way, a narrow footpath winding through the willow and birch trees lining the river. It's a journey I used to make a couple of times a week, back when I had a proper job teaching at a small and relatively obscure college. But I left the post, and it had been seven years since I last came this way.

The sky was that paradoxical cloudless grey, and the river gave back the same drabness. Strange, I thought, how silent it was. One thinks of moving water as noisy. Obviously, the paradigm would be a thundering rapids, or crashing ocean, but you'd have thought that even a wide, lugubrious river like the Thames at Richmond would make some kind of noise, a bubble or a burp. But when I closed my eyes, there was nothing, just the rustling of the dying October leaves, and the sound, somewhere, of children laughing.

Famously, the pre-Socratic philosopher Heraclitus – the same one whose bloated, dropsied corpse we'd left smeared in shit and eaten by dogs – says we never step into the same river twice. This has traditionally been taken to mean that everything is in flux, nothing is constant, nothing ultimately knowable, as by the time you've brought your attention to bear on one stretch of a river (or a life), it's gone. And this stress on volatility fits in with Heraclitus' belief that the basic matter of the universe, the fundamental reality of which all things were manifestations, was fire. Fire is both unstable and transformative. You find the river changed, but the fire changes you.

And this raises the issue of personal identity. Was it the same me returning to the river after all these years? Our cells die and are replaced. Old memories fade, as new ones are created. Our views alter, as the youthful radical becomes an old conservative, or the young prude finds that life widens her sympathies.

I remember going to London Zoo, and looking at the juvenile orangutans capering around their enclosure, frolicking and fooling, embracing each other one moment, play-fighting the next. And then, slumped in one far corner, I saw an old male, his thin arms crossed above a huge belly. The enormous, flat, leathery face had the look of one of those Celtic sacrificial victims that turn up in Irish peat bogs. He exuded a malevolent dignity, as if somewhere inside him he preserved a genetic memory of jungle fronds and wild fruits and treetop couplings with comely red-gold maidens, and knew the loss, and hated it.

One of the overly excited youngsters tumbled too close to the old despot, and he flicked out a long hand to cuff it, with great economy of movement, on the back of the head. Yet he too had once been like them. Where is the thread that binds them?

Such conflict between old and new, or young and old, is another central Heraclitan theme. War is everywhere, he says, and strife is justice. The only peace the world can attain is the temporary balance of forces: a bow pulled taut, the arrow notched, waiting to fly. That moment of perfect quiet and equilibrium before the release.

But some philosophers have begun to challenge this view of Heraclitus. He was a dense, dark, deliberately obscure writer, known to despise the common people, and what scraps of his work survive are difficult to interpret. His lines on the impossibility of stepping into the same river actually talk about the *water* changing, not the river itself. It could simply mean that with a river, as in everything else, there is both continuity and change, that indeed the continuity *requires* the change. If the waters didn't flow, the river would become a lake. That if a person doesn't change, then he isn't a person, but a rock.

So, coming back here now, it's the same river, the same me. Perhaps.

I slipped Monty off the lead, and he scampered back and forth to use up some of his suppressed train-energy.

'I've been thinking about our discussion the other day, the one about ethics,' I said, once he'd fallen back into step.

He looked up, as if to say, *go on.*

'And I think we reached a kind of conclusion, didn't we? If we're talking about the moral value of an *action*, then it makes sense to attend to the consequences, or the end, the *telos*, to which it is directed; and if we're looking to praise or blame a *person* for their acts, possibly handing out rewards or punishments, then it makes sense to probe at their intentions, and the extent to which they were following a rule or principle. It's a little untidy, I mean the fact we're stuck with two fundamentally different approaches to the question of good and bad, right and wrong, but it's the best we could manage.'

Monty shrugged his assent.

'There's a problem, though,' I said.

I thought there might be.

'The thing is, when it comes to the second of these, judging a person, as opposed to assessing the act, we've been assuming something rather crucial.'

That anyone cares?

'No,' I said, firmly, 'that we have a choice. That we are free to decide to do the right thing. Or the wrong thing.'

Monty gave me one of his puzzled looks.

'I'm sure that you can see how important this is. Let's imagine a situation in which I have to make a moral decision.' I looked around and picked up a slender branch that had fallen from one of the trees. 'I think we'd both admit that hitting a sweet little dog with a stick would, in the absence of certain strict criteria—'

Er, such as...

'Well, if it were to prevent some greater harm to you, say if you were about to run out in the road... But that's not important. This is hitting you with a stick for no reason that would, in the light of any of the ethical systems we looked at, be unacceptable.'

OK.

Monty still sounded unhappy about the being hit with a stick business, and I began to wish I'd come up with a different example.

'So, in general, I would expect to suffer blame, disapproval and possibly criminal prosecution for whacking you.'

Quite right too.

'But now imagine various circumstances in which my actions weren't free. I was either constrained, so that I couldn't do what I wanted, or compelled, in that I was forced to do what I didn't want to do. I'm sleepwalking, and in my sleep I dream I'm holding a magic wand, and I wave it around to conjure up a feast, or a beautiful ... let's keep it at feast. But in fact, I have this stick in my hand and I end up thwacking you with it. Or let's say that I'd contracted a disease that made me act in a violent or irrational way, without any chance of behaving differently. Rabies, say...'

Rabies?

'Oh, it's a disease you catch from mad ... Never mind, perhaps I've had a psychotic episode, and I think that rather than a dog, you are a man-eating tiger, and I'm trying to drive you away from Rosie...'

Monty emitted a low growl at the thought of tigers, whatever they were, trying to hurt his beloved Rosie, my daughter.

'Or in my delusions I think that you're on fire, and I'm trying to beat out the flames with my stick. Would you think I was to blame in any of those circumstances?'

Of course not.

'And in each of these cases you wouldn't blame me because I wasn't freely choosing to harm you?'

Yeah, that sounds right.

'But these are all special cases, aren't they? Usually when you commit an act, like whacking a dog, or telling a lie, you're not insane, and you're not trying to do something else. But what if, even in those cases where there were no formal constraints on your actions of the kind we discussed, you're still not free? What if freedom of choice is always an illusion? What then?'

Monty looked unimpressed. He cocked his leg on one side of the path, then cocked his leg on the other. It was his way of saying that we're free to cock our legs wherever we want.

'So, your position is that in the normal course of things, when I'm awake, and where no external forces, or inner derangement, stop me from doing what I want to do, or compel me to do what I don't, then I'm free to act in a moral or immoral way?'

Monty growled his agreement.

'That's the common-sense view, and one held, I'd guess, by most people. But it's a view that has to deal with some pretty serious objections.'

Object away.

'The first is that we live in a particular time and place, where certain things are thinkable, and certain things not. We have a menu, if you like. There are plenty of items on the menu, every kind of pizza you could want, say. And pasta: all the pastas. We've gone Italian. You're free to choose, of course. No one can make you have a marinara if what you want is a quattro stagioni. Anything on the menu is available. But the menu isn't infinite. No kitchen could cope with that. So, there's no curry, no rotted, fermented shark of the kind they eat in Iceland. Not the black soup made from pigs' blood that kept the armies of Sparta marching.'

Sounds rank.

'It was. One non-Spartan tasted it, spat it out and said, "Now I know why the Spartans do not fear death." You get where this is going. Our moral choices are in various ways circumscribed by the time and place we live. Three hundred years ago, in our own society, no one would think it an ethical issue to beat a dog. Men viewed women as intellectually and morally inferior. Children were worked to death in mines. Slavery was accepted, and the racism with which it was linked, almost universal.

You'll probably say that some individuals were able to break with these traditions and practices, to think independently, and that's why we've moved beyond these patently immoral views. But those revolutions in thought tended to come at a time when fundamental changes in society were occurring, deeper movements that opened up the possibility of new ways of thinking. Technological developments made slavery inefficient. The need to get women into the workforce facilitated female emancipation. Marxists contend the state of economic and technological development in any society determines the political arrangements and the ideas that circulate.'

Determines … ?

'I mean that they are caused by them, with nothing left over to explain or account for. The gods we worship, the type of government, the art we produce, the moral codes we follow, are all part of a superstructure determined by – caused by – the economic base, by the realities of how we make things and the relationships between the classes.

And even if you question the deterministic link between ideas and economic arrangements, you cannot doubt that ideas feed off ideas, and that ideas don't float around freely in space, but are embedded in certain historical periods. The work of all the philosophers we've discussed (with the possible exception of the earliest pre-Socratics), Plato, Aristotle, Kant, the utilitarians, emerged from traditions of thought, from existing conversations and debates. Kant was a professional philosopher, teaching the works of his contemporaries and predecessors. His ideas, while criticizing and going beyond theirs, couldn't exist without them. And it's the same on a more mundane level for us, here and now, making our decisions about the right thing to do. I, we, can't escape from Plato and Kant, and the Christian ethical tradition, and utilitarianism, even if we don't explicitly bring them to mind.'

So, we're not free because what we think has been thought before? Because it's not really 'our' thought at all?

'I'm just chewing this over. Actually, no, I don't think that. I think that the fact that we stand at the end of a long line of ethical thought makes us, if anything, more free, not less. We can consider Aristotle and Kant and Mill, compare and criticize their ideas, and then come to an informed choice about what is right. And you might argue that each of those figures is actually part of the same Western tradition of philosophy, so in fact I still haven't managed to think outside the limitations of my own culture. But we also have access to the philosophical thought of other cultures – Hindu, Taoist, Buddhist – which give a totally different perspective to ethical problems. And even within the Western tradition, which I accept is my main frame of reference, there's scope for thinking critically about the foundations of that tradition. So, what I'm saying is that even if we can't, logically, select a dish that isn't on the menu, the menu is extraordinarily wide, and does provide enough variety to make choice a reality.'

So, we are free! Hurrah!

Monty made one of his scampering, capering dashes along the river footpath and back. He used to do this a lot when he was younger, running in mad figures-of-eight until he collapsed from exhaustion. We called it a Monty-fit. It takes a lot to set him off on one these days.

'Not so fast,' I said when he'd calmed down.

Huh?

'We've only looked at one of the ways in which our ability to freely choose right and wrong might be limited. Usually, these days, when we speak about determinism, what we have in mind isn't the fact that the range of views open to us is historically and culturally delimited, but that, as individuals, we do not have the capacity to freely choose anything at all.'

Sounds serious.

'It is. And I'm afraid we're going to have to stray from philosophy into the world of science to get to the bottom of it. Classical physics, from Newton to Einstein, has done a pretty good job of explaining how the universe works. We live in a material world. The universe is made of stuff, of matter. Matter is made of molecules, and the molecules are made of atoms. Atoms in turn are made up of still smaller particles – protons, neutrons, electrons. At the subatomic level, other yet smaller particles exist – quarks, muons, neutrinos, gluons, photons. At the root of everything, there may be superstrings of vibrating energy.

Then there are a limited number of forces at play in the universe, which dictate how the stuff interacts. Two of these forces – the strong force and the weak force – only work at tiny distances, and they prescribe how subatomic particles behave. Then there's electromagnetic force, the power of repulsion or attraction that occurs between electrically charged particles. Whenever a current runs along a wire or a magnet sticks to a radiator, that's electromagnetic force at work. And last, we have gravity – the force that draws all bodies with mass towards each other.

That's pretty well it, for the universe. Scientists use the predictable and uniform ways in which matter and these four forces interact to construct laws – general statements derived from observations, which describe certain phenomena, and predict that given the same circumstances the same result will ensue. So, Boyle's Law says that the pressure of a gas is inversely related to the size of the container. Newton demonstrated that the force of gravity between any two bodies will be directly proportional to the product of their masses (it's stronger the bigger they are), and inversely proportional to the square of the distance between them (it's weaker the further apart they are). Einstein said that the energy (E) is related to mass (m) and the speed of light (c), such that $E = mc^2$.

For anything to happen in this universe of matter and forces and laws, it must have been caused by something preceding it. Nothing happens without a cause.

Taken together, these "facts" about our universe have tremendous predictive and explanatory power. If you have enough information about the state of the universe now, you could go backwards or forwards in time, predicting the exact state and position of every atom in the universe at any moment. We can make precise predictions about eclipses, send a metal box hundreds of millions of kilometres out into space so it will collide with a small moon going around a distant planet in the outer reaches of the solar system.

This view of the nature of physical reality is called *determinism* – because at every stage in the history of the universe the exact arrangement of every atom in that universe was determined by what came before it, no shirking, no dodging: there's no hiding from the laws of nature. No atom is "free": its precise movements and its position in space are dictated by the material conditions that surround and precede it.'

Monty isn't really into science, so I could tell that this was washing over him. He gave another of his shrugs, but this was more of a *what's this got to do with me?* shrug.

'That's *every* atom in the universe. Including the atoms that make up you and me. If truly all that exists in the universe is matter and energy, then that must include our minds and thoughts – minds and thoughts existing, like everything else, in the universe, as there really isn't anywhere else for them to go. And if we accept that everything in the material world is determined, that would mean that determinism applies not just to planets and comets and grains of sand, but to us, our bodies, our thoughts.'

I bent the stick in half until it splintered and snapped. Then I pulled back my arm, and threw one half of the stick out over the water. It splashed down, bobbed up and floated downstream with the current.

'When I threw that stick, physical laws determined exactly what would happen to it. The distance and direction it travelled were dictated by the force of the throw, the mass of the stick, the impact of wind and air resistance, the force of gravity. Anyone having full access to all the facts about the masses and forces involved could tell you exactly where it would land. And then they could tell you where the tides and currents would take it.'

But you chose where you would throw the stick. You threw it out over the river. You didn't throw it at me...

'Good point. Let's tease it out a bit. You think I was free to make that choice, that there is something about human will, the mind, that makes it different from everything else in the universe, prying it loose from the tight grip of determinism?'

Well, yeah. Why not?

'That view – that the mind is free from the chain of material causality, of atom colliding with atom – is premised on the idea that our minds aren't like everything else in the universe. It posits that there exist two different sorts of stuff: the material stuff we discussed earlier, made up of atoms and subatomic particles; and a mental substance, mind. The technical name for this view is Cartesian dualism, named after René Descartes, who gave it its most coherent form. It's got a superficial attraction—'

Superficial? Why do I feel this isn't going to end well for dualism?

'Hah, well, no, it doesn't. But, as I was saying, it does seem to accord with how many of us think about the world. Our minds, our thoughts, do simply seem to be a different sort of thing to tables and chairs and planets spinning through the cosmos. The attributes that we ascribe to the material objects – that they have extension, mass, weight, colour, etc. – don't apply to thoughts. Except, of course, as metaphors, and in reality a heavy thought and a light one weigh the same. And it feels to us that rather than these thoughts being caused by the material world, the causal chain works the other way. That by thinking something, I can then make things happen to the stuff around me. I decide to throw this stick. I move my arm, I send it out into the sky.'

I chucked the second half of the stick, by way of illustration. However, it got caught in the branches of one of the scrubby willows and dangled in a helpless sort of way.

'We'll talk more about this dualism thing on another walk,' I said. 'It doesn't really belong here. But what I would say is that no one believes it any more. I mean the, er, experts. Brain scientists, and philosophers of mind. The problems with it are too great.'

Like?

'What precisely is the mind made of, if it's not simply electrical impulses moving through the network of brain cells? Because if a thought can be reduced to those electrical impulses, then our minds are caught again in the material chain of causality.

And if mind and matter are fundamentally different substances, how and where do they interact?'

Easy, the brain.

'That's a where, but not a how. And where in the brain? Descartes believed that the soul (or mind) and body came together in the pineal gland, a little nugget of gristle right where your spine nestles into the brain. But that doesn't help us get over that fundamental problem, it just shifts the scale down. Somewhere a thing that is not matter has to communicate with a thing that is matter, and no one has the faintest idea how that might be achieved.'

So…

'So that leaves us with the conclusion that mind – consciousness, if you prefer – is just another effect of those physical particles and forces. A thought is nothing more than electrical impulses travelling around in an immensely complex network of neurons in the brain. And once we've decided on that, it must follow that those thoughts are determined, and that our freedom is illusory. When we think we're making a choice – to hit you or not hit you, to lie or tell the truth – we're no more free than that stick flying through the air. And if you take away freedom, how can you have praise or blame? How can you have morality at all?'

I still don't quite get how you go from atoms bashing about to a person not being free to choose whether or not to whack an innocent little dog with a stick.

'Well, a determinist would say that when a person comes to make a moral choice, the universe has put him there in that situation and given him certain capacities and experiences. Let's assume that human nature is formed partly from experience and partly from genes – but it doesn't really matter for the sake of this discussion. Either way, you're the kind of person you are, in this particular situation, at this moment in history, and your abilities, opinions, predisposition, must determine what you do, as surely as the laws of physics determine the trajectory of a thrown stick. You might think that you're doing something from a moral point of view, making a choice according to Kantian or utilitarian principles, but that's because the material forces that frame and form us have made you the kind of person who makes choices based on those kinds of principles. You haven't chosen to be a Kantian in any real sense, the world chose Kant for you. Or, if you're the kind of person who steals and murders, then that's because the world has made you like that.

And there's some force to that argument, when you look at the life histories of many criminals. Their background, upbringing and possibly their biological inheritance made it impossible for them to escape the life they were in. You can't choose to be a doctor rather than a burglar if you've been brought up by a family of burglars on a tough estate, and you went to a school where no kid had ever gone on to university. If you decide to whack the dog, it's not a decision you've made, but a decision made for you by the universe.

And there's even some experimental evidence that seems to back up the idea that our actions aren't willed by us. Psychologists have found that when performing various routine activities – reaching for a glass or checking the time – the muscles required have been triggered by nerve impulses before the thought "get the glass" or "look at your watch" has been formed. So, bizarrely, the conscious decision to act comes after the act has been initiated. If that's the case, how can we claim that what we did was a consequence of a free choice, made by a rational mind?'

Like dogs, really. I don't usually think, oh, I should have a pee now, I just find that I've had a sniff and a pee.

'Yeah, I guess. But many people would say that even given the fact that history and genetic predisposition have made you the kind of person you are, part of being human means that you can change. Maybe you can't go from being a burglar to a doctor, but you can go from a person who burgles houses to one who doesn't. And as proof of that, there are millions of people who have decided to become better, to reform, to give up the drugs or the booze, to stop being a shit. Isn't that evidence that we're free?'

Well, er, yeah, isn't it?

'Let's rephrase this, in a way that will show that this proof fails. To be morally responsible for our acts, we need to be responsible for the way we are, to have somehow chosen to be *this* kind of person. Fair enough?'

Monty didn't disagree.

'So, there was something in you that decided to be the kind of person you are. Let's say, to have changed from being a liar to a truth teller, and from now on obeying Kant's categorical imperative. You have now changed the kind of person you are, asserting your freedom, and with that freedom, taking on responsibility.'

Another nod from Monty.

'But that means that you must, at that point of choice, already have been the kind of person who could make that change. And we've agreed that to be morally responsible, you have to be responsible for the kind of person you were. So, you would also have to have chosen to be that pre-existing version of you, the one that decided to make the change, you see?'

Er, I think so.

'And how did that pre-existing version of you come into existence? Either it was formed by forces over which you had no control, or you brought it into existence by some act of will. If the former, we have no free choice, and no moral responsibility. If the latter, it was brought into existence by some pre-existing version of you … It's an infinite regress.'

A what?

'It's a concept I suspect we'll encounter a few more times on these walks. In philosophy, you find yourself sliding into an infinite regress whenever your reasons for believing something rely on reasons that can only be justified by further reasons, which in turn—'

I get it.

'In this case, the only way to stop the infinite regress would be to find what can't exist: a point of origin at which somehow you brought yourself into being through an act of free choice, as if God had created himself.'

We walked on in silence for a while. It seemed almost as if the birds had stopped twittering, and the leaves rustling, in dismay at where we were: a world without moral responsibility. Monty broke the silence.

Is there any way out of this? It just feels… wrong.

'You mean can we somehow reconcile our sense of being free to make choices – moral choices, choices about what to have for dinner, choices about which way to walk – with the brute reality of causation and determinism? Maybe. Let's set out the options. Is the physical world determined? The answer is yes or no. If it is determined, does it follow that our mental states are determined? If they are determined, is there any sense in which we can be said to be free? Let's have another look at each question, and see if there's any wriggle room.'

I thought we'd already decided the material world is determined. Atoms and whatnot bashing about … ?

'Well, there have been a couple of challenges to that view. One argument comes from the huge complexity of the physical world – a complexity that science tends to simplify – which means that we can never know enough to make determinism, in the sense of knowing what will happen, a reality. In the nineteenth century, the physicists James Maxwell and Ludwig Boltzmann had to resort to probability to explain the movement of gas particles in a container. There was just too much going on to ever predict what one atom would get up to. More recently, chaos theory similarly tries to explain certain complex systems – such as the weather, or the occurrence of earthquakes or solar flares – in which tiny variations in initial conditions lead to wildly varying and unpredictable results. Although chaos theorists can find recurrent patterns and areas of relative stability within the mayhem, they can never make the sort of absolute predictions that we think of as constituting "real" science. Modern computer weather forecasting may be much better than it was, but we'll only know for sure if I'll need an umbrella and you'll need your cute little jacket for tomorrow's walk when we're out in it.'

I hate that jacket. I get zero respect from the other dogs when you make me wear it.

'I disagree. You rock tartan. The trouble with both chaos and complexity of the kind we've been discussing is that even if they mean that in effect we can't predict the future with one hundred per cent certainty, that's simply a matter of the limitations of our knowledge. If we had a powerful enough computer, and an ability to feed in every detail about the state of the universe, then the precise effect of a butterfly flapping its wings in Borneo on the weather in Florida could be accurately predicted. We could foresee the movements of every atom in Maxwell's gas jar. So, ignorance doesn't get us out of the grip of determinism. We don't have to know exactly what the balance is of the forces that compel us, only that we are compelled.

But so far we've been talking about the universe as explained by classical physics – including the relativity revolution launched by Einstein. Einstein completely changed how we look at space and time, but his universe is still one that is absolutely predictable, as long as we focus on the big scale – a scale that goes all the way from galaxies to the atom. But things get very strange when we shrink the stage down to the subatomic level. And it's a strangeness that some have argued undermines that deterministic nature of the universe. Quantum theory tries – and largely succeeds – to account for the weirdness. This is hardly the place to discuss quantum mechanics, but I'm going to give a couple of very simple examples that should help to show the problem. When two billiard balls collide, we can predict exactly what will happen. When two electrons crash into each other, all that can be produced by way of prediction is a "probability cloud" – the electrons will be somewhere in that cloud. This is not the same as the problem of the atoms of gas in the jar, or of the unpredictability of weather. Those types of uncertainty are both down to our relative ignorance. With the electrons, there is simply no way in which the positions after the collision can be predicted. Quantum particles behave in ways that are not relatively, but *absolutely* unpredictable. This is linked to the notorious Heisenberg Uncertainty Principle. To predict the path of an electron, you'd need to know both its position in space and its momentum (the sum of its speed and mass). If this were a car or a stick or any other object in "our" world, there wouldn't be a problem. However, with quantum particles it is the case that we can know either their position, or their momentum, but never both.'

Why not?

'It's sometimes thought that this is a function of the so-called observer effect – the phenomenon whereby measuring something involves interacting with it in a way that changes what you were supposed to be measuring. An example from "our" world would be the fact that having your blood pressure taken often produces mild stress, which in turn raises your blood pressure. On the quantum level, measuring the position of an electron involves firing a photon at it. The photon collides with the electron, and inevitably changes its position and momentum.

However, quantum uncertainty is more profound than this. It has been demonstrated theoretically that uncertainty is an inescapable consequence of the wave-like nature of quantum particles. This has been backed up by experiments that proved, even when the measuring procedure does not directly interfere with a particle, measurement still changes the quantum state so as to render prediction impossible.'

So, wait, are we now saying that even the material world isn't determined?

'Some people have argued that.'

Some people? Not you, then?

'There are a couple of ways of evading quantum uncertainty for our purposes.'

Evading...?

'Answering. *Ish...* Firstly, it's not at all clear that quantum effects scale up, so as to manifest themselves on the level that impacts on our lives. Larger objects, from hydrogen molecules to hot air balloons, simply don't display the wave-like properties and indeterminacy of quantum particles. Quantum effects are lost on the larger scale due to a process called decoherence, a leaking away of the distinctive indeterminacy of quantum objects as they interact with the "normal" environment. It's been calculated that decoherence occurs within one billion billionth of a second – far too quickly for any meaningful effects to register on our scale.

Secondly, it's been argued, though not demonstrated, that the apparent randomness of quantum effects is just a sign that we haven't yet discovered the underlying principle that will restore predictability and determinism to the world (this was Einstein's view). Such a theory would enclose us once again in the web of necessity and determinism.'

Sooooo...?

'It's very hard to know what to make of these objections – particularly as a non-scientist. No one seems to quite know what the new unifying theory that would restore determinism would look like – it's simply that many scientists are unhappy with a world that escapes our ability to understand and predict. And although quantum indeterminacy isn't manifest in the world at the macro level, the fact that aspects of the world certainly *are* undetermined at least opens up cracks in the wall of necessity through which freedom, or something like it, might seep.

The rule *Everything is determined* leads on inescapably to the conclusion that our moral choices are determined. *Some things are determined* doesn't have quite the force. And despite the problem with decoherence, some scientists still maintain that consciousness is a function of quantum effects in the cells of the brain, and that this explains the undoubted oddness of consciousness, that feeling that a thought simply isn't like other stuff in the universe.

However, insofar as we're trying to establish whether or not we are free to make moral choices, quantum indeterminacy is of limited assistance. All that quantum mechanics can do is to introduce unpredictability and chance into the material world. The direction that one electron will take after hitting another is, it seems, genuinely random. If we try to read that knowledge across to our ability to make moral decisions, it is difficult to see how our situation is improved. Moral choice, if it exists, can't be about the operation of chance and randomness. Imagine if, when confronted with the choice of whether or not to hit you with a stick—'

What? I drifted off there for a moment. Why are we back with the stick thing again?

'Sometimes talking to your dog seems like a futile way to do philosophy… All I was saying was that if the physical world isn't fully determined, but lets in the possibility of chance, that doesn't move us on much in how free we are to make rational moral choices of the kind that allow for praise and blame, punishment and reward. So, imagine if, when confronted with the choice of whether or not to hit you with a stick, I took out a coin and tossed it. Heads I whack you; tails I throw the stick and you chase it.'

Not me, pal, as you know.

'OK, heads I whack you, tails I give you a doggy treat.'

Now we're talking. As long as you don't whack me.

'I'm not going to whack you.'

I scratched the stupid mutt behind the ear.

'But the point is, would you regard the outcome of this coin-toss as a rational, moral choice?'

No, of course not.

'Right. Einstein said God doesn't throw dice, and neither will we, when it comes to being moral.'

So, where does this leave us?

'On the balance of probabilities, the material world is determined. If it isn't, all that science can offer us as a respite from the grinding wheel of necessity is chance. But let's move on. Even given this bleak (or, sublime, I suppose) view of the universe as a huge machine, in which we are very small cogs, can we rescue any kind of sense of free will?'

I'm all ears.

'Determinists like to see themselves as hard-nosed, scientifically oriented realists, cutting through the wishy-washy nonsense about freedom and choice. But there's one big problem with determinism as a scientific explanation for the way the world is. Going back to whether or not I thwack you with my stick…'

Hah, bozo, you've thrown the stick away.

'It's a hypothetical boomerang, so back it came. Now, if I whack you, the determinist says that my *action* was determined. If I don't whack you, the determinist says that my *inaction* was determined. Whatever happens, the determinist says it was determined. So how could we ever disprove determinism? Every outcome is predicted. Nothing is ruled out. I used to know a girl at school. She had this catchphrase. Whenever you said anything, she'd reply, "I knew you were going to say that." And if you said, "No you didn't!" she'd say, "I knew you were going to say that." And this would carry on until you went insane or the bell rang for the end of break time.'

Annoying.

'Very. But just as scientific as saying that everything is determined. This is something we'll talk more about when we get on to the philosophy of science.'

Oh goody.

'It'll be fun, honest. But if determinism was a scientific theory, it should be able to make predictions that could be proved to be right or wrong. It should rule out certain outcomes, narrowing all the possibilities down to one. Determinism can't do that. So it isn't a scientific theory.'

So determinism loses, hurrah!

'Well, it can wriggle out of that one too by claiming that if we had perfect knowledge, we could make exactly the sort of predictions necessary to prove that it is a science. And perhaps one day there really will be computers clever enough to predict exactly what we'll have for lunch tomorrow. But for now, the claim of determinism to have the status of a scientific theory doesn't quite stack up. It's more like a theological belief.

But there are other reasons for holding on to our faith in freedom. Some philosophers aren't too concerned with material determinism. They think that you can accept everything that science has to say about atoms and quarks, but maintain that we are still, in a meaningful way, free. There's a term for it: *compatibilism*.'

Tell me more…

'Remember those things that we agreed affected our ability to freely choose? Being mentally ill, or asleep, for example.'

How could I forget? It involved me getting hit with a stick!

'We could add a few more things that would also interfere with our freedom to choose rationally. Let's say alcohol and recreational drugs. It would be fairly easy to arrange these in order of how far they impede our ability to act freely. And the extent to which that would then qualify moral responsibility. We could debate it a bit, but I'd say that the order might be something like, going from least responsibility to most: sleepwalking; severe mental illness, e.g. schizophrenia; milder mental illness, such as

119

anxiety and depression; drug use; alcohol. We can add or sub-tract other things that might affect us – being misled about the state of the world, acting in self-defence, etc. etc. I think it would be odd if a person denied that these sorts of things can affect our ability to act freely, and the consequent moral responsibility.

And this is a state of affairs mirrored in our legal system. Sleepwalking and madness are both defences under criminal law, which requires both the criminal act and the criminal intent. But if the determinist is correct, there can be no gradient of responsibility. Madness or drugs are irrelevant: we are all equally compelled to do what we do. And I think that the self-evident presence of the gradient must strongly incline us towards the idea that there are degrees of responsibility, and degrees of freedom.'

Monty wagged his tail.

'We have to go back to words and what they mean. When we actually use the term "free will", what do we signify by it? Most people instinctively take it to mean an absence of those impedi-ments we've discussed. Being free means being free from overt restrictions and constraints. If you precisely describe a situation of choice: say a man contemplating stealing a necklace from a jewellery shop, and you show how he is of sound mind, and capable of understanding right and wrong and the law of the land, and none of the other qualifications we apply are present – no one is holding his family hostage, and no one is covering him with a sniper rifle from a neighbouring rooftop – then this is precisely what we mean by free. Adding that there is a deeper force dictating our choices doesn't add anything to the explan-ation of what we do, and why.

Every day we make hundreds of small judgements. We thank people, tut at their selfishness, smile, nod, wave, ignore, rebuke, rebuff. We do these based on how we understand the actions and motivations of those around us. We assess in microseconds how guilty someone is. Someone accidentally steps on your toe. "Ouch," you say, then smile as she apologizes. Someone else parks her Range Rover in the disabled bay at the supermarket, leaps out and walks confidently to the store, not even bothering to put on a limp, and you curse her selfishness. To be human is to make these judgements. Some we get wrong. But we're good at it, and usually we get it right. The rather vague determinism somehow underlying the choices we make seems entirely irrelevant to our lives. Fate has certainly put us where we are. It has also equipped us with knowledge and intelligence. I can apply rational moral criteria to my decision making. I'll be influenced by many things, but that moment of choice, that hovering between options and deciding which way to go, can't be shirked or explained away. The huge dark shadow of determinism is so ubiquitous, so vague, so lacking in explanatory power that it can be cancelled out, removed from both sides of the equation.'

I looked down. Monty had wandered off into the trees. He looked tired. His limp was back.

'One last scientific interlude, before we have a rest. Evolutionary biology for a long time struggled to understand altruism in the animal world – altruism defined as reducing your own chances of surviving and reproducing in order to help another organism. Anything that reduces an organism's chances of having offspring ought to get selected out over time. And yet there are many examples in the natural world, the commonest being among social insects, where one member of a colony will sacrifice its life to defend the nest, and whole castes give up their ability to reproduce at all, in favour of the queen. But we see it in many species of mammals and birds too. Eventually scientists worked out that altruism in the animal world only exists in certain defined circumstances. Usually it was because the giver and receiver of the altruistic act were closely related, sharing genes. This is most glaringly the case with social insects. When a worker bee gives up her life defending the hive, it's a kind of selfishness, as all the female bees in the colony share exactly the same genes (they're essentially clones of the queen) so the sacrifice is worth it, in genetic terms, if it helps the colony thrive.

This shared gene hypothesis explains most but not all animal altruism. Some altruism occurs between unrelated members of the same species. Here the mechanism seems to be the promise of reciprocity. A vampire bat, returning from a successful hunt, will feed blood to another, unrelated bat that has been unable to leave the cave in the expectation that the favour will be returned when the circumstances are reversed. Several primate species help nurture unrelated young, again, storing up goodwill for the future.

Altruism of this kind is advantageous to the genes the organisms carry, and those genes dictate that the animals behave in this way. The behaviour is determined in the strictest sense.

Humans, of course, engage in both of these types of altruism. Parents will sacrifice themselves for their children – indeed, we are shocked when we encounter those rare occasions when a parent sacrifices the children to save themselves. And in social situations we're very aware of I'll-scratch-your-back-if-you-scratch-mine relationships. We remember the people who have treated us well, and we return the favour. If this was the full extent of our altruism, the rational explanation for it would be that it was also determined in the strongest sense, just as a bee has no choice but to sting you if the hive is threatened.

However, there are circumstances in which humans sacrifice themselves and their chances of reproducing without helping close kin, and with no hope of reciprocation. People have given up their places on lifeboats, or jumped into freezing water to save unrelated children. Soldiers have dived on hand grenades to protect other members of their platoon. Kamikaze pilots flew their planes into American warships. One way to account for this bizarre – from an evolutionary perspective – behaviour is that humans are unusually subject to group pressure. Those kamikaze pilots were influenced both negatively – by threats – and positively – by the promise of glory and honour. Are these not also factors that make these decisions determined? Not really. Not every Japanese pilot donned the white headband of the kamikaze. Not every man dives into the lake when the child is drowning. But some would say that often these types of altruistic behaviour occur in closed groups where even if we are not close kin, we will share many of the same genes, so could it just be a weak form of gene-selfishness?

But there are examples of human altruism where even this explanation won't hold. Many of us donate to charities helping to support those in the developing world. These are people with no close relationship to us, and people who are very unlikely to be able to reciprocate our actions. Humans are alone in performing these acts of "pure" altruism, and evolutionary scientists simply have no explanation for it.'

I suddenly realized that I was on my own. I looked back down the path. Monty was lying, exhausted, about ten metres away. I went back and picked him up.

'I forget how little your legs are. Anyway, the pub's right here.'

This was our destination: the quaint, whitewashed riverside pub I used to drop in at, alone or with a friend, all those years ago. I hadn't consciously known that this was my destination until I saw it.

'Let's have a drink,' I said.

And crisps.

It was still early enough for the outside tables to be free. I tied Monty up and went and got a beer, and a bowl of water.

You get the crisps?

'Of course.'

Cheese and onion?

We sat for a while. One of those impossibly thin rowing boats powered by eight oarsmen went past. Eight oarsmen with their muscles pumping, going blindly backwards. Were we really like that boat, driven by unseeing forces, unable to control or decide our course? Except, no, there was the little chap at the end. The one with the easy ride. He knew where they were going.

'What do you think, Monty? I mean about free will, the stuff we've been discussing.'

Monty had finished his half of the crisps. He licked the cheesy-oniony crumbs from around his mouth, giving himself time to think.

It's different for dogs. We just do stuff. Bark at the postman, pee on lamp posts, beg for snacks. We don't think, oh, is this right or is this wrong? We just do it. Or don't do it. It's why we're cleverer than you lot. You're like one of those computers you see in films from the olden days, you know, as big as a room. You ask it a question and lights flash on and off, and it makes a kind of whirring noise, and then out comes the answer. But we're state of the art. No waiting. Data in, action out.

I scratched his chin. Then he lay on his back with his legs in the air and I tickled his belly.

But give me a straight answer, for once. You guys. People. Are you really free?

'Well, I thought I'd answered that, at the end. The texture of our lives, the endless choices and judgements. That, I think, only makes sense if we're free. And the big, vague *everything determinism* just won't quite come into focus... But, OK, yes, I'll tell you what I think, and this is partly a rational philosophical belief, and partly a starry-eyed wish. I think that human beings are unique, in that we are suspended perfectly between two poles. It's possible to imagine us as pure ethical machines – an angel, if you like, programmed always to do the right thing. Utterly rational, coldly calculating. A Kantian machine, with pure reason, but no love. On the other side there is the ravening beast – no, not you, Monty, you're special – a ravening beast that acts always on impulse, eating, screwing, fighting, driven by forces it can't understand or control. An abominable thing, but one also with other, yet stranger impulses. Love and spasms of unnecessary kindness and wasteful pity. And then there's us in the middle. We have the urges of the beast – we want to do terrible things, and sometimes we do. But then there is the angel knowing what is right, guiding us. But the angel alone would be monstrous. What terrible things might the angel do, in the cause of good? But, sorry, this is meant to be about freedom. The beast and the angel are both unfree, one blinded by the light, the other by the darkness. But there, between the two, there is that tiny possibility of freedom. What was it that Heraclitus said? The equilibrium of the bow. That moment when the diver springs from the board, and hangs in the air, utterly free, gravity vanquished for a moment...'

And then down you go...

I laughed. 'Home time?'

Have another beer.

'Well, OK.'

A Very Short Logical Walk

On this walk, I have one job: to explain to Monty the type of logical argument called the syllogism.

We were out of milk. Milk is one of my responsibilities, along with turning lights off and dealing humanely with spiders in the bath.

'Fancy a quickie?' I said to Monty. 'Just down to the shops and back?'

Sure. Er, is this just a walk-walk, or is it a talk-walk?

'Seems a shame to waste it, so let's chat.'

OK, but keep it snappy.

'Right. Mostly we've been taking on the big questions, but maybe we can make this one a neat little, self-contained package. We could do the syllogism.'

Which is … ?

'… a type of logical argument developed by Aristotle. It can be very useful.'

Hit me.

We were out in the streets by this time.

'Right, a syllogism is made up of two propositions, which are called premises, and a conclusion. The classic type of syllogism has a major premise, which is usually a general proposition, a minor premise and then the conclusion.'

It's just noise until you give me an example.

'Okey-dokey. Let's stick with the classics:

All men are mortal. (Major premise)

Socrates is a man. (Minor premise)

Therefore Socrates is mortal. (Conclusion)

Got that?'

I think so.

'Before we go on, we should throw in a few more special terms.'

Oh goody.

'Don't worry, these are quite simple. A premise can be *true* or *false*, which is something you can establish by observation or enquiry, though we'll talk more about that later. The conclusion can be *valid* or *invalid*. A valid conclusion is one that follows unavoidably from the premises. An invalid conclusion is one that—'

Let me guess, does not follow necessarily from the premises?

'You're all over this one. If the premises are true, and the conclusion follows logically, then our syllogism is described as *sound*. Here's an example of a sound syllogism.

All dogs are mammals. (Major premise)

Monty is a dog. (Minor premise)

Monty is a mammal. (Conclusion)

If you accept that all dogs are mammals, and if you agree that Monty is a dog, then you just can't wriggle out of the conclusion that Monty is a mammal. You still with me?'

127

Yeah, you've proved I'm a mammal.

'You'll notice that the major and minor premises both have one term in common, which is known as the *middle term* – here it is "dog". And the conclusion will wrap together a term from both the major and minor premises, here taking "mammal" from the major and "Monty" from the minor.

This type of syllogism may seem curiously rigid, or formal, like some ornate, courtly dance. And it is also, undeniably, rather limited, in that the usefulness of the whole elaborate machine is dependent on the truth of the premises. It's a classic case of garbage in, garbage out. And so, all a syllogism can really do is help you organize what you already know, and draw the right conclusions from it. But when it works, it really works, and it can help you to clarify what seems like a hopelessly muddled situation. So, often you'll come across arguments where the conclusion doesn't follow from the premises. Or there are other situations where the truth of the premises is accepted, but the conclusion, even though valid, is rejected. In either of those situations you can win the argument by pointing out that your opponent is being illogical.'

Great. Though I've got to tell you that not many dog arguments turn on logic...

'Perhaps this type of logic is most useful in showing you when you've taken a wrong turn. Let's imagine this argument.

1. Monty is a dog.
2. Monty barks.
3. All dogs bark.

This is one of those cases where both the premises are correct, but the conclusion is not valid. Nothing in 1 or 2 entitles us to conclude that all dogs bark. What's gone wrong here is that both the premises are "minor", in that neither makes a general claim, yet the conclusion does make such a general claim, thereby going beyond anything we could deduce from the premises.

And, as we've said, the truth of a syllogism depends on the truth of the premises. Take this case:

All dogs bite postal delivery workers. (Major premise)

Monty is a dog. (Minor premise)

Monty bites postal delivery workers. (Conclusion)

Here the argument fails because the major premise is factually incorrect. Not all dogs bite postal delivery workers. So even though the argument is valid, in that the conclusion does follow on from the premises, the conclusion is false.

And that's the syllogism done and dusted. Wasn't too bad, was it?'

I'm still not convinced it's something I'm going to use much when I'm fighting over a Nando's wrapper with that mental whippet.

'It'll come in handy later on when we discuss the theory of knowledge. And, anyway, sometimes it's just nice to have something in your head that wasn't there before, don't you think?'

The streets were filling up with laughing children on the way back from school, their various carers busy on their phones, so Monty answered me with one of his mute but eloquent shrugs.

I bought a bottle of wine, and forgot the milk.

Walk 6

Metaphysics 101: The White Stuff in Bird Poo

O n this, the first of two thematically linked walks, Monty and I talk about metaphysics, encompassing those questions that deal with the fundamental nature of reality. The first walk introduces the subject, and we then move on to looking at what the very first philosophers, the pre-Socratics, said about the basic material constituents of the world, and how they were arranged and organized. And Monty finally finds out what 'ontology' means.

Sometimes a walk has a purpose, a goal. You have a destination in mind, a place to be or some task to perform. The philosophical term for this end-directedness of an action was, you'll recall, *teleological*. I said that teleology derives from the two Greek words *telos*, meaning end, and *logos*, meaning reason. But there's a bit more to logos than that. Logos, in its simplest sense, means word, or statement, or something said. No problems there. But then the meanings start to expand and slither away from any strict definition. In one of the few surviving fragments by our excrement-smeared friend Heraclitus, logos is used to mean something like *my explanation*, or *my account of why things are the way they are*. And then, by transference, it came to mean not just the explanation, but the thing that explains, i.e. human understanding and reason.

And now all things were possible, for logos.

The Stoics saw the entire natural world as inhabited and controlled by an intelligent entity, a spirit of universal reason, the Logos. Christianity gave this spirit of reason a human form, and called him Christ: In the beginning was the Word (*Logos*), and the Word was with God, and the Word was God. Here logos retains the idea of an intelligible statement, in that Jesus was the part of the Trinity that had been sent to bring the ineffable and incomprehensible majesty of God within the scope of our limited human understanding.

Er, hello.

'Oh, sorry. So sometimes a walk is teleological and sometimes—'

It's just a walk.

So Monty and I were on a non-teleological walk, except for the fact that dogs *have* to be walked, especially when you live in a flat. Non-teleological, then, in the sense that if even we had a purpose (the avoidance of having to clean the floor under the dining table, which has become Monty's last-resort, emergency bathroom), we didn't have a destination. It was just a directionless early-evening amble through the dull, damp streets of West Hampstead.

Though, of course, for a dog, the streets are never dull. They are alive with excitement, the smells spilling out and coiling everywhere like jazz in New Orleans. And every other dog encountered is a source of endless delight or fraught anxiety. The sniff, the growl, the kiss, the snap, the cringing retreat, the assertive thrust, the attempt to mount, the passive acceptance of mounting. It's all very much like a publisher's party or book launch. Although the dog-walk has the added complication and awkwardness of the owners having to dance around each other, disentangling leads and engaging in the great English pastime of competitive apologizing.

So what's this evening's topic?

'Hmmmm. Well, broadly you could split the core of philosophy into three major parts. There's the philosophy that tries to tell us how we should live…'

Ethics. Been there, done that.

'Then there's the philosophy that examines how it is we come to know anything, and what counts as knowledge. That's epistemology. We'll talk that over on a future walk.'

And this evening?

'Finally, there's metaphysics, which has become a catch-all category used for the sorts of topics that don't fall neatly into the other great branches of philosophy. So, the big, vague questions of what exists in the world, the nature of space and time, even what might be thought of as primarily theological issues, such as the existence of God: these have all been regarded as metaphysical. *Why am I here, and just what the hell is here?* might well sum it up.

Originally the meaning was more specific. Metaphysics was a name applied by later philosophers to a number of thematically linked books by Aristotle. Its literal meaning is "after the Physics", the *Physics* being Aristotle's books on natural science, which were mainly concerned with motion and change in the natural world. Metaphysics could mean either that these books go beyond or transcend Aristotle's works on physics, or perhaps just that they should be read after them. It's possible it just means that they followed them on the bookshelf.

Aristotle's own term for the matter dealt with in the *Metaphysics* is *first philosophy*, which he defines as the study of *being as such*. To put this in different words, the subject is existence: what exists, what categories of things there are in the world. Aristotle also says that he is studying "that which does not change", which makes a contrast with the "science" of change examined in the *Physics*. He also says that his subject is the "first causes of things".

This more limited subset of metaphysics, i.e. the question of *being*, is now generally called *ontology*, which is a lovely word, the utterance of which alone is enough to make you sound intelligent. Give it a go.'

Ontology.

'There – don't you feel smarter?'

Monty's ears pricked up. *Actually, I do...*

'It's a tricky and slippery idea (you'll be forgiven if *being* strikes you as an altogether amorphous concept), but it might be useful to contrast *ontology* – the study of what is – with *epistemology* – the study of what counts as knowledge, and how we come by it. So, Monty, if you ask me "What's for dinner?" that question exists in the ontological sphere. And if I reply "I don't know. I'll look in the cupboard when we get home," that's an epistemological answer.'

One more go?

'OK. What's the white stuff in bird poo? That's an ontological question. You're enquiring into the nature of the substance.'

Got that, I think.

'How can I discoverer what the white stuff is in bird poo? That's an epistemological question. You're asking about the nature of knowledge, not about the nature of stuff.

But the truth is that ontology and epistemology are intimately wrapped up in each other. As we'll see, the kinds of things that you believe to exist (ontology) dictate what tools and principles you apply when you're looking for them (epistemology). And if you have certain views about epistemology – say that you believe truth can only be revealed through the application of reason or, conversely, that knowledge is only discoverable through the senses – then that suggests a theory about what kind of stuff is waiting out there to be discovered. Yes?'

Er, what's for dinner?

'Bird poo.'

What!?!

'Oh, no, sorry. I was following our earlier train of thought. It's just that I think of ontology as starting off with a question about, well, bird poo. Specifically, what is the white stuff in bird poo?'

I'm so not with you.

'You know, some people look at bird poo and just see bird poo. Other people look at it and wonder what the white stuff is. Wondering what the white stuff is is the beginning of metaphysics. And possibly science.'

Really?

'Sure. What sort of stuff there is in the world, and how that stuff is organized and arranged, was the question that obsessed the earliest people we now describe as philosophers.'

Tell me more…

'Philosophy, as we know it, began in two main intellectual hotspots in the sixth century BCE. The first was Ionia, a strip of land along the Mediterranean coast of modern Turkey. From about the tenth century BCE, Greeks from the area around Athens had colonized the region, founding city states, such as Miletus, Colophon and Ephesus, which eventually grew rich on trade and commerce. That wealth created a culture that gave time and opportunity for some of the citizens to pause from their labours and look around them and begin speculating. They dug their hands into the earth and let it fall through their fingers; they watched sunlight sparkle on the water; they gazed at the moon; and they asked, "What is all this stuff really made of?"

What makes these first speculations *philosophical* was that rather than accepting the existing religious or supernatural causes for phenomena – thunder, for example, being the unfailingly lethal weapon of the god Zeus, or earthquakes being caused by his brother Poseidon's enraged thumping of the ground with his trident – they tried to find rational, natural explanations. And they backed up their speculations with evidence, or, in the absence of evidence, *reasons*.

Many of these so-called pre-Socratics (because they came before Socrates, although some overlapped with him, and a couple of them even met him) were practical men – the very first of them, Thales of Miletus, was an astute politician, a student of the natural world and an astronomer, who may (I'm actually a little doubtful about this) have predicted an eclipse of the sun in 585 BCE.

There's a nice story about Thales. Like many philosophers, he was too occupied with pondering deep matters to have the time to make much money. This made him something of a figure of fun to the worldly Miletans. He was mocked for his scruffy clothes and distracted air. He was compared to the fox that claims that the grapes are sour merely because he cannot reach them. And then he used his meteorological knowledge to work out that a bumper olive harvest was likely, bought up or rented all the olive presses for miles around and minted it when the harvest came in and, having a monopoly on the presses, he could charge what he liked. The point was to show that he scorned money not because he couldn't get it, but because he valued philosophy more.

But it is the pre-Socratics' theorizing, rather than their practical skills, that makes them interesting to us. Almost all the pre-Socratics came up with elaborate cosmologies, complex pictures of the structure of our universe, along with explanations for its origins. For Thales, the Earth was a disc floating on some vast expanse of water. Anaximander (610–546 BCE) posited an infinite space, with a sort of drum-shaped Earth at its centre. We live on the drum skin, the flattened top, on a landmass surrounded by an ocean. Anaximander's version of the Earth was the first to see it floating free in space, allowing room for the sun and stars and planets to orbit beneath it. Anaximander's answer to the question why the unsupported Earth didn't fall "down" through space shows how the pre-Socratics tried to think their way out of problems. As the universe is infinite, extending infinitely in all directions, the Earth has no particular reason to move in any one of these directions. In Anaximander's words, the Earth is "indifferent", like a fussy child rejecting her peas, carrots and fish fingers. This may be the first appearance in philosophy of the *principle of sufficient reason*, the argument that everything that happens occurs for a reason, is *caused* and can be fully explained by those causes. In Anaximander there is no good reason for the Earth to fall, and so it floats.

Anaximander had a follower of his own, Anaximenes. His Earth was a flattened disc of thickened air, drifting like a leaf in the void. For Parmenides (born c. 515 BCE), all of reality is a sphere, in which there is no variety, no change, no beginning, no end.'

Huh?

'Yeah, OK, Parmenides isn't quite like the others. Apart from anything else he wasn't from Ionia. He was from the other great centre of pre-Socratic thought that I mentioned, the Greek cities in southern Italy and Sicily. For some reason these residents of what was known as Magna Graecia tended to be a bit less tethered to reality than their Ionian cousins. Parmenides was the first philosopher to say that we shouldn't trust what our senses tell us about the world, but that we should begin with rational principles, and follow those principles through to the end, no matter how strange that end is. And where Parmenides takes us is Weirdsville.

He begins with what is for him the key distinction between *being*, by which he means all the stuff there is, and *non-being*, which is, well, everything there isn't. He claims it's literally impossible to conceive of a thing not existing, and therefore non-being cannot exist. With me?'

Er, ish...

'And if non-being doesn't exist, that has certain strange but unavoidable consequences. Being, i.e. everything there is, cannot ever have come into existence, because that would have meant there was a time before that when there was non-being – and we've already agreed that non-being is inconceivable and therefore impossible. And it can't end, for the same reason – because that would entail non-being. So our universe is eternal, without beginning or end. And not only does it stretch backwards and forwards in time, it must also be infinite in scope. To imagine that the world has a limited size is again to imagine the unimaginable: a place of non-being beyond its boundary. But the weirdness has barely begun. In everyday life we perceive around us discrete shapes and objects: people, dogs, lamp posts, cars. But to "see" these different objects must be another of those illusions.'

Really?

'Yes, because for me to stop being me and you to start being you means there must be a gap, a place where there is not me and not you. A not-being. And ...'

Not being is impossible!

'Good dog! There can't even be different types of stuff, wet stuff, dry stuff, heavy stuff, light stuff. White bird poo and black bird poo. Substances, if you like. Because if there were more than one substance, there would have to be that same gap, where one substance stopped being itself. So our universe is timeless, infinite, changeless, and there's only one kind of stuff, one substance.'

Nuts.

'Oh, yeah, and there can be no motion. If we move, it must mean that you enter a place where nothing else is, a place of non-being. So movement is as much an illusion as the existence of separate bodies.'

Some of the implications of Parmenides' assertion that time and motion and indeed the very idea of plurality are illusions are brought out in the paradoxes of his pupil, Zeno. There were originally forty or so of these paradoxes, of which only a handful have come down to us. One of the best known is Achilles and the Tortoise. Achilles, famously fleet-footed, has rashly agreed to take part in a race with a tortoise. I suppose he should have known that if a tortoise challenges you to a race, he has something up his sleeve. But poor naïve Achilles gives the tortoise a head start. They both set off. Before Achilles can catch up with the tortoise, he must reach halfway to it. In that space of time, the tortoise has trudged a little further on. Achilles must now go half this smaller distance. When he reaches that point, the tortoise has again progressed slowly. Once more Achilles must reach halfway. Again the tortoise has moved. The distance, it seems, will keep on shrinking, but Achilles will never catch up.'

Monty looked highly sceptical about this.

'I know what you're thinking. Of course Achilles would have caught up with the tortoise. All of the paradoxes seem vulnerable to a common-sense refutation. One says that a fired arrow will never reach its target. To reach halfway, it must first reach a quarter of the way; to reach a quarter of the way it must reach an eighth of the way; to reach an eighth, it must first reach a sixteenth. And so on forever.

Our old friend Diogenes the Cynic "refuted" Zeno by silently getting up and walking out of one of his lectures. Whenever I read this story I always imagine the grumpy sage lifting up his skirts and waving his hairy old bottom at Zeno in a final dismissive gesture. But the whole point of Parmenides' system is that you can't rely on "common sense" or on our perceptions of reality. Only reason can guide us to the truth, so the paradoxes have to be solved with reason and logic, and not by flapping your skirt and storming out of lectures.'

And the solution is … ?

'In truth it's still making people scratch their heads, even now. But there are two ways of making the problem go away. There's a mathematical solution, using calculus, which didn't exist back then – it had to wait another two thousand years to be invented by Leibniz and Newton, so no shame there. There's also a solution based not on maths, but on physics. All of Zeno's paradoxes assume that both motion and time can be divided up into an infinite number of individual static moments, almost like the film in a movie camera. So, if you stop the film, a moving body can be frozen at a particular time in a particular place. But in reality these static moments don't exist: it simply isn't what motion means: the moving body is always in a process of moving somewhere else. As soon as the granular texture of motion envisaged by Zeno is replaced by the fluid version, then the possibility of infinite regress disappears. But that's more detail than we need on Parmenides and Zeno. Though they'll be back...

What unites all of the pre-Socratics is the urge to explain the way things are in terms of simpler elements, to find an under-lying principle, or a first cause, the thing or things out of which all the other stuff is made. So those entertaining cosmologies, the drums floating in infinite space, and so on, are all con-structed by establishing first what the most basic elements are, and then arranging them in a logical way. Or so they thought. For Thales it was water: everything else came from water, either solidified as the earth, or rarefied as air. After Thales, all the other pre-Socratics had a go at the same game. Anaximenes thought it was air, which could be thinned to make fire, or suc-cessively concentrated to make clouds, water and rocks. Xenophanes (c.560–c.478 BCE) – another of our Ionians – thought that the history of the universe was of an epic struggle between wet and dry, each taking it in turns to dominate, with life only possible during the wet ages. Life – including human life – has been regenerated endless times over the course of this struggle. Anaximander took a different approach. He saw the various elements that had been championed as secondary products of some greater entity that he called the Infinite.

Empedocles (c.490–430 BCE) incorporated ideas from several of the earlier thinkers, constructing a theory that, because it was taken up and modified by Aristotle, was to be hugely influential down to the birth of modern science in the seventeenth century. For Empedocles the universe was made up of four elements, earth, fire, air and water, brought together or torn apart by two eternal forces: Love and Strife. These forces would combine and split the elements in an endless cycle.

As well as their theories on the material world, the pre-Socratics had interesting and challenging views on the nature of the gods. The Greek gods had always been seen in anthropomorphic terms...'

Eh?

'Oh, it's when you give things that aren't humans human-like qualities.'

Seems a strange thing to do.

'It does. But hard, it seems, to avoid when we're talking about the gods. So, the Greeks saw theirs as larger-than-life superhumans, their divine powers intermingled with the all-too-human frailties of lust, greed, anger. It's hardly surprising that the pre-Socratics, who tried to uncover the truth behind appearances, were not content with gods who seduced girls in the shape of swans, or were henpecked by their jealous wives or who tormented humans for their own amusement. Thales imagined a universe suffused with a divine mind, or, according to another interpretation, in which everything is possessed by gods. And was it not a mistake to see life only in animals and plants? Did not the ability of the magnet to draw iron show that it has within itself an animating force, a soul? Xenophanes claimed that there was only one god, and that he was incorporeal. He laughed at the human tendency to create gods in our own image. It was Xenophanes who said that if cows and horses or lions had hands and could draw, they would draw the forms of gods as cows or horses or lions.'

Dogs… ?

'Ah, well, Xenophanes doesn't explicitly mention dogs, but, yeah, sure. And slightly pulling in the other direction, our friend Empedocles claimed that *he* was a god, able to cure the sick, bring favourable weather, escape from the hands of death itself.'

So he's still with us, is he?

'Hah, no, I suspect Empedocles was a bit of a charlatan. There's an amusing story about him. He'd claimed that as a god he could not die, which came to prey on his mind as he got old and ill. The Ancient Greeks were very much concerned with their reputation after death – as we've seen, Aristotle thought that your personal happiness was a broad enough concept to include what happened to you after you were in the grave, and no man could be happy who had become a posthumous laughing stock. So if Empedocles died a normal death, and his body was found, suffering the usual indignities of corruption and decay, then his reputation as a god would take a bit of a beating. And so, feeling that his time was near, he secretly hauled himself to the top of Mount Etna – his handy local volcano – and threw himself in, hoping that his disappearance would confirm his divinity. Unfortunately, one of Empedocles' distinctive brass-soled sandals was found, either regurgitated by the volcano or left politely on the lip, the way you might slip your muddy shoes off in the porch. A less cynical reading of the end of Empedocles has him throwing himself into the volcano to prove his belief in reincarnation. "I'll be back," he cries, as he hurls himself into the fiery depths.'

Monty turned and gave me another of his Doubting Thomas looks. *You know an awful lot about these guys who lived a very long time ago*, he seemed to say.

'Fair point. Although I'm confidently expounding the views of these thinkers, we actually only possess fragmentary and second-hand knowledge of most of them (the exceptions being Parmenides, of whom we have extensive sections of his major work, *On Nature*, and Empedocles, of whom we have a few hundred lines from his two long poems, *Purifications* and yet another *On Nature*). What we know about them mainly comes down to us through later philosophers who quoted them, arguing, agreeing, disagreeing. Most important among these was Aristotle, who mainly quoted them to point out where they were wrong.'

Sounds like they were wrong most of the time...

'We shouldn't underestimate the pre-Socratics' radicalism, or their importance in trying to make sense of the physical world. Their method was to understand by analysing, in the strict sense of breaking down something complex into its constituents, and showing how when combined or transformed these constituents make all the familiar things we see around us. And in many ways what they achieved was pretty impressive. They didn't accept the account of the world handed down to them and believed by most of their contemporaries, but looked and thought and reasoned, and tried to come up with better answers than just "the gods made it thus". You could argue that what they were doing was more akin to science than philosophy. And that is both their triumph and their tragedy. Nobody believes their fascinating and bizarre cosmologies, the drums suspended in space, the discs floating on water. Zeno's paradoxes still tax clever minds, but no one studying sports science thinks they can employ the methods used by the tortoise to keep ahead of Achilles to improve athletic performance today. Science moves on, leaving old theories behind in a way that philosophy never really does. In philosophy, the old theories never quite get shaken off. Perhaps the answers might not satisfy, but the questions stay fresh.'

And that's a good thing?

'That the questions in philosophy never seem to get a decisive answer? No, I don't think it's a good thing. But maybe it isn't entirely a bad thing either. And don't roll your eyes at me, old dog. The questions that philosophy poses just might not be the sorts of questions that ever have a single, straightforward answer. And the ones that *were* amenable to a factual answer, such as the one about the nature of the cosmos, well, they got answered. Modern physics tells us pretty much all we need to know about the sort of stuff there is in the universe, and modern astronomers know what shape the universe is, and how it began, and how it will probably end.

Modern science is only possible because of the power of mathematics, which itself was once a branch of philosophy. Perhaps the most enigmatic of all the pre-Socratics, Pythagoras (c.570–c.500–490 BCE), is now remembered mainly for his mathematical theories, and less for his belief in the transmigration of souls, or the deleterious effects of eating beans. Plato was greatly influenced by Pythagoras, and had the words "Let no one ignorant of geometry enter" inscribed over the doorway to his philosophical school, the Academy. Descartes and Leibniz were both brilliant mathematicians.

So perhaps philosophy is like an insane asylum: we house all the lunatics, until they get well, and they leave us. We don't get the credit for curing so many because they've gone out into the world to live productive lives.'

Monty said nothing, but I sensed his disdain for this line of reasoning.

And then I remembered another of the pre-Socratics.

'Most of the quasi-scientific theories we've been discussing are now curiosities in the history of thought. But one had legs. Democritus (c.460–c.370 BCE) was another of those Ionian Greeks, who tended to be a bit more grounded than their more speculative colleagues in Magna Graecia and elsewhere. Following on from ideas concocted by his teacher, Leucippus, Democritus proposed that matter was made up of tiny, invisible particles, moving in a void. All the properties of the world about us were created by these *atoms.* An atom was what happened when you divided matter, cutting it down, using an imaginary scalpel, until you reached a point at which it could no longer be divided, no matter how sharp your blade. Here was your undividable, indestructible and eternal atom. The atoms came in different shapes, and these shapes determined the qualities of the substances formed by them. Heavy, dense metals such as iron and gold were made from atoms that hooked closely together. Water atoms, on the contrary, were slippery and only loosely bound together. Both fire and the soul were composed of active, circular atoms.

Democritus was a materialist, meaning that for him the atoms, and the void in which they moved, were all that there was. No strange non-material substances, no heavenly realm, no gods were permitted in his universe. Indeed, Democritus is supposed to have been the first to say that rather than gods creating men, men created gods.

Although Democritus' theory in some ways looks very modern, and certainly comes closer to what science regards as an accurate picture of reality, it's not really a scientific theory in the modern sense. Democritus didn't conduct experiments, or subject his hypothesis to rigorous testing. He looked at the world and speculated.

His argument went something like this: everything around us is subject to decay; living creatures die, rocks collapse and crumble, waters evaporate, wood rots. And yet there are still living creatures, rocks, waters, woods. This must be because the ultimate matter from which they are composed persists. And over time it will reform, and all these substances will be recreated. Democritus imagined a universe that was full of worlds like ours, endlessly being destroyed and reformed.

It may be that if Democritus' theory had won out in the Classical battle of ideas, it would have resulted in something like the birth of modern science. But it lost. A universe composed of the four elements of Empedocles, fire, water, earth and air, a universe without a void, meaning that even outer space was filled with "ether", remained the standard model right down to Newton.

One of the main reasons for that was the advocacy of Aristotle. Aristotle's works on physics – heck, his works on nearly everything – shaped how the Classical and medieval worlds saw themselves. Only one person rivalled Aristotle in both genius and influence. It's time we talked Plato.'

It's time we talked dinner.

Ah, I'd wandered too long in the backstreets. The street lamps and car lights were on, casting complex shadows on the world. The first of the returning commuters were clipping along the pavements. It was no time to be talking philosophy.

'OK, boy, home it is.'

And dinner.

'And dinner.'

Metaphysics 101: The White Stuff in Bird Poo

Just one thing, though.
'Yeah?'
What is the white stuff in bird poo?
'Ah, well, that's bird poo, too.'

Filling Out the Forms and the Problem of Universals

O n our second metaphysical walk, Monty and I discuss Plato's theory of Forms, and the related 'problem of universals'; in other words, what is the relationship between the general idea of a dog and any particular dog? Do general ideas have a real existence, or are they nothing more than useful words? We also talk about seagulls.

Even when young and sprightly, Monty never showed much enthusiasm for his last walk of the day, especially in the winter months. These days he bitterly resented being dragged out into the cold. I called out the usual bright 'Walkies!', but rather than the eager clipping of his nails on the floor, there was only silence, and I had to go and track him in his lair. I found him asleep on our bed. He'd made a sort of nest from my pyjamas. He was kept company by his toy lamb, and the dental floss box, which was his favourite chew toy. I made a mental note to buy more floss, knowing that I'd probably forget, and remember only when I realized that I was flossing my teeth with something that tasted like Monty's breath.

'Come on, fella,' I said, 'we haven't done with metaphysics.'

He gave me a mournful look, suggesting that only a sadist would drag him out in this filthy weather.

We walked down to the Green on the corner, dark and deserted at this hour. In the hot summer we'd just had, rough sleepers made beds of flattened cardboard boxes and slumbered under the trees. But now we were alone. I sat on a bench bathed in a dim neon pool cast by a nearby streetlight, while Monty sniffed at the tired trees, and peed in a desultory fashion. And then he came over and put his front paws up on my knee.

'Up you get then,' I said, expecting him to jump the rest of the way. But he just looked at me, his black eyes reflecting the streetlights, so I lifted him on to my lap, and he nestled there warm in the night chill.

'Comfy?'

He sighed and burrowed further into me, worming his way under my jacket.

'We've seen how the pre-Socratics tried to make sense of the world by breaking it down into the elements or constituents that formed it, and then constructed various elaborate cosmologies to explain our place in the universe. Some of it is interesting, some of it crazy. Not much of it survived for long as a living tradition. And we've also met Plato, and his teacher, Socrates, on our earlier walk. Discussing ethics, we saw how Plato proposes that there is an entity, the Good, that exists in a mysterious realm outside our world. Plato argues that any action we perform is only good insofar as it "partakes" in this entity, the Form of the Good. Back then we concluded it wasn't actually very useful, in terms of helping us to decide how to behave ethically, but now let's examine the wider theory into which Plato's ethical thinking slots.

We're also going to be discussing a related problem – in fact, Plato's theory of Forms is an attempt to solve this problem ...'

And the problem is ... ?

'Dogs.'

What?

'The thing about dogs is that you come in all shapes and sizes. No other animal exhibits such morphological exuberance, such variety. An alien visitor would never put all these diverse quadrupeds into the same species, based on appearance alone. Only your genetic code, and I suppose your willingness to get cosy with each other ...'

Embarrassing.

'... reveals your kinship. So then the question is, what makes a dog a dog?'

Huh?

'I mean, why do we decide to put all you guys in one group, and call you dogs, and then have different groups for foxes, cats and whatever?'

It's obvious. A dog is a dog. A thing like me.

And then Monty did a quick woof, whether for me or at the scent of a lurking fox, I don't know.

'Good effort. Let me translate that for you. Your definition is that a dog is a quadruped that barks. Perfectly OK for a first stab. But let's subject it to a bit of the old dialectical method. If Socrates were here, walking up and down in his sandals, with his chiton wrapped around himself, he would now give examples of dogs that don't bark, showing that your conditions are not *necessary*, and of quadrupeds that bark but which aren't dogs, such as sea lions, showing that your conditions are not *sufficient*.

150

This might be a good time to have a little digression on *necessary* and *sufficient* conditions, as they come in useful more often than you'd think, not just in philosophy, but in everyday situations. Let's concentrate on our barking dog.

For a dog to be a dog, there are certain things that have to be true about it. For example, it must be a mammal. And it must be in the family *Canidae*, along with its cousins the jackals and foxes, and the genus *Canis*. You might also want to say that it must be, or at least has been, alive. And that it exists. These properties are *necessary* conditions for doghood. Without them, whatever we have before us, we cannot conclude that it is a dog.

But none of these count as a *sufficient* condition. By that I mean that none of them on their own would be enough for us to say that whatever we have is definitely a dog. There are alive things that aren't dogs. There are mammals that aren't dogs. There are members of the family *Canidae* that aren't dogs.

And now I think about it, I'm not sure that there are any single *sufficient* conditions for being a dog, other than a tautological one to do with specifying its precise genetics.'

Stop! Tautological…?

'A tautology just means you're saying the same thing twice, using different terms. And it might be clumsy and stupid, like the US president who said "We must come together to unite", or it could be useful, helping to tease out some half-hidden truth, or clarify part of a definition. If I say that all men are mortal, that's a tautology, because mortality is part of the definition of man, but it's still a useful reminder.'

Thanks, got that.

'Back to barking dogs. Let's say that dogs *were* the only animals that barked. In that case, barking would be a sufficient condition for us to conclude that Monty is a dog. Perhaps we

should veer away from dogs for a moment, to nail down suffi-
ciency. A number being divisible by ten is a sufficient condition
for it being divisible by two. OK, that's a bit dry. Leeds is in the
county of Yorkshire. So, a man being born in Leeds is a sufficient condition for his being a Yorkshireman. (But in this case,
being born in Leeds is not a necessary condition for being a
Yorkshireman, because Yorkshire is a greater entity than Leeds,
and you are just as much a Yorkshireman if you're born in
Bradford or, heaven help us, Sheffield.)

Where were we? Oh, yes, we were talking about the abstract
idea of "dog". Is there a sense of the word "dog" that applies not to
any specific dog, this shi tzu or that Labrador, but to dogs in general? And if there were such a thing, it would have very different
qualities to a specific, individual dog. Because it could be in more
than one place at the same time – in a dog here in London, and
another dog in Beijing. And yet even though it existed in those
different places, it would still be one thing, and not many things.
So already we have something slightly curious, no?'

Monty seemed to agree.

'As an individual dog, Monty, you have certain qualities, your
beauty and courage…'

No need to be sarcastic.

'And then there is the Rottweiler we meet on the Heath, who
has different qualities…'

Monstrous, stupid, smelly.

'And then the poodle from the Green…'

She loves the smell of her own pee, that poodle.

'Quite so. Lots of different individuals, with an almost
infinite variety of attributes. But is there a quality of "dogness"
that covers them all? And if there is such a general *form* or *idea*
of dogness, what sort of thing is it, and where does it live? What

is the relationship between this idea of dogness and actual dogs?'

I don't know, but I've a feeling you're about to tell me.

'I'll try. But this is another of those philosophical problems that have perplexed philosophers almost from the moment such a thing as philosophy came into existence, and it still perplexes them now. It's called the *problem of universals*. I can tell you what solutions have been put forward, and what looks like the best of a not entirely satisfactory lot. But it's going to be a longish walk…'

Monty didn't object, so I began.

'As we've seen, in the early dialogues, Socrates ties his debating partners into knots as they try to define certain key concepts, such as courage, virtue and beauty. Whenever anyone tries to find a common link, a definition that covers all the instances of the quality at issue, endless complexities and contradictions emerge, and our hapless searchers after knowledge go home defeated. We are looking for one thing, yet all we find are multitudes.

Plato's answer to the muddle we get into when we try to define these general terms is to argue that we are looking in the wrong place. Staring at the confusion of the world around us will get us nowhere. In fact, this very confusion is a clue that there is something "better" and "truer" in a world beyond ours. Plato's most famous account of this other world, and its relationship to ours, is his metaphor of the cave, in the *Republic*. In it he says that humans are like prisoners chained facing the back wall of a cave. Behind us, beyond the mouth of the cave there is a fire burning. Figures pass in front of the fire, and their shadows, fleeting and weirdly contorted, briefly play on the wall before our puzzled eyes.

The objects we apprehend with our senses in the world around us are just such shadows, copies of the true reality, lurking just beyond our ability to fully grasp it. The *real* entities that make up this higher reality – the figures passing outside the cave – are the Forms, or Ideas. These Forms are not simply ideas in our minds, but have a reality, a true external existence. They are unchanging, eternal, perfect. It is only by coming to know the Forms that we will achieve true knowledge and wisdom and, with it, happiness.'

I looked at Monty. He looked back at me. I sensed I was going to have to work a bit harder to bring Plato's theory of Forms to life.

'In the *Phaedo*, Socrates asks us to imagine three sticks.'

You and your sticks. It's an obsession.

'Pay attention, this is important. And it's kinda cool that one of the most important arguments in the whole of philosophy involves sticks. So, are you imagining the three sticks?'

I need a bit more detail on the sticks before I can imagine them properly.

'Two are yay long, one is a little longer.'

Got it.

'Now, thinking about the two sticks that are the same length. We would say that they are equal in length, or, put another way, that they have the property of being equal, just as they have the properties of being made of wood, of being brown, of having fallen from a tree. I'm going to use a bit of jargon here, but it's not too bad, and might be useful later on. In philosophy – especially in logic – we use the term "predicate" to mean something you can say about something. In a sentence, you will have the subject and the predicate. For example, in the sentence *Monty is white*, you, Monty, are the subject, and white is the thing we've said about you, the predicate. Returning to our sticks, the predicates *wood*, *brown* and *equal* (along with lots of others) can all be applied to them, agreed?'

I guess so. At least to the two that are equal...

'Great. But now, as you've already surmised, if we compare the two equal sticks to the longer one, they are now *unequal*. So, the predicate *unequal* applies to them just as much as the predicate *equal*. We might wonder how a thing can be both one thing and the opposite of that thing. Plato makes a similar point about heat: something can be hot in relation to one thing, and cold in relation to another. So, heat isn't some straightforward predicate. It is instantly caught up in a complex network of relationships.

And going back to our roughly equal sticks. If we measure them precisely, we'll find, of course, that they aren't exactly equal. One might be 22 centimetres, and the other 21.5 centimetres. And other objects we reckon to be equal, even rulers or tape measures that we regard as exactly the same length, if we measure them using yet more precise measuring instruments, we'll find that they aren't exactly equal, but vary by tiny degrees.

And all around us, Monty, there are geometric shapes. You see how the eaves of the houses here form triangles? And the windows are various types of rectangle or square?'

Monty had a quick glance around, and didn't dispute the point.

'We see them as triangles and squares and so on, yet if we measured them, they would turn out to be slightly *out*. The angles would be a little wrong. Nothing is quite what it seems.

A number of questions then present themselves. The first is that given all these things that aren't quite equal, or aren't quite triangles, how do we recognize them in the first place as triangles or equals? We never, in fact, experience a *true* triangle, or *true* equality. Yet we have the idea, not just of *vague* triangularity, but of *perfect* triangularity. And it might well seem that we recognize all these near-misses as triangles or squares or equals only because we have the idea for a perfect triangle or square or equality to compare them to. And if we've got that idea of a perfect triangle, where has it come from, given the appalling lack of perfection in the world around us?'

Dunno, said Monty, or I think he did.

'There's another of Plato's dialogues, the *Meno*, in which one of the characters – well, actually, it's Meno – puts a paradox to Socrates. Let's say I want to find out what a lion is. If I have no idea what a lion is, and I go wandering about in the world trying to find one, how will I know when I meet one?'

Because to find the lion, I must already know what a lion is. Neat.

'Put another way, if you know the answer to the question, why ask? If you do not know the answer, then you would not know the right answer even if it bit you on the bum.

Plato's theory of Forms is his answer to this and other related problems: the question of how we know anything, and, more specifically, the problem of how we define certain general terms. When we recognize something as beautiful or large or equal or triangular, it's because we have a prior knowledge of these things as perfect Forms, and so can recognize the shadows before us.'

Like the Form of the Good? From our ethics walk?

'Exactly.'

So, these Forms, if we're here, and they're there, wherever there is, and all we ever have here is the shadowy reflections, or whatever, how do we ever get to know what they are?

'Great question. And Plato's answer is, if I'm honest, one of the most embarrassing things in the history of philosophy.'

Say what?

'It's true. I honestly believe it's the worst argument ever put forward by an otherwise sensible person. The argument is linked to another of Plato's obsessions – the idea that our souls are, like the Forms, eternal. He believed, as do many religious people, that our souls lived before us, and they survive our death. It's one of the reasons Socrates was so sanguine about taking the hemlock – his husk would fall away, leaving the vital part of him, the true Socrates, unharmed.

But how to prove it?

Easy. What Socrates does in the *Phaedo* is to question an uneducated slave boy about certain abstruse mathematical concepts. It takes some sensitive and patient probing, but finally he manages to get the poor boy to come out with some complex theories that he simply couldn't have learned in his intellectually impoverished life on Earth. The only possible reason for this, Socrates claims, is that he learned these mathematical principles before he was born. There was a time when his soul was in contact with the Forms, and although the memory of that time is lost when we are born, the knowledge of the Forms remains. This is his answer to Meno's paradox. We can find the lion because we, or rather our souls, encountered the Form of the Lion before we were born into this world of strife and confusion.'

You're right. That sucks.

'Doesn't it? Plato has "proved" that something exists by inventing a character in a work of literature, and putting words in his mouth. It's as if I proved that dogs can perform opera, by describing how you now stood on your back legs and sang "Nessun Dorma".'

That's stupid. It's for tenor and you know I'm a baritone.

'So we have an unconvincing argument put forward to defend a truly strange proposition, i.e. that certain abstract ideas have a real existence in another realm, and our own understanding of the world is based on our prior acquaintance with those entities.

But let's not dismiss Plato's Forms just yet. There are elements of the theory that do seem to solve genuine puzzles. The issue of how we get to the idea of a perfect triangle or perfect equality when these things don't exist around us is a real one. To take part in any form of mathematics involves manipulating perfect ideas, circles, triangles, squares. Even the numbers themselves exist as ideal entities. The number three does seem to have an existence separate from all the instances of *threeness* in the world. It has a timelessness and purity that will surely still be there after our world has been eaten by the sun, and our universe finally collapses back in on itself. And if three can exist in this perfect way, then why not the idea of beauty, or of love or of justice?

But so far all we have is the rather vague notion of what the Forms are and how they relate to the material world around us. It has to be said that Plato scatters clues to his meaning throughout the dialogues, without ever quite nailing things down. Perhaps the best place to start is with his dialogue the *Parmenides*. In this work, a young Socrates discusses an early version of his theory of Forms with an old Parmenides. Parmenides goes to town on it, pointing out various problems and contradictions.'

So giving Socrates a taste of his own medicine!

'Quite. And the truth is that this shows Plato at his best, prepared to subject his own theory to a vigorous critique. There's not much else like it in the whole history of philosophy.'

And look at you being nice about Plato for a change!

'I try to be fair... Anyway, Parmenides takes three different tacks. He first tries to get Socrates to say exactly what sorts of things have a Form. Oneness, he says, Justice, Beauty. Fair enough. But what about slightly more commonplace things? What about humanity? Is there a Form of Man? Or what about fire?'

The Form of the Dog?

'That isn't mentioned, but, yep, our guy would have to answer that, too. Socrates isn't sure of the answer here. In other dialogues, the idea of a Form is widened to include relatively mundane things, such as beds and chairs, but the young Socrates of the *Parmenides* isn't quite there yet. But what about still baser things? What about dirt and hair? Definitely not, replies Socrates, which amuses Parmenides, who thinks he's being too prissy. If the Forms are the general terms that give meaning to particular instances, surely everything that is part of a larger group must have a form?

But Parmenides has far more important criticisms to make. According to the theory, we have the Forms existing in their eternal realm. And we have their reflections around us in our reality. So how, exactly, are they connected? What is it about the Form of the Good that unites it with a good act performed in Athens? Parmenides uses the example of largeness. There are many large things around us, mountains and elephants and oceans. If the largeness of these large things is explained by the Form of the Large, what exactly does that entail? Does a small piece of the Large somehow reside in these earthly large things? If so, how could a small piece of the Large make a large thing large? Or is the Large like a huge sail that covers all the large things? None of these possibilities seems very enticing. We are left with the unsatisfactory idea that the individual instances of largeness somehow "partake" in the Form of the Large, or that they "resemble" it.

But resemblance is a strange sort of thing to say about a substance without material form. I find it helpful to substitute the idea of a colour for some of the vaguer examples Plato uses. So, he's saying that all the instances of blue in the world are blue because they have something in common with the Form of the Blue.

But now Parmenides has what is often taken to be a knock-down argument against the theory of Forms. It's one of the great arguments in philosophy, and we're going to have to concentrate on this one, though it's quite simple when you get it.'

Says you.

'It's called the Third Man Argument, because when Aristotle explained it, he used the example of the Form of Man. In the *Parmenides*, Plato uses largeness, but I'm going to stick with the Form of the Blue. Let's say I have compiled a list of blue things. The sea, the sky, a sapphire necklace, the eyes of my beloved, a kingfisher's wing, a line of mould in a Stilton cheese. The theory of Forms says that these are all blue because they *partake in*, or *resemble*, the blueness of the Form of the Blue. Got that?'

Monty grunted his assent.

'But now we have this group of things that are blue by virtue of the fact that they resemble the Form of the Blue. And we also have the Form of the Blue. But how can we know that the Form of the Blue resembles this group of blue things? By the same logic that grouped together the blue things, we must now have a second and greater Form of the Blue, which unites the first Form of the Blue and all the blue things. Still with me?'

Monty looked at me, and didn't obviously signal that I'd left him behind.

'But now we have the original Form of the Blue, plus all our blue things in one group, and the second Form of the Blue on the other side. They must resemble each other, mustn't they? And if they resemble each other, it must be in relation to yet another – our third – Form of the Blue. And, of course, this will go on forever, an infinite regress of Forms. You with me?'

I honestly don't know if I understand or not. Try harder? Be more doggy?

'OK. Let's say we have a load of delicious bones. We know they are all bones, because we have a picture of a bone, the sort of thing you'd see being eaten by a dog in a cartoon. A perfect, Platonic bone. We use this picture to assess whether the various things that might be bones actually are bones. But now we have a group made up of the bones that pass the test, plus the picture. How do we know that the picture and the bones resemble each other? Why, we have another picture that the bones and the picture of the bones resemble. And how do we know that the original bones, the picture of the bone and the second picture of the bone belong together? Why, we produce yet another pictorial bone.'

Monty shook his head, and said, *Nuts.*

'Well, yes, nuts. It's an argument that Plato never really escapes from. As soon as you say that blue things are blue *because* they resemble a greater entity, the Form of the Blue, then you're on the slide to the infinite regress. Does Socrates have an answer to it, in this dialogue? Not really. Except that Parmenides concludes by saying that Socrates is definitely onto something, and that all of his objections can be overcome.'

What do you think?

'Hmmm… well, as you've seen, I've been a bit reluctant to commit myself so far, in most of these debates. But I can tell you unequivocally that I think Plato's theory of Forms is nonsense. It's nonsense that was to go on to have a long history. The theory fell out of fashion for a few hundred years after Plato's death, when other philosophical schools moved to centre stage in Athens and then Rome. But it came bursting back with Plotinus (204/5–270 CE) and the Neoplatonists, who were important in the formation of the ideas underpinning Christianity. The idea that there are perfect Forms dwelling on another plane of existence chimed beautifully with the views of the early Church Fathers, and God became associated with the ultimate Form of the Good. Although it had to compete with Aristotelian ideas, Neoplatonism remained a key undercurrent in the philosophy of the Renaissance, and lurks in many of the greatest works of art ever produced. You can find it in John Donne and Shakespeare, indeed wherever a contrast is made between the humdrum world of the everyday and a plane of higher existence, which is considered to be more true, more real. But, no, it was basically bullshit, and gets us absolutely no closer to understanding the true nature of the world.'

Cripes. So what next?

'A quick reminder, because we've covered a lot… We're still trying to get at the meaning of general terms, like "dog" and "triangle". Plato had a fair crack, and failed. And after Plato we have…'

Aristotle, perchance?

'You've spotted the pattern! OK, with Plato we have the idea that we only understand individual examples of a thing, in fact only recognize them as the kind of thing they are, because we already have the abstract idea of that thing. I've got that photo of a perfect bone, and whenever I think I might have a bone I check it against the photo, and if it resembles the photo, then bone it is. Aristotle's answer to the problem of universals was that, yes, there is such a thing as a universal, a general idea, but that we come by it in a very different manner, and that it exists in a very different way.'

Do tell.

'*The School of Athens*, the famous fresco by Raphael in the Vatican, portrays a scene bursting with the joys of intellectual debate. Many of the great philosophers of the Ancient world are there, including several we've already bumped into here – Parmenides, Heraclitus, Epicurus and Socrates – all chatting merrily away. It's a philosophy party you'd really love to be at, though there aren't many women (I count one: philosophy's great female pagan martyr, Hypatia, sliced to pieces with sharpened oyster shells by a Christian mob in 415 CE), and the wine hasn't yet begun to flow.

At its centre are two figures deep in conversation. One is Plato, who is pointing up towards the heavenly realm of his Forms. *Look up: that's where the truth is*, he says. The other is Aristotle. He is gesturing downwards, with an open palm. *Not in the heavens, but on the earth, will we find the truth of things.* It's a brilliant summary of the rival metaphysics of the two philosophers.

Aristotle is the most modern of all the Ancients. His range of interests was vast – he wrote on biology, geology, physics and astronomy, as well as the more conventional philosophical areas of logic, metaphysics and ethics. His method was always to begin with the evidence of the senses. All knowledge began for him with what we could see. After gathering the raw data of the senses, we could then apply logic and rationality to construct laws and generalizations.

Unsurprisingly, then, Aristotle looked for the origin of general terms in the world we can perceive. He began by rethinking universals as predicates (remember those?) that could be applied to many subjects. So, of the various things we could say about you, Monty, some are specific and apply only to you: your name, your exact size and weight, your particular smell. The things that make you, you. But then there are some predicates that apply not only to you, but to lots of things. The colour white and the species dog, for example. These are *universals*. Plato said that these universals have a separate real existence, outside any earthly bodies. This position is sometimes called *extreme realism*, despite the fact that I think it's extremely unrealistic. Aristotle's position is that the *whiteness* and *dogness* are real things, but that they only exist when embodied in an object. So we really can talk about "dog", meaning a quadruped with certain characteristics, the characteristics of dogness, but that dogness only lives in specific actual dogs. The same would go for blue. Blue is a real thing, but we shouldn't think of it as living in a special realm with the Platonic Forms, but only in a blue sky, blue sea or blue eyes. Furthermore, insofar as we can talk about a universal dog, or triangle or blue, it is by abstracting from the manifestations of these qualities in real objects.'

Sounds not unreasonable.

'In Plato, we recognize the imperfect triangles around us by virtue of their resemblance to the perfect triangle we remember from the pre-existence of our souls; in Aristotle, we look at the imperfect triangles and are led by them to understand and recognize the ideal perfect triangle.

Aristotle's view is known as *hard realism*, and it was the most widely accepted notion of the nature of universals from the Classical world right the way through to the Middle Ages.

Let's get a little history out of the way. The philosophers we've been talking about – the pre-Socratics, Socrates, Plato and Aristotle – were part of a clear tradition. They knew each other's theories, often knew each other directly as friends, rivals, masters and pupils. And this tradition carried on, with the schools formed by Plato and Aristotle continuing to flourish for hundreds of years, competing for attention with the Epicureans and Stoics and the various flavours of Scepticism and Cynicism. And then, after almost a thousand years of vigorous life, it sometimes seems as though philosophy went into a long sleep with the fall of the Western Roman Empire, battered by internal strife, external assault and catastrophic plagues. The philosophical schools of Athens were closed by the Christians, for whom philosophy was inextricably linked to the old pagan ways. And, besides, what use were scholars arguing about the relationship between the general concept of bone and any particular bone, when the barbarians were at the gates, threatening to make bones of them all?

But the thread was never quite cut. During Late Antiquity, as the period from the decline of the Classical world under the assault of the barbarian invasions through to the emergence of a more settled world in the Middle Ages is generally known, the torch was carried by a few diehards, such as St Augustine (354–430) and Boethius (477–524), Platonists both, who continued debating the issues that had preoccupied the first philosophers. Muslim scholars preserved many texts that would otherwise have been lost, and specialized in working through the consequences of Aristotelianism. When learning flickered back into life in the Middle Ages in Europe, it was often these Arabic texts that gave philosophers access to the classics. Philosophical enquiry also persisted in Byzantium, where the Eastern Roman

Empire endured, with periods of glory and ignominy, until 1453, when the Ottomans finally captured the city. Many Aristotelian and Platonic texts that had been lost even to the conscientious erudition of the Arab and Persian scholars were saved by the Byzantines.

So philosophical problems, just as they are hard to solve, can be hard to kill. And one that survived to perplex the greatest minds of the medieval world was our old friend the problem of universals. Scholasticism, as the philosophy that thrived in the new universities at Paris, Oxford and Cambridge and elsewhere in Europe became known, was about much more than debating the number of angels that could dance on the end of a pin. Theological issues were, of course, a vital part of the Scholastics' intellectual world, and although the question of how many angels could dance on that pin is a later myth, concocted to ridicule the thought of the medieval period, the greatest of the Scholastics, Thomas Aquinas (1225–74), and others, certainly did discuss whether angels could have a material form, and whether they could eat or have sex. However, much of the work of the Scholastics wasn't theological. A clear doctrine was developed by Aquinas, distinguishing between matters of faith, where church teaching was dominant, and areas where reason, combined with scientific observation, was appropriate.

Building on Aristotelian and, to a lesser degree, Platonic principles, Scholastic philosophers made important contributions to all the branches of philosophy, from logic and ethics to the theory of knowledge. Almost every modern philosophical position can be found to have its roots in the work of the Scholastics. And one problem they kept returning to was that of universals.

One way in which the problem was solved was a kind of blending together of Platonic and Aristotelian realism, Christianity forming the binding agent. Like Plato, Boethius and Augustine and the later Scottish philosopher Duns Scotus (1266–1308) thought that the Forms, or general ideas, were real entities. But rather than shuffling about as blobs of pure Beauty, Goodness, Largeness and Dogness, in some nebulous otherworldly realm, they considered them to be ideas in the mind of God. From Aristotle they took the view that these ideas could be discovered by abstracting their essence from the world around us.

It seemed then that realism, in this modified form, had won the day. But the Scholastics, being academics with little else to do, lived to argue. Anything that wasn't set down unambiguously in scripture was ripe for dissection, analysis, destructive critique. One of the most effective debunkers in the history of philosophy was the Franciscan monk William of Ockham (1287–1347), who devised a brilliant tool for cutting through nonsense.

"Ockham's razor" is one of those philosophical terms that has entered the everyday vocabulary. Most people have a vague idea what it might mean. Often it is used in the sense that where there are two explanations, and you can't decide between them on other grounds, you should always choose the least complicated.

So, if I get up in the morning and find that my favourite biscuits have been removed from the cupboard, the packet roughly opened, the biscuits devoured and crumbs scattered all over the section of the sofa …'

I'm pleading the Fifth, whatever that is …

'… where Monty always takes his goodies, and that, surprise, surprise, there's a moist puddle of vomit in the corner behind the curtain, then rather than postulate that we've been burgled, and the burglars felt a bit peckish so had a snack break, and sat on the Monty-warmed part of the sofa, and worked their way through the whole packet, and then decided to puke behind the curtains, and then changed their mind about robbing us and quietly went their way home, I'd say that Monty it was that done the crime.'

You'd think I was the only person who ever pinched a biscuit and then had a little accident behind the curtains.

'And viewed in this way, Ockham is a useful guide in many situations. There are also times when choosing the simplest explanation isn't, in fact, the right course. I might be wearing a hat not because my head is cold, but because I got drunk during the day and tried to cut my own hair using a pair of nail scissors, meaning to snip away only a few wild strands from around my ears, but found myself progressing via small but fatal steps to a patchy hair apocalypse. Again.

In Ockham's original formulation, the razor is not principally about choosing the least complicated, or most obvious, solution to a problem. In his writings, Ockham argued that in trying to explain something, "entities must not be multiplied beyond necessity". In other words, don't add unnecessary complications. If you are trying to account for a phenomenon, trim away with your razor anything that does not need to be there.

Ockham took this approach to the problem of universals. When he surveyed the world, all Ockham could see was individuals. Individual dogs. Individual blue things. Individual beautiful things. That's both all it is *possible* to say, and all we *need* to say. Adding another mysterious element – the eternal Form of the Blue or the Dog or the Beautiful – complicates the matter without actually taking us anywhere useful. Claiming that they are bound together by their partaking in or resemblance to another thing, the idea or form or universal, whether residing in all the examples of the thing, as Aristotle said, or in another world, or in the mind of God, is unnecessary and confusing.

So if we use Ockham's razor to cut away the idea that universals have a real existence, what is left? The options are that the universals are simply words – hence the name given to this theory, *nominalism*. We conveniently call a number of individual carnivorous quadrupeds "dogs", because they resemble each other. Another group we call "cats". The word is a mere convenience: all the world really contains is the myriad of individuals.'

OK, just let me try to get this straight. Ockham's razor means that we don't need any kind of big spooky concept of dog *or whatever. We just have individuals that might resemble each other, but that doesn't signify. So, bang goes – what was it? – extreme realism, which says the general idea exists before the specific thing, and bang goes hard realism, which says the general idea resides in the specific thing... I can live with that. I'm tired. Can we go home?*

'Nearly, we're almost there. But not quite. Just because realism had taken a beating, it didn't yet mean that nominalism had won.'

This is what I feared.

'Nominalism struggles to explain the mechanism by which we come to allocate the name dog or red or blue to a group of things. One answer has been to try to use set theory. Let's say that we will apply the word "dog" to a certain group of animals that resemble each other. We don't claim that there is any deeper connection between them other than this resemblance. So we begin to collect the set of these "dogs", based on resemblance.

After a while we have lots of dogs. The nominalist says that set is all that we mean by the general term "dog". But there is also something that troubles us. One of the members of our set resembles the rest of the set in several ways, but differs in others. It is roughly dog-shaped and dog-sized, but it has very pointy ears, and a very pointy snout.'

Does it have a bushy tail?

'It does.'

And is it red?

'It is.'

It's a fox, isn't it!

Monty gets quite excited about foxes. He often picks up a scent on the street and goes into a frenzy of sniffing and scrabbling and barking. I don't suppose he could do much damage to an actual fox, but in his mind he is the fox's worst nightmare made flesh.

'On further consideration, you decide that despite the resemblances, the red thing isn't a dog and you kick it out of the set. Now, on what grounds have you decided that some of the common features are more important than others, certain features that qualify you for the term "dog"? Surely it must be that you had a general idea of dog, a template? And is this not, then, realism?'

I'm lost. So realism is stupid, and nominalism either makes no sense or turns into realism? Or are you about to hit me with the third option?

'There is another contender for the crown. A third way, between realism and nominalism. What if those general ideas weren't in the mind of God, as the medieval Platonists contended, but in our human minds? *Conceptualism* is the belief that universals exist as, well, *concepts*. Concepts are a way of applying a general idea to more than one object. The concept *dog* really does cover, it seems, you, Monty, and all the other dogs. The concept *green* applies to leaves and limes and the colour of my comfy chair. We can't deny that we have these concepts. "Green" is real. It just isn't in the stuff, or in the heavens, but in our heads.'

Please tell me this is the one…

'I think superficially…'

I hate that 'superficially'.

'… conceptualism is very attractive. It sits nicely in the space between realism, which a little thought is enough to throw into doubt, and the rather bewildering idea of nominalism, which appears to deny something we rather take for granted – that *blue*, and *dog*, and *beautiful*, mean something. Ideas live in our heads. Ideas for the specific dog, Monty, and the general dog, Dog. So can we accept this happy compromise?'

Please, please, please…

'Sadly, no. Say I have the concept *dog* in my mind, and I apply it to two things, you and the sausage dog down the street. But I decide that the leftover hot dog in your bowl is not a dog, in the same sense. If I am applying the concept correctly, it must mean that I am saying that there is a quality that you and the sausage dog have in common, and which is lacking in the hot dog. This is exactly what realism has asserted – the presence of a third thing, separate from you and the dachshund, in which you both partake. So conceptualism also collapses into realism.'

My head hurts. Everything is wrong. Are you now going to tell me that there is no dog, that I don't exist?

'I think our problem is that we are trying to apply a conceptual framework based on language to a world that is too complicated to be completely caught under the net. You remember the sorites paradox? How many grains make a pile?'

How much you'd pay to snog Hilda…

'It was how much I'd have to be paid, actually. Anyway, my point is that the reason it is a paradox is because the word "pile" is a *fuzzy* term. Its meaning hasn't got sharp edges, just like the words "bald" and—'

Snog.

'… "*dog*"! They are all in some way vague, or fuzzy. In most situations, the context provides enough information for us to know what is meant, despite the fuzziness. There will be a family resemblance (the expression is Wittgenstein's) between the different circumstances in which we use these words. So, "*dog*" might be used to refer to a single cute, if sometimes cranky, Maltese terrier, and it'll be used about a big, not very bright Rottweiler, and it'll be used about a sausage dog, and it'll be used about a type of sausage, and it'll be used as an insult, and it'll be used as a verb, meaning to follow a person's steps. And even though each example will have a link to other parts of the family, it's impossible to give a definition that covers every possible use. The complexities here are just too great. There's the complexity of the world out there, there's the complexity of the human mind that tries to understand it and there's the complexity of language that tries to negotiate between the two. This is something we'll talk about more, on our epistemology walk.'

Hang on, are you saying that this whole exercise was pointless, that the idea of a universal is so fuzzy that we can never answer the question 'what is a dog?'?

'In a way, yes. On the other hand…'

Here we go again.

'I'll finish our story on the way home. You want a carry?'

I can manage. Actually, maybe, thanks…

So I picked Monty up, and cradled him in my arms for the walk back, murmuring into his floppy ears.

'If you're asking me straight am I a *realist* (extreme or hard), a *conceptualist* or a *nominalist*, I can, in fact, give you an answer. But it's going to be by way of an example. Quite often the problems of philosophy can be cleared up by a close, detailed study of what happens to be the case in the world. For the medieval philosophers, one of the drivers for believing in universals was the fact that they believed that there were discrete species of animals, which had been created by God. If he had created them, they must have existed first in the mind of God as an idea. Therefore universals must exist.'

God first thought up 'Dog', then made some dogs. I get it.

'Good. And until Darwin, the idea that each species was quite separate from every other was still a powerful argument for universals. Of course there is a black bear and a polar bear and a grizzly bear, each as a separate and complete thing.'

Doesn't sound unreasonable…

'Let me tell you about the herring gull. It's a big, impressive gull, with a pale grey back and a yellow beak, and murder in its eyes. Then there is the slightly smaller lesser black-backed gull. It looks a bit like a herring gull, except it's got a—'

Let me guess, black back?

'Precisely. They are two quite different species, which don't, in the UK, interbreed. However, if you look at how the two species are distributed around the northern hemisphere, you discover something quite odd. For most of their range we find not clear lesser black-backed gulls and herring gulls, but various more or less intermediary stages. No one seems quite sure how many species there might be – some ornithologists say just two – herring gulls and lesser black-backs – some say eight. But, essentially, you have a hotchpotch, not quite a blending, not quite a separation.'

Interesting, but I'm not quite sure I…

'I think that this just shows how arbitrary our general categories are. We want there to be proper, nicely delineated species. Many organisms give that impression, and reproductive isolation does, to an extent, occur. But evolution tells us that we all slither and slide into each other. We'll carry on using general terms and thinking of universals, but the truth is they're just words.'

Monty raised his head and licked my face, as a sort of thank you, I think.

Walk 8

What Do I Know?

On this walk we begin to talk about epistemology, or the theory of knowledge. We start with the Greeks, touching on the different theories of knowledge put forward by Pythagoras, Plato and Aristotle, and then discuss the Sceptics, who denied the possibility of ever gaining sure knowledge of the world. Then we work our way through the ideas of the rationalists: Descartes, Spinoza and Leibniz.

'Walkies!' I called from the hallway.

Classic error.

Monty came bounding from wherever he'd been lurking. Well, perhaps not quite a bound. His bounding days were over. But he could still scamper, in a limping sort of way. He picked up his lead in his mouth (does this count as a trick, I wonder? If so, it's his only one …), and gazed at me, the excitement making his whole body thrum like a plucked guitar string.

The trouble was that there was going to be another five minutes of me trying to locate things: wallet, keys, poo bags, shoes. I shouted out to the family, asking if anyone knew where they were. No one answered. They've learned to ignore my anguished cries in these situations. Mrs McG calls it my 'wheresma rant', as I get increasingly irate, stamping about, yelling, 'Wheresma keys?' 'Wheresma wallet?' & co.

Eventually I found them. The keys were on the tray, where they're supposed to be (I don't expect things to be where they should be, so never check there until all other possibilities are exhausted). My wallet was in a jacket I could have sworn I hadn't worn for months, but I suppose I must have. My shoes were outside the front door. I've no idea why. I checked the soles just in case… but they were clean enough.

All the time I could sense Monty's annoyance and frustration grow. He interspersed a couple of plaintive whines with impatient barks.

Why do you never know where anything is?

'What? Oh, well, knowing is never as straightforward as you think. And right there, I believe, we have our topic for the day. Where do you want to go?'

That place with the animals…

'Good choice. Today we're going to be doing the theory of knowledge, and we might need some distractions.'

'Who are you talking to?' came a sharp voice from the kitchen. It was the sort of tone that, although still just in the normal register, could easily be modulated up into an actual reprimand. Of course I didn't need to see her to know who it was.

'No one. I mean, just me. See you later.'

'He only pretends to listen, you know.'

'Who?'

'Monty.'

Monty and I looked at each other, shrugged and quietly slipped away.

'The place with the animals' was Golders Hill Park. It's a part of the Heath that's been tamed and landscaped, with a children's play area, a decent café and a surprisingly extensive menagerie. I suppose in a fully joined-up world the café would serve up the wallabies and cassowaries that passed away (through natural causes, of course), but they were never on the menu when I was there.

The playground was a life-saver when the kids were small. I'd take them up every morning to hack away at the frozen crust on the sandpit with their little plastic spades. Then, when their hands were numb, and tear tracks began to show on their grimy faces, we'd go and have a hot chocolate in the café.

The downside of Golders Hill was that Monty had to stay on the lead, but that was compensated for by the novel smells and sounds – it's not often a pampered English pooch gets to catch the whiff of capybara on the wind, or hears the haunting cry of the sacred ibis.

We walked up there, Monty still limping a little. I took pity on him and carried him some of the way, tucked under my coat.

'We'll have to get you checked out,' I said. Monty didn't reply. He hated the vets. You couldn't really blame him…

We reached the park and I found a bench with a view over the cages full of exotic waterfowl. Beyond the aviary there was a paddock with lounging fallow deer, their breath clouding in the cold air. Smaller than you'd think, in the flesh. I imagined riding on one, rodeo-style, and realized how silly it would look as my legs would almost reach the ground. Perhaps more cruel than silly. Among the deer were two or three rheas, the South American cousin of the ostrich. They wore that expression of wide-eyed, tight-lipped moral outrage typical of their kind.

'It's got a name, of course.'

Monty looked up at me, forgetting that this was one of our philosophical rambles.

'Epistemology. The theory of knowledge. How we come to know things. What knowing means. The kinds of things that can be known. How do you know that you know? All that jazz. It's always been one of the key concerns of philosophy. It's sometimes described as "under-labouring" – the job of clearing away the rubble and rubbish from a building site before you can get to work constructing your palace. But that's not to underestimate its importance. Unless you can establish a clear foundation for knowing, then whatever you construct on top of it is doomed to collapse. And it's one of those areas where there's a fundamental disagreement about the basics.'

One of those areas? Is there anything you people don't disagree about?

I chose to ignore that one.

'There are those who think that the path to knowledge is through pure thought, using mathematics and geometry as a kind of template for knowing. They tend to be called rationalists, because they put reason on a pedestal. Then there are the empiricists, who think that the only things we can know are what we learn from experience, using our senses. And then there are the sceptics, who think knowledge is an impossible dream.'

And don't tell me, it all began with the Greeks?

'Of course.'

Plato?

'I'm going to go back a little further, to one of those pre-Socratics we mentioned on an earlier walk, Pythagoras. Pythagoras was the first philosopher to argue that mathematics and geometry were the ideal form of knowledge, and that the best way to attain knowledge was through disengaged contemplation, cutting out the distracting nonsense of the everyday world.

The Pythagoreans developed the view that mathematics could deliver its own eternal truths about itself, but also that those truths could be applied to the world "out there". Learn the secrets of squares and triangles and circles, and you will also be delivered of knowledge of reality. This is because the world is built on geometric principles, constructed from those ideal shapes and figures. All subsequent attempts to prioritize pure thought above the grubby business of digging up facts about the world can be traced back to Pythagoras, although that is principally because of the way Pythagorean ideas were incorporated by Plato.'

I knew it. So, what did he have to say about all this, then?

'In one of his most important dialogues, the *Theaetetus*, Plato focuses on the *What is knowledge?* question. Socrates' main companion in the dialogue is the eponymous Theaetetus, a bright young mathematician, described as being almost as ugly as Socrates himself. Socrates says his role in philosophy is to act as a midwife, drawing forth the ideas of others, and asks for Theaetetus' help in understanding what knowledge is. Theaetetus gives a list of things he believes count as knowledge – arithmetic, geometry, astronomy and musical theory, as well as certain crafts and skills such as making shoes.

Let me guess, Socrates says that Theaetetus has just listed examples of knowledge, without actually defining it?

'Good dog! So then Socrates does his midwife act, and nudges the boy into proposing various possible theories—'

Which Socrates immediately accepts, and the dialogue ends with dancing and laughter?

'Which Socrates rejects. He first has to deal with the idea that knowledge is perception, i.e. that knowing something means nothing more than to see or sense it in some way. We know from the parable of the cave why Plato is likely to be dissatisfied with this view. Perception can only be of the world of shadows. In the *Theaetetus*, his attack begins by eliding the concept that knowledge is perception with the idea, associated with the pre-Socratic philosopher Protagoras, that "man is the measure of all things", in other words that all judgements must begin with the subjectivist qualification, "from my point of view".'

Are they the same?

'Plato argues one follows on logically from the other. If we all have our own individual perceptions, and perception is the only basis of truth, then we must all have our own individual truths, and any objective standard of truth or reality is lost. If truth and knowledge are linked solely to an individual viewpoint, it's impossible for a person to be wrong. If I say the sky is green and the tree is blue, then that is right for me, in the same way that saying I like marzipan or sushi is right for me. So, Plato spends a lot of energy rebutting the Protagorean viewpoint. And he has some fun with it. One of his arguments is that if we all have our own truth, then someone who disagrees with Protagoras must be correct. So if Protagoras is right, he's wrong!'

Nice.

'He makes another similar but broader argument. If we accept that we all have our own truth, that means that nobody can be wrong or have false beliefs. But some people do think that false beliefs exist in the world. If they are correct, then there *are* false beliefs, and knowledge isn't simply what anyone thinks.

If they are wrong, then they have a false belief, proving again that false beliefs exist.

And Plato also tries to show that many of those things we most want to know are beyond perception – not just things like pure mathematics, which many people accept to be the result of reasoning rather than perception, but also the "big issues", the nature and meaning of existence, and so on. If we take a rose, we might see the colours and smell the aroma. But we also would want to say that the smell and the colour and, indeed, the rose exist. But this quality of "existence" is something beyond our senses. The same applies to qualities such as sameness or difference. These are simply not the sorts of things, Plato contends, that can be picked up by our senses. The argument here is similar to one we'll encounter later when we discuss Kant's epistemology, i.e. the idea of existence isn't something that we take from the world, but one we bring to it.

Another sort of argument concerns poor old excrement-smeared Heraclitus, and his view that everything in the material world is in constant motion. This motion applies both to the world "outside" and also to the perceiver herself. So, if we have a universe of radical flux in which neither the perceiver nor the perceived is the same from one second to the next, how can there ever be knowledge of anything? I'm changing, it's changing. As soon as you think you've grasped something, it's gone.'

Not sure I'm entirely convinced by that one. OK, so maybe the river is changing, and those deer never stand still, but there's also continuity. This bench we're on, it's not moving around, is it? It'll still be here tomorrow…

'A couple of points. The bench is made from atoms. Atoms are in constant motion, flying off in all directions. At a molecular level, tomorrow this bench will not be the same—'

Pfff!

'OK, I take your point, and it's one I agree with, as I'll come to later on. But if you want perfect knowledge, which Plato thinks is the only kind there is, that means we can never "know" this bench unless we know all of its atoms, and that's impossible. But there's the other half of the equation. Tomorrow you and I will be different, and so the bench we see will be different. Let's imagine another bench, in a different park. Two lovers meet on it. She tells him that they have to part. What had been a beautiful bench becomes for him a place of desolation and anguish. And every time he sees it again, it has changed. The sadness of the bench is lessened, as time dulls the pain. Or, perhaps the pain grows. You never know with these things. Some pains ease with time, some get worse... In either case, the bench is never the same.'

Monty is not an especially sensitive dog, but he looked up and licked my face, in a consoling sort of way.

'So,' I continued, clearing my throat, 'knowing can't be the same as perceiving. Plato then examines the next idea that young Theaetetus puts forward: that knowledge means believing a thing to be true that is, in fact, true. So, if you think your favourite chew toy is under the cushion on the sofa, and you go and look, and find that it really is there, that must be knowledge, mustn't it?'

Been looking for that dental floss for ages... Er, but yeah, this sounds like a good one. If you think something is true, and it is true, that's knowing it.

'Although it sounds promising, Plato, being Plato, is not entirely happy.'

Surprise, surprise.

'We might have a case where both conditions – believing something and it being true – are met, but we wouldn't want to say that we had real knowledge. Let's say my friend calls me up, and complains that I hadn't been in touch for a while. I reply that I hadn't called him because I've lost my address book with his number in.'

Which is a bare-faced lie?

'Precisely. When he rings off, I look for my address book, and discover that I have, in fact, lost it. Now, my friend, when I told him about losing my address book, believed that I had lost it, and in fact I *had* lost it. But he didn't have knowledge, in any real sense, did he?'

That sounds like an illustration to one of our other talks. The ethics one.

'OK, a more straightforward example. I toss a coin. I am convinced that it's going to come down heads. I don't know why, I've just got this gut feeling. It does come down heads. Again, we wouldn't say that the belief and the truth of that belief were the same as knowledge, would we?'

No. It was just a lucky guess.

'So Plato says that what we need are three things: a belief that something is true, the trueness of that belief and a rational justification for the belief. For Plato, that third point was where the theory of Forms comes in, with knowledge ultimately being knowledge of the eternal and changeless Forms. As I've already said, I think that sucks, so we'll leave it there. But we should grant that Plato helped to focus attention on the problem of knowledge, and suggested some of the ways of addressing it, which was helpful to later philosophers, even if his own solution was flawed.'

I suppose it's Aristotle next...

'You know my methods too well. Aristotle thought there were various ways you could go about the search for knowledge. The first two – *induction* and *demonstration* – were quite closely linked. The inductive process begins with sense perceptions, in which Aristotle, unlike Plato, has a basic faith. These sense perceptions or observations can then be stacked up to produce more general statements – this is what we mean by induction, the way of going from noticing several particular instances to stating a universal principle. So, you see many examples of men being mortal, i.e. you see them alive and then you see them being dead, and you reach the general conclusion that all men are mortal. That's induction.'

Are we happy with that? It sounds like the kind of thing you'd criticize…

'All in due course. For now, let's just accept it. So, we've gone from the specific to the general. You can then feed these generalizations and other, more specific observations into the structure of the syllogism, and what pops out is knowledge. You remember the syllogism, don't you?'

Sure. Big premise, little premise, conclusion. Easy.

'So, knowledge equals observation, plus logic. Its aim is to understand things in as general a way as possible, formulating broad principles and laws.

Let's see how this works. You're a biologist interested in the reproductive habits of animals. You make various observations. You compile some of these into a syllogism:

Only mammals suckle their young.

Dogs suckle their young.

Dogs are mammals.

You're happy with this, and try another one.

All mammals give birth to live young.

The platypus lays eggs.

The platypus is not a mammal.

But then you do more observations and realize that the platypus has much more in common with other mammals than reptiles or birds, and so must be a mammal. So you reconfigure your syllogism.

The platypus lays eggs.

The platypus is a mammal.

Not all mammals give birth to live young.

And that's *demonstration*. You've rearranged what you know from observation, to make a new and general claim about the world.

The Aristotelian system had plenty of competition in the Ancient world, and in the popular vote it lost out to the Epicureans and Stoics; but it fought back and became the dominant way that knowledge was thought of in the Middle Ages, and right up until the dawn of modern science in the sixteenth century. You begin with reliable first principles, derived from observation, apply sound syllogistic logic to it, and achieve knowledge of universal truths.

As well as demonstration and induction, Aristotle also thought we can get at knowledge in two other ways, although these might best be thought of as adjuncts to the first two. One was *dialectic* – by which he meant discussing the matter in hand with knowledgeable people.'

A bit like you and me...

'Just like you and me. Truth emerges in the give-and-take of a debate. Aristotle, although no fan of democracy, was actually the first person to talk about the wisdom of crowds, the idea that the more people who are involved in making a decision, the better it will be.

Finally, there is the *aporetic* method, which focuses on problems in existing theories. Wherever there is a problem or contradiction, or an awkward gap in our knowledge – an *aporia* – it acts as a signpost. It tells us that this is precisely where we need to focus our attention.

These last two methods anticipate two of the key areas of modern science. Dialectic is simply the peer-review process – the way science works by publishing the results of experiments, or new theories, which are then discussed freely in the scientific community. The wider and more freely the issues are debated, the better the chance that the truth will out. And the idea that new theories emerge only because an existing one starts to fail, throwing up *aporia*, is central to contemporary thinking on the philosophy of science – something we'll be probing on a future walk.

Just a final word or two about what knowing means for Aristotle, and the whole Scholastic tradition that followed him. To really understand something, you needed to know its *cause*. For Aristotle, this was a far more convoluted prospect than it would be for us. Aristotle defined four types of cause: material, formal, efficient, final. The *material* cause is what something is made from, the *matter*. So, the material cause of you, Monty, is the blood and bones and muscles and all the other cells in your body. Simple enough. The *formal* cause is the way the matter is arranged. So, in you, it's how all those cells are put together to make a cute little dog. The *efficient* cause is pretty much what we think of as *the* cause – the thing that brought it into being. So for you, Monty, that would be your mother and father.'

My what? How did they…?

'Ah, we never had that conversation, did we…? Moving on, the *final* cause is the purpose, or end of a thing. OK, that one's a bit hard to attach to a dog. Perhaps your final cause is to be my best friend.'

Awwww.

'Maybe a simpler illustration might help. Take a table (one of Aristotle's own examples). The material cause is the wood, the formal cause is the shape and structure of the table, the efficient cause is the carpenter who made it and the final cause is so I can eat my dinner off it. To know a table means knowing all those things. Got it?'

Check.

'So, knowledge for Aristotle, and for the Scholastic tradition in the Middle Ages, is reasonably complex, but also achievable. With observation, logic, induction and debate, we can get to know the causes of things, and that is knowledge.'

Sounds good. Are we done?

'Not even nearly. There have also always been those thinkers who doubted the very possibility of knowledge. On our previous walks we've talked about most of the Ancient philosophical schools, but we haven't yet met one of my favourites, the Sceptics. The Ancient Sceptics came in various flavours, but they almost all aimed to achieve the same thing: a state of tranquillity, brought about by a deliberate suspension of judgement on all matters. Happiness was *not* knowing. Or, rather, not deciding.

Many Sceptics looked to Socrates as their intellectual precursor – the Socrates of the early dialogues who irritated the heck out of everyone he spoke to by exposing the threadbare state of their reasoning. However, the first true Sceptic is generally accepted to be Pyrrho of Elis (360–270 BCE – so born some forty years after Socrates' death). Pyrrho was one of those almost self-parodic, head-in-the-clouds philosophers. He had trained himself so thoroughly in the ways of Scepticism that he would reject even the plain evidence of his senses, leading him to walk blithely towards precipices and oncoming road traffic. Only the intervention of his disciples could save him from plunging down onto the rocks, or from the wheels of the ox-carts.

Pyrrho and the other Sceptics set themselves against the various philosophies of the age that claimed to have found the key to knowledge – the followers of Aristotle and Plato, of course, but even more so against the Stoics. The Stoics, as we've seen, were materialists, believing that only matter existed. And matter could be perceived through the senses. Although sometimes the senses could be misled, certain perceptions were so strong, so clear and vivid, that the mind grasped them securely. These they termed *cognitive impressions*, and they provided the Stoic with a secure foundation for knowledge.

The Sceptics were having none of this. They developed a sort of toolkit for taking apart the philosophical arguments of the dogmatists—'

Dogmatists? I'm liking the sound of that.

'Sadly, dogmatism hasn't got anything to do with dogs, any more than catastrophe is a bad thing that happens to a cat. It comes from the Greek word *dogma*, which means *that which you take to be true*. A dogmatist, from the Sceptics' point of view, was anyone so rash as to hold firm beliefs about pretty much anything. The Sceptics' toolkit was divided into a number of "modes". The idea was that whenever you encountered anyone taking a dogmatic position in a debate, you ran their arguments through the woodchipper. Some of the modes adapted arguments from relativism and were intended to undermine the belief in the reliability of the evidence of the senses. So, perhaps we find perfume attractive, but dung beetles find it repellent (and of course the reverse for dung). A healthy man finds honey sweet, but one with jaundice finds it bitter. There are many cultural practices that we find vile (or good) that at other times and places were found good (or vile). The point was that there wasn't a single simple proposition that couldn't be confronted with its equal and opposite, if you searched hard enough.

Other modes showed how to destabilize your opponent's arguments. Let us say that we have managed to show to your dogmatic challenger that there are a variety of possible views on an issue. How then do we settle it? The dogmatist has various options (and anyone with a family will have encountered variations on these...). He can simply jut out his chin, and insist that he is right, which is no sort of argument at all, and is tantamount to conceding defeat; or he can give reasons. If he gives reasons, those reasons in turn can be disputed by the Sceptic. If further reasons are given, to back up the first, then again the Sceptic will be able to find counterarguments. Thus we are in an infinite regress, and the original position can never be grounded.'

Again an illustration might help...

'Fine. I say that humans are better than dogs. You begin by answering that some people hold different views, and regard dogs as far better than humans. So now I can either restate the original position, saying *oh yes they are* to your *oh no they're not*, or I give a reason. So then I say that humans are clearly more intelligent than dogs, and more intelligent is the same as better. You can either dispute this, arguing that the fact that dogs get humans to feed them and pick up their poo in little bags means they are more intelligent; or you could say that I've now substituted a different sort of quality – "intelligence" for "better". Who says "more intelligent" is the same as "better"? In both cases whatever I say to back up my point can be challenged, and we'll be in that infinite regress.

Another possibility is that, to avoid an infinite regress, I'll find myself arguing in a circle. So I'll say that humans are better than dogs. You'll demand evidence. So I'll say that humans are more intelligent. You'll ask how I can prove that, and I'll say it's because they're better. So we've finished where we began. Or in an example the Sceptics actually used: *God made the world.* How do you know? *Because here is the world that he made.* How do you know God made it? *Because it is perfect.* How do you know it is perfect? *Because God made it, and all he makes is perfect.*

There's one more argument from the Sceptics that I'd like to go through. A philosophical conundrum for you. It's called the *problem of the criterion*, and it's still a real head-scratcher. It's usually formulated as the following two questions:

1. What do we know? (Or what is the *extent* of our knowledge?)
2. How do we know? (Or what is the *criterion* of knowing?)

The problem is that to answer 1, i.e. what things we know, we need to have an answer to 2, i.e. what counts as knowing. But to answer 2, we need to have some instances of 1.'

Monty looked up from my knee, his little face wrinkled in puzzlement.

'You want an example, of course. OK:

1. What are the best breeds of dog?
2. How do we decide what breeds of dog are the best?

To answer 1, and identify the best breeds of dog, it seems we need a theory, or criterion for what counts as the best. So we need an answer to 2. But to answer 2, i.e. establishing a theory of best dogginess, don't we need examples of the best dogs to base it on? And it doesn't just work with dogs. Perhaps we're trying to decide on which are the greatest novels ever written. To decide that, you need a theory of greatness in literature. But how could you come up with such a theory without having some great novels to base it on? So how do you locate those great novels to base your theory on? Round and round we go.

Don't leave me hanging – there's an answer, right?

'There are a couple of half answers, but nobody's nailed it. The responses usually involve shuffling forward, making some provisional answers to each question, and continually revising them, until we are more or less satisfied. But my point was just that this is another of the strategies adopted by the Sceptics to undermine our faith in knowledge.'

And you said Socrates was annoying. These guys…

'Hah, I take your point. But I'd like to go back to where we came in. The Ancient Sceptics were not aiming to annoy and frustrate. They were trying to bring peace and sweet relief. If all disputes could be argued equally on both sides, then there was no point getting het up or in a state about them. Take a breath, relax. By all means enjoy the discussion, but remember that nothing ultimately turns on it. Reach for that state of tranquillity – the Greek term is *ataraxia*, also translated as imperturbability or equanimity. The things you think are good may well turn out to be bad. The things that are bad might end up being for the best. We can't know. Pyrrho faced storms at sea with *ataraxia*, as all those around him panicked. And though he did once cringe from the teeth of an attacking dog, he answered that although "it was not easy entirely to strip oneself of human weakness", nevertheless, "one should strive with all one's might against facts, by deeds if possible, and if not, in word".'

He probably annoyed the dog by denying the reality of his bone, or something.

'The reason for the attack is not recorded, sadly. Although the Sceptical doubt was banished first by the Stoics and then the Aristotelians, their influence came to be felt when their texts were rediscovered in the sixteenth century. The great essayist Montaigne (1533–92) helped to trigger the rebirth of Scepticism, inspired in part by the endless religious disputes that tore France apart in his lifetime. Confronted by fanatical Protestant reformers and entrenched Catholic diehards, Montaigne found solace in the old Sceptical injunction to withhold judgement, to rise above disputation and to accept that we cannot ever be sure enough about the truth to shed blood over it. Montaigne had a medallion cast, engraved on one side with *Epecho*, the Greek for "I abstain", and on the other *Que sais-je?*: "what do I know?"

Ancient Scepticism, in the version espoused by Montaigne, was all about using the possibility of doubt to help the doubter find a way to a state of calm acceptance, but our old dog-tormenting friend René Descartes (1596–1650) used a radical and disorienting scepticism in a very different way. For Descartes, questioning everything was a matter of stripping away the tangle of weeds and briars that obscured the path to truth.

Did you say dog-tormenting…?

'Oh, er, you weren't here for that part, were you. It's… probably best to skip over that whole episode… So, Descartes was one of the great geniuses of history, excelling not only at philosophy, but also at maths and the sciences. He invented co-ordinate geometry – the idea of mapping two-dimensional space on X and Y axes – and began the process of overturning the outdated scientific and cosmological views of Aristotle that was to culminate in Newtonian physics. So it's ironic that someone who knew so much, and advanced knowledge in so many areas, began by doubting everything.'

Everything?

'Everything. Descartes begins by doubting what his senses tell him. His target there was the whole system of knowledge developed by Aristotle. As we've seen, the syllogism, to produce knowledge, needs true premises, and true premises assume that we can rely on the accuracy of our perceptions. Yet a tower seen from the distance appears small, and then, close up, *voilà*, it is huge! (I've never been quite convinced by this – the rules of perspective suggest that the senses here are accurately conveying the real state of the world to us – we should, indeed, doubt them more if the tower appeared large when it was far away, and small when near.) Descartes looks and sees that he is sitting in a room by the fire, wrapped in his dressing gown. Is this not certain? He can feel the warmth of the fire, and the sensations of his dressing gown, see the walls and the roof. But he has dreamed before that he was up and out in the world, when he was in fact naked in his bed. Mad people imagine that they are seeing things that are not there. We've all had dreams in which we fly or find ourselves speaking in front of an audience quite naked.'

Yeah, but we usually do know, don't we? When I chase rabbits in my dreams, as soon as I'm about to grab them they jump into the air and fly away, like birds. That's when I realize that these aren't normal rabbits…

'Of course, generally we can tell the difference between dreams and waking. But can we always know? If there is ever a time when we cannot tell, or get confused, how can we ever have complete confidence in the material reality of the tree or dog or wallaby we see before us? Descartes is determined to dismiss everything that he does not know with absolute certainty, and the possibility, however remote, that he is mad or dreaming means that he cannot place his full confidence in the senses. And so out they go.

But what of mathematical or geometrical knowledge? That 2 + 2 = 4 is not dependent on the easily deceived senses, is it? A triangle will always have three sides. These things are not sense-dependent, but analytic truths, determined by the definitions of the terms.'

There's no doubting that, is there?

'But could it not be that there was an evil demon planting these erroneous ideas in my head? How can I know I'm not a brain in a jar, fed a stream of nonsense? This evil demon could confuse and muddle me whenever I begin counting the sides of my triangle, making me think three, when the truth is eight. Once again, it is not that Descartes is saying that these various deceptions are probable, merely that it is impossible for us to entirely rule them out.

Descartes' radical scepticism is genuinely challenging. His goal was to show that almost everything we take for granted is based not on solid ground, but soft and treacherous marshland. For the Ancient Sceptics, this was the place they wanted to be. Own it, they said. We can't know, so get on with enjoying life without knowledge.

But Descartes' doubt is only the first step, not the last. He's taken us down into the depths of doubt, now he leads us up again, into the light of sure knowledge.'

Hurrah!

'And the place he finds illumination is not in the shifting and uncertain world of perception, but in pure thought. We can doubt everything, except that we are doubting. Because to doubt that you doubt is still to doubt. To doubt is to think. Even if you are thinking something that isn't true, you are still thinking. And thought cannot exist independently: there must be a thing that is thinking. And that thing is I. *Cogito ergo sum*. I'm pink, therefore I'm spam.'

What?

'Just checking. *Cogito ergo sum*. I think therefore I am.'

Better. What is spam, anyway?

'It's, er, well, it's what we used to eat before there was food. So, the mind is the one certain thing, more certain than the existence of the external world, more certain than matter. This introduces one key element of Descartes' thought – the idea that mind and matter are two quite different things. This will create problems for Descartes, as we'll see. But for now, he has shown that his essence is thought: he is a thing that thinks.

But the job of rebuilding isn't yet over. Descartes has proved his own existence, but he wants more. What is it about the *cogito*, he wonders, that so struck him as true? If he can identify this "signature", then he can search for other ideas that have the same quality. He concludes that what distinguishes the *cogito* is that it is *clear* and *distinct*. This, then, becomes the touchstone – if he can find other ideas that are equally clear and distinct, these will also be true.

One idea that fits the bill is, a little surprisingly, the idea of God, which he finds there, fully formed, inside his mind. Where has this idea of God come from? The options are either that he has invented it, that it has somehow come from without, through the senses, or that it is innate. As for the first, the idea of God is of a perfect being, infinite in scale and power. The ideas of perfection and infinity could not be conceived of by an imperfect, finite being, because like must be caused by like (this is an old Aristotelian concept – motion can only be imparted by motion, heat by heat, etc.), and it is all too obvious that humans are not perfect. So God cannot be the creation of man. The idea of God also could not have come from my senses, as we have already established that all the knowledge we get from the senses can be doubted.

This then leaves only the possibility that the idea of God is innate within me, planted in my mind by him at birth (or conception). This is Descartes' "trademark argument" for the existence of God – so called because it's as if God left a trademark in our mind, to let us know that he was here.

Once we have proved the existence of God—'

Er, have we?

'Descartes trips out various other arguments for God that satisfied him and many other people at the time, but that don't convince many people now. Let's just assume that Descartes has satisfied himself that God exists. After that, the rest of his scepticism falls away. A good God takes the place of the evil demon, guaranteeing, rather than undermining, the validity of perceptions, and our deductions about mathematics and geometry. He is happy to confirm that the material world of bodies – defined as that which has *extension* – causes ideas in the mind, and those ideas are an accurate representation of the outside world. All is well. Doubt is defeated! We have our solid foundations. We know!'

This all seems a bit too easy...

'It is, and most modern philosophers are more impressed with the sceptical half of the equation than the positive edifice built upon it. Descartes' non-sceptical foundations rest on God, and his positive arguments can be, and have been, dismantled. One line, adopted by John Locke (much more of him, soon …), is that it simply isn't true that we all have an innate idea of God. Locke thinks we don't have any innate ideas at all – as we'll see, shortly – and certainly none of God. There are tribes and cultures without a concept of God, and many more with very different ideas of deity, which don't involve infinity and perfection. And, if an imperfect mind cannot concoct the idea of a perfect being, isn't it equally as true that an imperfect mind couldn't grasp such an idea, even if implanted by that perfect being?

Without the hand of God, stretching down to lift him up, there is nothing within Descartes' epistemology that allows him to escape the scepticism he has so persuasively put forward.

The strongest legacy of Descartes' philosophical thought was the importance it gave to pure reason as the route to truth (and potential certainty). The defining features of a "true idea", such as that of the existence of his own mind, and the existence of God, are that they should be clear and distinct. The paradigmatic cases of clear and distinct ideas are those of mathematics and geometry, and so these came to be seen as both a model for truth and a means of attaining truth. The philosophers who followed in this tradition – the rationalists, most famously Spinoza and Leibniz – reinforced Descartes' distrust of the body and its senses, and like him tried to ground knowledge purely in the operations of the mind, using mathematics and geometry as the ladder to truth.

Descartes also bequeathed a major headache to the following rationalists. You remember our walk where we discussed the mind–body problem, in relation to the idea of free will?

Yes. Sorta.

'OK, recap. For Descartes, body and mind were fundamentally different substances. And that mind–body dualism, as it is known, makes a kind of sense: a thought and a sandwich are two quite different things. One has mass, colour, taste; the other doesn't: the thought exists only as a disembodied mental entity. The trouble is that these very different things have to communicate. The material substance of the world has to find its way into the world of thought. The sandwich out there must become the idea of the sandwich in my mind. And then my mind – a mental thing – has to make my arm – a physical thing – reach out, pick up the sandwich and put it in my mouth.

Descartes' solution to this problem – how the mind and matter can interact – is famously awful. Rather than tell us *how*, he tells us *where*. A cruder thinker might well have said it happens "in the brain", but our vivisectionist has an intimate knowledge of anatomy, and is beyond such vulgarities. He claims that it happens in the pineal gland.'

Yes, now I remember. The thing in the brain.

'Exactly. Of course, all this does is to shrink the problem down, without making it go away. The pineal gland is still a physical thing that has to somehow interface with a mental thing. In fact, the problem of substance is even more complex, as Descartes has three separate substances – body, mind and God, although the God problem is easy to solve, as long as you decide that God, by definition, can do anything... But still, we have three quite different substances floating around that somehow, if we are going to really understand the universe, we have to comprehend.

Let me turn it into a sporting metaphor. For Descartes, the world is like a football team. There are the players, who are "body", characterized by having the property of being extended in space. Then we have the ball. But this ball is not made of leather, but of light – it's a hologram. Then there's God, who is the team manager. There's a big problem for anyone trying to kick a hologram football – it has no mass, so how can it be moved by the player? Descartes' non-solution is to say that he moves it with his foot. Or, rather, his toe. I think we can all see that if we accept that the foot and the ball are different substances, one material and one not, the hologram ball just isn't going to budge.

One of Descartes' most gifted followers, the notorious dog-kicker, Nicolas Malebranche—'

WHAT?

'Oh, nothing, honestly. It's not important—'

If this guy was a notorious philosopher-kicker you wouldn't say that.

'Fair point. Anyway, Malebranche thought he had the solution. He accepted Cartesian dualism, and saw the problem quite clearly. The physical foot could never move the mental ball. So Malebranche said that the team manager – God – used his magical powers to make the ball move when the foot connects with it. Even in the intimacy of the individual human mind and body, the heavy lifting was done by God. You may think your finger wiggles because you've made it wiggle, but Malebranche says that God picks up the thought *wiggle* and conveys the intention to the muscles, and makes the finger wiggle. If you prick that same finger with a needle, the (mental) pain is not caused by the (physical) needle – such interactions are impossible – but by God.'

I find that I am not convinced by this.

'Quite so. You might well object that this is a funny sort of job for God to be doing. And if you accept the Christian view that all those born before Christianity must be damned, it meant that God spent a long time animating human puppets that were then condemned to burn.

Such were the absurdities that followed from mind–body dualism.

Baruch Spinoza's solution to the problem was rather cunning. He decided – indeed, proved, in his own way – that there were not three substances but one. The footballers and the ball were nothing but different aspects of the manager. The team was one thing, and the team was all there was.'

This is getting crazier and crazier…

'It gets worse before it gets better, believe me. Spinoza (1632–77) was actually one of the more attractive figures in the history of philosophy.'

Dog-kicker?

'Not him. His radical views on religion meant that he was shunned by his own Jewish community, and never really accepted by Christian society, even in the relatively tolerant world of seventeenth-century Holland. He lived most of his life in poverty, but refused any financial help from his friends, preferring to maintain his independence by living in cheap digs and scratching a living grinding lenses for scientific instruments. He was modest, brave, brilliant and, most of all, prepared to go wherever his reason led him, no matter what the consequences. And it took him to some very strange places.

Spinoza argued that there are four types or levels of knowledge. There are things we take on trust because we are told them, but never experience them. Then there are the things we learn from experience, such as that my toe will hurt when I bash it on the step, and that my thirst will be quenched by cool water. Next there is a slightly more rational level of knowledge, but still based on experience: working out that some things are small because they are far away, and some things are small because they are, er, small. All of these ways of knowing are unsatisfactory, and prone to error. Which is why we need the fourth level, which is understanding and knowing the essence of a thing, that which is necessarily true of it. And, of course, the ideal here is—'

Let me guess, sums?

'Yes! Well, geometry. Geometry gives us real knowledge, knowledge that cannot be wrong. And as Spinoza wanted to bring the same certainty to philosophy that Euclid's *Elements* (which for two thousand years had been the standard textbook on the subject) had brought to geometry, he chose that as his model for his masterpiece, *Ethics*, published posthumously in 1677.'

Hang on, ethics? Wasn't that some other walk…?

'With Spinoza, even more than the other thinkers we've been discussing, it's all connected. *Ethics* does deal with, well, ethics, but his moral principles follow on inevitably from the metaphysical and epistemological groundwork. Anyway, Euclid's *Elements* starts out by offering various definitions ("A point is that which has position but not dimensions"), axioms ("Things that are equal to the same thing are also equal to one another") and postulates ("A straight line may be drawn from any one point to any other point"). Beginning with these statements, which any rational person will accept as true, and using nothing more complicated than a ruler to draw straight lines and a compass to draw circles, Euclid constructs the whole beautiful palace of geometry, each step following logically and inevitably from what has gone before.

Spinoza tried to do the same for philosophy, building up from basic definitions and axioms, to construct complex propositions, which in turn were backed up by his "proofs". The whole system of definitions and proofs is internal – he never points to anything out in the world to illustrate what he asserts, in the same way that you don't need to check Euclid's propositions about triangles by rushing out and measuring actual triangles in the world.

Ethics is dense and complex, the mathematical structure making it a forbidding book to tackle, but the outline is fairly simple. A substance is defined as something that causes itself, i.e. nothing outside it causes or influences it in any way. There is only one substance, which is infinite and ageless, and that substance is God. God is everything that exists. God has two attributes: thought and extension. We are part of God. Everything that happens is absolutely determined, which means that there is no free will. Humans strive selfishly to promote their own interests, but this striving is ultimately futile, as we can't change anything. The best we can do (and this is the ethical part of *Ethics*) is to reconcile ourselves to *what is*.'

Reminds me of something…

'It's very close to the Stoic world view – that composite world–mind–god thing, bundled together with the determinism. And it's a view of the deity that isn't much like any kind of Christian or Jewish God. In fact, it's a kind of God that isn't really a god at all. God in Spinoza is nature. Everything in nature is part of God. So not a great surprise he wasn't Mr Popular with the organized religions of his day.

Although all this seems like a very strange conception of reality, and at the time it was seen as utterly shocking, it's actually less startling than it once appeared, and amounts to little more than reconceptualizing what we already know. Spinoza draws an analogy with the body. On one level, the body is made up of innumerable separate entities – organs, blood, hair, skin, etc. (Spinoza didn't know about the individual cells, which weren't discovered until a little after his death, though it would have helped his argument.) However, we can see that it makes sense to regard this as one thing, made of many parts. In the same way, though we perceive that we live in a world of variety, both material and mental, a shift in perspective reveals it as one thing – God, or, if you prefer, Nature.

The idea that mind and body are just attributes of God (or Nature), rather than separate substances, may involve a change in perspective, but it's not clear that it means very much in practice. What it does do is to bring thought and matter closer together, thereby getting round the problems with Cartesian dualism. The modern way of resolving the mind–body problem is to see thought as an epiphenomenon of matter, not a different substance at all. They are two sides of the same coin, and that is close to what Spinoza was saying.'

Spinoza sounds quite cool.

'Yeah, well, he's definitely interesting, but there's also a kind of darkness there. Spinoza was a lovable guy, but his system isn't lovable. The world doesn't care about us. It's just this huge engine, or organism, of which we're helpless parts. All we can hope to do is understand the mechanism, and accept it.'

Monty jumped down from my lap and had a stretch. His lead reached as far as a birch sapling, and he had a quick pee on it.

I'm a bit lost here. Remind me again what we're getting at?

'We've been looking at the answer to the question *What is knowledge?* We checked out the Greeks, and now we're looking at one of the two great modern traditions in epistemology: the rationalists, who thought pure thought was the way. Then we'll look at the empiricists, who thought perception and experience should be our guides.'

Does this mean we're only halfway?

'More than halfway. But I'm getting hungry. Let's finish the rationalists, then we'll get home. You ready?'

Monty climbed back on board.

'Our third—'

And last…

'… great rationalist, Gottfried Wilhelm Leibniz (1646–1716), was a very different character to Spinoza. Like Descartes, he was a spectacular polymath, a historian, diplomat, and perhaps the finest mathematician of his age. Affable and eager to please, he lived a comfortable life, mainly in the court at Hanover, toadying to the rich and powerful. He seems to have been the sort of courtier who strove to ingratiate himself, without ever quite managing it, rendering himself just a little ridiculous. And he was a bit of a tightwad. Whenever a young woman at court got married, his wedding gift was a little booklet of helpful advice and tips for the new bride.'

Nice touch!

'The latter part of his life was soured by a long-running and bitter dispute with Isaac Newton over who had invented calculus. Newton won the PR battle, not least because he secretly chaired the committee judging the issue, but it seems most likely that they both came up with the idea independently, which is perhaps the single most striking example of great minds thinking alike (and for once the minds really were great).

Genius though he undoubtedly was, Leibniz concocted perhaps the oddest and least plausible of all metaphysical systems. The starting points were reasonable enough, as long as you accepted the rationalist view of knowledge. He thought that all truths were analytic, i.e. that every true premise was already contained in the subject.'

Oh, you know I always get confused when you talk about the subject and the premise…

'OK, well, there are obvious cases. Everything true that you can say about a right-angle triangle is already contained in the concept of a right-angle triangle – it has three sides, the angles add up to 180 degrees, the square on the hypotenuse is equal to the sum of the squares of the other two sides, etc. So all the truths about it are analytic – which is to say that they are *inside* the concept. Or, again, with the syllogism *Monty is a dog; all dogs are mortal; therefore Monty is mortal*, all of the "truth" in the conclusion is analytic – we're just bringing out the latent truth content.

But we think it's different when it comes to most statements about things in the world. There are true things about you that aren't contained in the concept of *Monty* – these are *contingent* things, things that you might or might not do. You might chase a ball if I throw it to you—'

Fat chance.

'You might go off your food tomorrow. You might pee on this lamp post, rather than that lamp post. All these truths, or premises, are *synthetic*, which means they are not contained in the subject, but reside outside it. Leibniz thought that all truths, even these apparently contingent ones, were analytic.'

Huh?

'Well, he says that if you know enough about a subject, whether it's a garden wall or a dog or a person, then you'll understand everything that has happened or will ever happen to it. With enough knowledge, all truths are analytic – we all contain everything that will ever happen to us. Now, in reality, that sort of knowledge is only available to God, but it's still, logically, there. This rather crushes the possibility of free will – if whatever we do is already waiting inside us, then what hope freedom? However, unlike Spinoza, Leibniz shied away from the deterministic consequences of his thought, at least in his published writings, as he was always afraid of controversy.

The second plank of Leibniz's philosophy is carved from our old chum substance. Leibniz agrees with Spinoza (and Aristotle) that the essence of substance is singularity – every substance must be a single thing: that's simply what substance means. But *extension* – which Descartes had said was the essence of matter or body – is multiple; there are many things, with different shapes, each separate from the others – tables, chairs, raindrops, dogs, cats, people. Spinoza looked at the many and saw one. Leibniz looks at the many and sees… many.

For Leibniz, each player in the team, *and* the ball, *and* God, are all separate substances. The Cartesian problem of how different substances interact is now multiplied massively. And embraced. The world for Leibniz is made up of an infinite number of separate entities – he terms these *monads*. A person is a monad, but so is every cell in his or her body. Every apparently physical thing is also a monad. And each monad is, in Leibniz's term, *windowless* – they do not connect or interact with the other monads. And we shouldn't think about these monads as having physical properties – they occupy no real space – space and matter as we think of them don't exist.'

I suppose you did warn me about the weirdness but this is very…

'It is. Leibniz's monads are arranged in a hierarchy with, at the top, the human soul. And this soul is the source of all knowledge. Leibniz set himself firmly against the idea that knowledge comes into the mind through the senses. There is no "coming in" in his system.'

No windows.

'Exactly. So everything important that we know is a function of the soul coming to know itself, understanding its own analytic content. The soul has substance, and so it comes to possess the idea of substance through self-reflection. The soul has being, and so it comes to know of being. It can reason, and so it possesses the beauty of mathematics and geometry. Here is everything we need, a little world, like a goldfish bowl, for our mind to swim around in.

But if monads can't interact, what about our football team? How can they score? That ball has to be propelled towards the opposition goal. Heck, it *is* propelled. The crowd roars, the ball hits the back of the net. How so, if the monads don't have any connection to each other? And how can I even see the ball, if I'm a blind monad?'

Let me guess – God?

'Oh yes! Back of the net for Monty. This is Leibniz's most famous concept – well, second most, we'll come to the first in a moment. The world does appear to work in a certain way, with people chatting to each other, billiard balls colliding, dogs barking at cats, dropped plates shattering as they hit the floor. But Leibniz has shown, by careful argument, that it cannot be this way – the infinite number of separate substances can't really be communicating in the way we think we see.

There can only be one answer to this dilemma. God has created a universe in which things appear to be caused by other things, but in fact they are simply *harmonized*. Imagine two clocks, he says. They have no connection, but chime at the same time. It might seem to an observer that they are linked, that the

How to Teach Philosophy to Your Dog

How to Teach Philosophy to Your Dog

chiming in one causes the chiming in the other, just as a feather causes the itch—'

Talking of which, could you just scratch the chin, there… yes, just there, thanks.

'But this is simply God's *pre-ordained harmony*. He has designed the world to give the appearance of working through causal interactions between the elements in it, but that's nothing but a show.'

Er, why would he do that?

'That leads us on to Leibniz's actual most famous idea. His God is constrained only by the laws of logic. Within those laws God could have made an infinite number of worlds. The one he picked on has the optimal amount of good in it. This is the best of all possible worlds.'

But all the crap that happens… war, disease, cats…

'God could have made a world without those things in it. But those bad things result in good things happening. Evil provides the opportunity for good. A world without disease is a world without carers for the sick. Every evil is not just counterbalanced by the good, but swamped by it.

And God could easily have made humans into robots, only capable of doing good. He could have programmed us all to be good Samaritans. He could have taken away our ability to do selfish, evil, stupid things. There was a popular TV series called *Buffy the Vampire Slayer*, featuring a character called Spike, a sort of semi-reformed vampire. What reformed him was being fitted with a chip in his brain that delivered an excruciating shock if he ever tried to harm anyone apart from demons and other vampires. God could have given us all the virtue chip. But then we would be in a world without free will, and that is a world without the possibility of good. So what he has given us is not a perfect world, but one with the greatest surfeit of good over evil.'

Sounds like a load of rubbish.

'It's certainly provoked ridicule. Voltaire wrote *Candide* in 1759 to satirize it. A hundred thousand people were killed in the Lisbon earthquake of 1755. Many of those killed were sheltering in churches. Was that really counterbalanced by the good it achieved – one presumes the charitable acts of the rescuers? What could possibly counterbalance the agonizing death of a child?

So, no, it hasn't won over many people. But, logically there's nothing wrong with it. There's no way we can know for sure that this isn't actually the optimum world. It's the sort of thing that can never be decided. But its plausibility is, shall we say, low…

I should say that the idea about this being the best of all possible worlds is actually logically independent of Leibniz's arguments about blind monads and pre-ordained harmony. Many contemporary theologians hold a view that this is the best world, in terms of the balance of good and evil, without signing up for all of the courses of the full Leibnizian banquet.

But we've strayed away from our main theme today, the theory of knowledge. Leibniz's system is a marvellous concoction, and the deductive steps to get there may follow logically from the philosopher's views on substance and truth, but the absurdity of the conclusion alerts us to the fact that what he says about substance and truth must be nonsense.

We must also question the underlying epistemology that has led us, like a faulty satnav, to this odd place. Can we rely on the cogitations of that windowless brain, admitting nothing from without, and reflecting only on what is already contained within it? It is like an agoraphobic, terrified to go outside or even open the curtains, and subsisting on whatever is already in the house, the desiccated scraps in the kitchen, the old and broken ornaments above the fireplace, the fading photographs of the dead.

And it's an interesting fact that though there are a few Spinozans still around, and Descartes remains at the centre of many live philosophical debates, and our next philosopher, Kant, has never got old, there are no disciples of Leibniz. So let's open those curtains, and see what comes in …'

You said we could do this on the next walk. My little brain is all full up.

'Oh, sorry, Monty, of course. Can you make it back on your own legs?'

Let's see how we go.

And so we left the wallabies and the capybaras and the sacred ibises behind us, and walked home. I carried Monty for the last part.

Walk 9

Empiricism:
Sensing is Believing

On our second epistemological walk (although it's not so much a walk as a lie-down), we discuss the empiricists of the seventeenth and eighteenth centuries, Locke, Berkeley and Hume, who thought that knowledge must come from experience.

The next day the rain beat in waves against the windows, so we had the briefest of walks down to Monty's favourite tree, and then settled back on the sofa in the empty flat. In truth, now that his youthful effervescence is over, it's Monty's preferred way to pass the time. I lie on the sofa, and he lies on me, in a neat line along my sternum, like a large hairy slug. If the book I'm reading isn't too heavy, I can rest it gently on his back. If I fidget too much, he opens his eyes and gives a quick tut.

'You ready to tackle epistemology, part two?' I said, when we were settled.

Monty breathed out, heavily. More a huff than a sigh. But he didn't climb down and seek refuge in one of the other rooms, so I took it as a *yes*.

'Yesterday we considered Ancient theories of knowledge, and then looked at the sceptical tradition, and finally how the rationalists banished scepticism by the power of pure thought. Today we'll look at how the rival tradition of empiricism tried to build firm foundations for knowledge not on thought, but on experience.

Although we can see that there are elements of empiricism in Aristotle, and some Italian Renaissance thinkers and artists had explicitly stated that experience is a better judge of truth than either reason or ancient authority, empiricism really got under way with the English thinker Francis Bacon. But I want to hold off on Bacon until another walk, as he's mainly considered a pioneer of the philosophy of science. Thomas Hobbes put forward a crude but clear version of the theory in his political masterwork, *Leviathan (1651)*. There he states that everything in our heads got there originally through our senses. Memory, imagination, reason are dependent on that original sensory input. Knowledge means knowledge of facts: the things out there in the world. The only way that you can know something is to see it happening.

Hobbes's great successor, John Locke (1632–1704), brought empiricism to a height of common-sense plausibility. Reading his main work on philosophy, *An Essay on Human Understanding* (1689), the clarity of the writing (usually) and the relative straightforwardness of the thought mean that, again and again, you nod, thinking, "Oh, that sounds about right."

Yet Locke's empiricism contained a fatal flaw, and it was to have implications that, in the hands of his successors, Berkeley

and Hume, were as strange as anything in the wondrous im-
aginings of the rationalists.'

*You're trying to make it sound a bit more exciting than it really is,
aren't you?*

'Maybe. Just a bit ... Although Locke rejected the certainties
of the rationalists, he is no sceptic. His starting point is that we
clearly do have knowledge of the world, so the question is how
we came by it. His main target is Descartes. As we've seen,
Descartes thought our mind contains certain innate ideas: of
our own existence, and that of God, which lead us on in turn to
a reasonably sure knowledge of the external world.

But for Locke (as for Hobbes), we enter this world with
nothing, no ideas in our heads at all. The mind at birth, he tells
us, is a *tabula rasa* – a blank slate. Although devoid of knowledge, the mind has certain aptitudes. It possesses the ability to
think and reason. But it contains no *ideas*. Idea is the term Locke
uses for whatever is in our heads. Ideas are mental objects,
which correspond to the physical objects out there in the world
that cause them.

Locke's arguments against innate ideas have already been
examined in relation to God. But the same arguments applied to
those who held that the mind contains innate moral feelings, or
ideas of good taste, or mathematical concepts such as equality or
difference. Having said that he wasn't one, Locke uses essentially
the same strategy employed by the sceptics in demolishing innate
ideas. He points out that if these ideas are innate in humans, they
should be i) universal; ii) the same everywhere; iii) present from
birth. A quick anthropological survey strongly suggests that different cultures vary greatly in their ideas of religion, and good
conduct, and even mathematical knowledge. And furthermore,
anyone acquainted with the young will affirm that children do not

possess these notions until they are taught them. Plato may have claimed that Socrates could draw out the knowledge of geometry lying latent in the mind of a slave boy, but Locke says that the mind is an empty bucket, waiting to be filled.

If ideas are not innate, where do they come from? Locke, like all the empiricists, points to experience. Our senses feed sensations into our minds, where they become ideas. Once there, the mind actively considers and combines them, turning the *simple* ideas that result directly from sense impressions into *complex* ideas. I'm looking at you, Monty, lying on my chest. I stroke you...'

Stroking is nice...

'I smell you...'

Hey!

'... which feeds into my mind the simple ideas of weight and size and warmth and grubby whiteness and softness and hairiness and a slight musty pong. These simple ideas are assembled into the complex ideas of *dog* and *give him a bath*.'

But I had one last month!

'Locke gives a more straightforward example. Roundness, redness and sweetness are all simple ideas, which come together to form the complex idea of an apple.'

Not that complex. Even I know what an apple is.

'Complex only in that it is made up of several different simple ideas, combined to form a single complex one.

So we have simple and complex ideas, but Locke also differentiates between those original simple ideas. Sticking with you, Monty, Locke argues that some of those qualities that I perceive, your shape, your weight, your position in the world, the fact that you are a solid, and not, usually, gaseous, and the fact that you are sitting still and not moving around, can be said to genuinely be *in* or belong to you. And some of them, your colour, your smell, your, er, taste if I were to lick you, the fact that you feel warm on my leg, these things are more properly thought of as being in *me*.'

Eh? I don't really like the idea of any of me being in you... And, frankly, the licking thing is gross.

'It'll all make sense, soon. The qualities that Locke thinks belong to you, your mass, weight, shape, solidity and so on, he calls *primary qualities*. These things are actually present in the object you're observing, and inseparable from them. I couldn't even conceive of you, Locke says, without you having a shape and size. You wouldn't be *you* at all without these things.

However, it's quite different with those properties like smell, taste and colour. I can conceive of a Monty that isn't dirty white, or who smells less funky. These qualities aren't essential in the same way. And they really do seem to be in my mind more than they are in you. If you ask me "Where do I smell Monty?" it makes sense to say that I smell him in my mind.

So Locke calls these *secondary qualities*. The secondary qualities are a product of the primary qualities, and caused by them, but the actual sensation of colour or of smell is in my mind. We mentioned on another walk the difference between subjectivity and objectivity. For Locke, the primary qualities are objective: they are independent of the opinions of any particular person or group of people. If we didn't exist, a lump of coal would still be a lump of coal, with a certain weight and particular dimensions. If two people disagreed about the weight of the coal, it is open to an independent check, and the two parties would be forced to agree to abide by it. But the coal's blackness does require the perceptions of people, as the blackness only exists in the brains of those perceiving it. And the same applies to the orange flames, and the warmth the coal produces when it is burned. The secondary qualities are subjective, dependent on the individual perceptions of the observers. And if one person says the coal is black, and the other says it isn't black but actually a sparkling chromatic world of infinite variation and gradation, then fair play to them. Such is the nature of subjectivity.

The primary qualities can be identified in part by the fact that they can be detected using more than one sense – you can see and feel that an object is moving, for example, whereas the taste of a dog treat isn't something you can see—'

Ah, talking of which, you don't happen to have a…

'Maybe I do… let me look … yes, here you go.'

Thanks.

'There are one or two cases you might consider borderline. Heat, for example, you might think of as a primary quality – the fire is hot, surely, in and of itself. Locke's answer is that it's a mistake to think that the fire contains in itself anything like my *idea* of warmth. It would be as much to say that the pin contains my idea of pain, when it pricks me.

So now the brain has been furnished with ideas – simple and complex – but this is not quite the same, for Locke, as "having knowledge". Knowledge requires the mind's active capacity to find connections between ideas, to see agreement or disagreement between them. The eye delivers to the mind, for example, the simple ideas of black and white. The mind compares these two ideas, and sees that they are different. This understanding of difference is knowledge. The rationalists had considered concepts such as *difference* or *sameness* as being innate – they were categories just waiting to be filled up with data from the senses. But for Locke, without the experience there is no concept.

The various senses deliver us the complex ideas of cat and dog, and again we can see areas of difference, but also areas of similarity. From the fact that they are warm blooded and suckle their young, we can work out that cats and dogs belong to the same *class* – they are both mammals. Looking at their teeth, we then see that they are part of the same *order* – they are carnivores. But from the differences, the fact that—'

One is an evil psychopathic killer, and one your loving companion?

'Hah, maybe, whatever the differences, we see that you are in different *families* – one a canine, one a feline. This is knowledge, the proper sorting and arranging of the data supplied exclusively by our senses.'

Sounds great. What's wrong with it?

'Locke's ambition was to sound reasonable, to appeal to common sense, to eschew the paradoxical and the strange, but his very reasonableness gets him into a muddle – a muddle that empiricism has never quite managed to fix. I rather glossed over the mechanism by which Locke is able to say that the ideas in our minds are connected with objects in the external world. In the *Essay* Locke says that our mind contains only ideas, and that knowledge consists in comparing these ideas to see if they agree or disagree. I always imagine a little person in my brain carefully monitoring a bank of computer screens, on which various images are received. These images can be stored and retrieved to facilitate Locke's business of comparing and judging. But the trouble is that this little scene takes place entirely within the mind of the philosopher. How is she to know that anything on the screens relates to the world beyond? On what grounds is she able to say that there is any connection between the two, if the ideas in the mind are all she has to go on?

Locke later claims that simple ideas are both *caused by* and *resemble* the objects they represent, but how can this be known from those images on the computer screens, which we have already been told are the only things that the mind contains? In limiting knowledge to what we experience, Locke finds himself in a vicious circle. All that experience can tell us is that we are experiencing our experiences. By definition it cannot tell us what lies beyond experience, as a *cause* of experience. As we'll see, David Hume had a way out of this bind, but it wasn't really a philosophical one. Locke's way is to brush it quietly under the carpet.

But Locke's problems don't end with how experience can be grounded. You quite often find that what looks most solid about a theory is its weakest point.'

Do you?

'Well, OK, not really. The weakest part of Descartes' theory is pretty obviously God. And the weakest part of Leibniz's theory is the whole damn thing. I'll have to work on that … But, anyway, the weakest part of Locke's theory is that very reasonable-sounding distinction between primary and secondary qualities. The difficulty was pointed out by a brilliant young Irish philosopher called George Berkeley (1685–1753).

Berkeley appeared at first to be working solidly in that same empiricist tradition as Locke and Hobbes (and, later, David Hume). He begins by restating the Lockean view of the subjectivity of secondary qualities. It's helpful to remember that Locke had established that all the mind has access to are ideas, which are caused in some way by the things out there in the world. So the objects of our knowledge aren't the, er, objects, but the representations of those objects in our heads.

But then Berkeley pushed it further. Even those primary qualities – the dimensions, the solidity, the weight, the motion – do we not also only have access to them as ideas, as perceptions existing as images in the mind? What gives us the logical right to suppose that they exist independently of us, any more than colours, smells and tastes? And the same examples that Locke uses to show that colours and tastes can vary from person to person can be used to show that primary qualities are just as dependent on the perceiver. The lump of coal is a mountain to an ant, and a tiny pebble to an elephant.

And if now all of the qualities, primary and secondary, can be said to exist only in the mind of the perceiver, where does that leave the object itself? According to Berkeley, it leaves it literally *nowhere*. Berkeley makes the startling and disconcerting move of declaring that there are no objects outside of consciousness. When we say that a table or a chair or a little white dog exists, all we are saying is that we have, at that moment, those ideas in our mind. It makes no sense to talk about anything beyond that, something somehow causing those perceptions. To be is to be perceived.'

But that's… that's…

'Insane, but logical, if you accept those oh-so-reasonable positions adopted by Locke. Common sense says that if Berkeley is right, then when I close my eyes and open them again, the world has, in the gap, ceased to exist. Can we really contemplate a world that flickers into and out of existence like this?

Berkeley's answer to this objection is that it never arises, as the world is always being observed. His view was encapsulated rather wittily in philosophy's most famous pair of limericks (the first by Robert Knox, the second anonymous):

There once was a man who said, "God
Must think it exceedingly odd
If he finds that this tree
Continues to be
When there's no one about in the Quad."

Dear Sir,
Your astonishment's odd.
I am always about in the Quad.
And that's why the tree
Will continue to be
Since observed by
    Yours faithfully,
God

So, then, it is the omniscient eye of God that guarantees the continued existence of the external world, by observing it even when all human eyes are closed or averted.'

Convenient.

'This view – that the only things that have a real existence are ideas in the mind – is called *idealism*. The opposite view – that the material world does exist – is called *realism*. Annoyingly, this is only vaguely related to the nominalism–realism debate we examined a few walks ago. Nominalism may reject the idea that the generalized term *dog* is a real thing, but it in no way entails a belief that there are dogs only in my head.

We can see why Berkeley's views appealed to the aged Leibniz. Reality for Berkeley, as for Leibniz, exists in the mind, not "out there". And just as importantly, what gives the world its continuity is God.

Empiricism: Sensing is Believing

The last of the great empiricists, David Hume (1711–76), on one level has little truck with the notion that there is no real world out there. Hume was a great believer in common sense. He acknowledges that the philosopher might, for a few moments, convince him or herself that when you walk out of a room it ceases to exist, and that there is no actual world of objects outside the mind. But then the philosopher realizes the absurdity of this view, smiles and carries on as before, assuming the solid reality of tables and chairs and little dogs.

Yet Hume's analysis of what our senses can truly tell us about the world was far more destabilizing than Berkeley's whimsical idealism.

Much of Hume's empiricism, put forward first in *A Treatise of Human Nature* (1738–40), and later in a revised form in *An Enquiry Concerning Human Understanding* (1748), is a familiar rehashing of Locke. Whatever is in the mind Hume calls a *perception*. Perceptions are either *impressions* or *ideas*. Impressions are the more vivid, being either sense perceptions, emotions or feelings. We reach up and pluck the red apple, bite into its crisp flesh, taste the sweet sharpness of it, feel a surge of joy. The red, the crispness, the sweetness, the joy – these are all impressions. When we later recall the experience of eating the apple, the redness and other qualities that we experienced with such intensity are now pale reflections of the original experience. They are ideas. But though ideas lack the force and vivacity of the first impression, we have gained an ability to manipulate and combine them in various ways, using the imagination. Imagination enables us to come up with things we haven't experienced, forming, for example, the idea of a unicorn by adding together that of a horse and a horn. Although the imagination can manipulate and merge ideas freely, it can only bake with the ingredients delivered by the senses.'

Slightly annoying they couldn't all agree on the words for the stuff in your head.

'You mean the way an *idea* means something slightly different in Locke and Hume? Don't sweat it. The differences aren't important. For each of them they are entities in the mind, more or less what we all think of as an idea. So far, Hume is pretty close to Locke. Hume's radicalism begins with what comes next. All knowledge falls into two categories. On the one hand there are *matters of fact*, in other words something we perceive with the senses out there in the world. On the other, there are *relations of ideas*. By this he means those same analytic truths discussed earlier, the laws of mathematics and geometry, and tautological statements, such as "all men are mortal".

One key way of distinguishing the two is that to deny a true relation of ideas is to contradict yourself. If you say that a triangle has not three, but four sides, or that the square root of nine is not three, but four, you have shown that you do not know the meanings of the concepts involved. However, to deny a matter of fact never involves a contradiction of this kind. It is always possible that the opposite might occur, and the only way to find out is to use experience. No experience will ever change the number of sides a triangle has, and there really wouldn't be any point in sending out a scientific expedition to try to find a four-sided one in the Himalayas or the Amazon. But, however unlikely, there's always a chance that we might discover somewhere a blue-haired dog, or a potato that looks exactly like Winston Churchill.

This division between relations of ideas and matters of fact is known as Hume's fork, and if anything fails to be speared by one of the prongs, it cannot be, for Hume, a thing that it is possible to know. Such a thing is *causation*. Causation seems to most of us to be simply a thing we see happening all the time in the world. I kick a stone and it skitters away across the road; I strike a match, and the flame comes. And so many things depend on or follow from causation. All of science assumes causation. Human life depends on it. And there it is, happening right in front of our noses. Surely nobody could doubt the reality of such a thing?

Well, Hume can.'

I thought he probably would.

'First of all he points out that causation is not a truth like the truths of mathematics. Denying the reality of causation wouldn't involve a contradiction, like saying a triangle has four sides.'

Fair enough, but surely it's the other sort of knowledge, the matter of fact part of the fork?

'Well, you'd think so, but he has none of it. Hume says that all we see when one billiard ball hits another is that one thing happens – the approaching ball collides with the target ball; and then another thing happens – the target ball rebounds away. I see the match strike the match box, and then I see the flame atop the match. I click the button on the remote and then I see the telly come on. What I don't see is causation. What we see is what Hume calls a *constant conjunction*: A is always, or nearly always, followed by B.'

But this is just playing with words!

'Hume doesn't think so. He's not saying that we shouldn't expect B to follow A. Humans are ruled by habit and customs. We see one thing following another a number of times, and we expect that it will always happen thus. Hume thinks this is dandy. Common sense and habit and custom are exactly the sorts of things that should be governing our behaviour. But that doesn't change the fact that causation isn't a matter of fact or a relation of ideas: it's just a thing we've learned to expect.

Causation for Hume is a specific example of a wider phenomenon. We've mentioned the concept of induction before, in relation to Aristotle. The basis of induction is the idea that the future will resemble the past. We collect a number of examples of something, say of white swans. Then we construct a general law, e.g. that all swans are white, which in turn enables us to make predictions about future events, e.g. that the next swan we see will be white. But, again, inductive reasoning is not a relation of ideas: there is no contradiction in postulating a black swan. Nor is it a thing we can observe. Induction makes predictions about the future, and the future is something we can't observe.'

But don't we see the future eventually? I mean, you keep saying din-dins, and I run to my bowl, and my food is always there... ?

'Well, let's just look at this. What we want to test is whether inductive reasoning is a good basis for drawing conclusions. In other words, will the future resemble the past? We've found that inductive reasoning has been successful on various occasions. Therefore it must be useful in the future.'

Yeeeeeees....?

'So we're assuming exactly what it was we were trying to prove in the first place.'

Run that past me again.

'Induction is the idea that the future will resemble the past, in such a way as to enable us to construct laws and make predictions. Yes?'

Yes.

'We find that induction works on a number of occasions. Therefore we assume it will work in the future.'

Yes.

'Which is what we were trying to discover in the first place. You've used induction to prove induction.'

Ah. I see. I think. But, still, my dinner is always there…

'For once the logical objection isn't empty point scoring. Induction isn't always right. Famously, despite all the millions of white swans observed over the years, the theory that all swans are white was disproved when someone brought back a black swan from Australia. And Bertrand Russell has an amusing story that concerns animals expecting to be fed…'

I suspect I'm not going to like this…

'In the retelling it usually becomes a turkey, but Russell's original was actually a chicken. Anyway, every day the turkey gets fed at 9 a.m. This happens on 364 mornings. The turkey quite sensibly uses the logic of induction to arrive at the theory that he will always be fed at 9 a.m. The next morning is Christmas and the farmer wrings its neck.'

Cheers.

'You're welcome. Hume's critique of induction may well have been influenced by his reading of Ancient Scepticism – indeed Hume was, despite his occasional demurrals, a good reincarnation of the old Sceptics. One, Sextus Empiricus, had included arguments against inductive reasoning in his anti-dogmatic toolkit. If your dogmatic opponent tries to establish the truth of a general rule from a list of many observed particulars, they have a couple of possibilities. Either they can select a limited number of examples, or they can try to list all the examples. If they choose the first course, you can say that they've deliberately left out the examples that undermine their case. And if they try to list all the examples, the list will never end, as the number of possible examples is infinite. This isn't quite Hume's argument, but certainly inspired him to question the logic of induction.

So, Hume has established that causation (and induction in general) cannot be a matter of fact – it is never directly observed, merely inferred. And nor can it be a relation of ideas. Saying that striking "causes" the match to light or that the sun will rise tomorrow simply aren't analytic truths of the mathematical or geometric kind, something confirmed by the sad tale of the inductivist turkey. No logical contradiction is entailed in the idea that striking will not cause the match to light.

Where does that leave us? As ever, with Hume, custom and habit come to the rescue. We have got used to one thing being followed by another. It is likely that this habit will carry on being useful. We can't "know" it, in the way we can know certain other facts about the world, or demonstrate it, the way Euclid demonstrates a proof in geometry, but we can "use" it.

Hume's moderate scepticism about general tendencies or, in other words, *laws of nature*, is epistemological rather than ontological: he doesn't question their existence, he merely undermines the basis on which we claim to know them. One of the reasons Hume doesn't challenge the idea of a law of nature on a more fundamental level is that his scepticism, paradoxically, requires it.'

Huh?

'Oh, you're still awake? Sometimes this feels a little like talking to myself.'

Yeah, I was just resting my eyes. Paradoxically, you were saying… ?

'Yes, you see Hume was a great critic of religion, or at least of religion as it was practised in his time. He had a particular aversion to miracles. He defines a miracle as any event that goes against a law of nature. Bodies heavier than water ought to sink. People who have died shouldn't come back to life. Five loaves and seven fishes can't feed a crowd of five thousand people and leave over as crumbs a greater mass than was present at the outset of the experiment. So you can see why he needs to have the concept of a law of nature in the first place: without the law, there is nothing for the miracle to break. Experience may not have equipped us to say that laws of nature are infallible, but constant conjunction, combined with habit and custom, means that we have come to rely on them.

A wise man, he asserts, proportions his belief to the evidence. So what would count as good evidence for a miracle that breaks those laws on which we have come to rely? The criterion Hume puts forward is that disbelieving the witness must be more difficult, more *miraculous*, than believing the fact that a law, attested on so many occasions, has been broken. And we know that even when sincere, human beings are supremely fallible as witnesses. When we add that most miracles took place at a time of general credulity, among uneducated people, or those who had very good reasons to exaggerate or lie, then the rational man must conclude that there is no reason to accept the truth of miracles. And given that Christianity requires the belief in miracles, it was hardly surprising that Hume was widely attacked in his day for being an atheist.'

And was he?

'Yeah, I think so. Anyway, Hume, coming at the high point of the empiricist tradition, regarded religion as unproven nonsense, thought that our belief in causation and natural laws was grounded on nothing more firm than custom and regarded all moral and aesthetic beauty as not in any sense "real" things in the world, but as mere sentiments, living only in the human mind.

We began with the common-sense realism of Locke, who thought that our senses could deliver reliable knowledge. We have ended with something close to complete scepticism, relieved only by Hume's good-natured acceptance that habit and custom will see us through.'

Monty's head came up off my chest.

Someone's coming.

'What, really?'

Yeah.

He sniffed.

The Alpha female.

'Let's resume this later.

What's next?

'Kant.'

Gulp.

Walk 10

Kant and Fuzzy Logic

On our third epistemological walk, we tackle the Big One: Immanuel Kant argued that the mind has an active role in shaping our knowledge of the external world. We then look at the role of language in determining the limits of knowledge. Finally, we conclude that what counts as knowing depends very much on the context, and return to the useful notion of 'fuzziness'.

In the event, it was a few days before we got our next decent walk. I had a couple of out of town meetings, and Mrs McG took charge of the dog care. She brought him to the vet to see about his hip, and other problems. It wasn't the best news. The kind of news you don't really want to think about. So, for a treat, I took him on the bus to Primrose Hill, one sunny morning. He always liked it there, and would sit and gaze out across the vacuous glass towers of the City, as well as the gentler shapes of the old churches. We lay together on a blanket on the slope near the top of the hill, out of the wind.

'You remember where we got up to? It was a while ago...'

Kant, I think. You left it hanging over us, like a threat.

'OK, let's summarize. The rationalists believed that the human mind was the source of all real knowledge, and they distrusted and dismissed the evidence of the senses. The empiricists allowed that some knowledge, such as that of mathematics, may be arrived at by the mind working independently (although Locke denied even that), but for the most part they believed that we know what we know because our senses have transmitted information about the world to our minds, which were otherwise blank slates. The rationalists offered us sure knowledge of what is unbelievable, and the empiricists offered us only doubts about what we thought we knew.

What was needed was, of course, a way of combining the two views, giving due weight to each. The person who achieved this great act of synthesis was Immanuel Kant. Kant's account of the way the human mind comes to know the world, and what the limits of that knowledge are, is one of the greatest achievements of philosophy. The work in which he published his theory – *Critique of Pure Reason* (1781) – also happens to be one of the most difficult books ever published, the profundity and complexity of the thought mirrored by the knots and contortions of the language. (Reading it in German doesn't help – many German scholars have claimed it is easier to understand in English.)'

You're really selling it...

'One problem with Kant is the technical language he uses. Kant was trying to be as precise and accurate as possible, using words in highly specific and novel ways to avoid the possibility of misunderstanding. But in trying to avoid misunderstanding, he often entirely bypassed understanding. He was working within an established tradition of metaphysical thinking, taking its language from Aristotle, Descartes and Leibniz, to which he added his own terms, usually defined within the text, but often defined in ways that seem to take you further away from, rather than closer to, comprehension. All these things make reading Kant an extraordinary challenge for any non-professional philosopher. However, it is just about possible to present Kant's key ideas in a way that simplifies but does not distort them, although it must leave out much of the richness, as well as the mind-boggling trickiness.

Kant claimed that he had been awakened from his "dogmatic slumbers" by reading Hume. Hume's scepticism challenged him to find a way to precisely delineate what could be known. As well as Hume's scepticism, Kant was stimulated by the role that Hume gave to the mind in making sense of the data supplied by the senses. But Kant also wanted to avoid the idealism of Leibniz and Berkeley: there was a real world out there. The question was, how do we grasp it? So Kant's project was both to bring certainty to what could be known, and to properly theorize the role of human consciousness in the process of knowing.

I've tried to avoid most of Kant's most difficult technical language, using terms that I hope are familiar, but we'll have to begin with a few definitions.

As we've seen, before Kant, it had been assumed that there were two types of possible knowledge. There were those things that you could know from having experienced them – Kant terms this type of knowledge *a posteriori* (meaning "from the later"). And there were those things that you could know without experience, by reasoning, which he calls *a priori* ("from the earlier").

Most a priori truths are analytic – the truth is already in the propositions, and the reasoning process simply brings it out. The syllogisms we looked at earlier are examples of this. Though a priori knowledge can help clarify what you know, it is not really "new". So, once you define what a triangle is, all the other interesting things you can say about it – the square on the hypotenuse type stuff – is already locked up in there just waiting for you to unpick it. A posteriori truths come from experience. They are *synthetic*, in Kant's term, meaning that they create *new* knowledge – they bring before the understanding things that were not there before.

In *Critique of Pure Reason*, Kant set himself the challenge of demonstrating that there can be such a thing as synthetic a priori knowledge.

Hey, you said no jargon!

'I said I'd try to keep it to a minimum... But this is pretty straightforward, if you focus your little brain. Synthetic – meaning containing new stuff; a priori – meaning not learned from experience.'

And is there, er, any of that stuff?

'Does he pull it off? I think he does, yes!'

For Kant, the mind has two faculties involved in the production of knowledge. *Sensibility* is the mind's receptivity, its ability to take in sensory information from the outside world. *Understanding* is the mind's capacity to organize and manipulate the ideas that originate with the sensibility. Both of these sound similar to the way Hume envisaged knowledge to be generated. However, Kant's intention was to go far beyond Hume's relatively superficial account of the relationship between the mind and the world.

Kant's first step is to see that the acts of perception and understanding are precisely that – *acts*. Sensibility and understanding are not matters of passive reception, but active processes. Together they turn the chaotic jumble of sensory impressions, which Kant calls the *manifold*, into the logical and comprehensible world of our experience.

Beginning with sensibility, Kant never disputes that the sensory data that enters the mind relates to something *real* – he argues that there is simply no meaning to the idea of an appearance without having something real that appears. So he has no truck with the idealism of Berkeley, who maintained that perceptions have no reality outside the mind of the perceiver. The colours and sounds and smells of the world are representative of something *out there*, just as they were for Locke. For both Locke and Hume, our minds work on the incoming data, combining and interpreting it in various ways. Kant argues, however, that this act of organizing by the mind happens not passively, once the images have been received, but actively. Our perceptions have a structure from the outset, and that structure is imposed upon them by our consciousness in the very act of perception.

So what is this structure? Kant strips away both the raw data, the flashes of colour and flurry of action, and the later, more complex work of arranging and organizing done by the understanding. What he finds left are two concepts that had previously always been placed "out there" in the world, but which Kant now moves back into human consciousness: space and time.'

Whoa! So space and time are in our heads?

'Exactly. We don't observe space or time. They are not empirical concepts derived from our experiences. These are the *preconditions*, Kant argues, of any kind of perceptual experience. Kant's way of putting this is that space and time are *a priori intuitions*. To see an object is already to have the idea of space and time written into them. It is impossible to imagine something that isn't already organized spatially and temporally. We cannot think of objects other than as occupying some space, and as having qualities such as separateness, or connectedness.

This is what Kant means by that idea of the *synthetic a priori*. Usually something before experience can only be analytically, or tautologically, true. But here we have something that comes before experience, and yet contains real knowledge.

To the person who argues that we do simply perceive space "out there", Kant replies that even the idea that space exists outside us presumes the existence of the spatial concepts of inside and outside, so the argument is circular. Similarly, the idea that things exist either in a chronological sequence or simultaneously is a structural principle that helps us to make sense of the world, not a thing we actually find out there.'

I'm trying here, but I've only got a little doggy brain.

'It's not just you. It's genuinely challenging to force the mind to think of space and time as being projected from consciousness rather than being passively perceived by them. It might help to think about them as being the rules of a game. If you watch a football match or two people playing chess, what would otherwise be utterly baffling and random movements are, if you know the rules, entirely understandable. And it's not that we passively receive the images of a person kicking a ball or moving their queen, and then subsequently interpret these movements: the game itself is structured by our consciousness – we read the rules *into* the match.

And this active making sense of the world is very much in accord with modern psychology, which fully endorses the view that the brain works hard to give the chaotic muddle of sensory perception a form and meaning. Just one very basic example.

When we look at something, the image of that thing hits the retina. Because of the structure of the eye, the image on the retina has been flipped upside down. One of the first jobs the brain has to do is to flick it the right way up again. But that whole flipping business implies an innate knowledge of spatial relations.

It's impossible for us to think of a world without time or space. That moment before the Big Bang, when space and time come into existence? The human mind literally cannot conceive of it. We have the words "before the Big Bang", which seem to mean something, but there is nothing, no image in the mind that corresponds to them. To think of any object is to place it in space. To imagine it moving involves not only an idea of space, but also of time, which passes as it moves.

So, even *sensibility*, the first stage of acquiring knowledge through the absorption of sensory perceptions, is structured by qualities of the mind. The next stage in the process of knowing now takes over: the *understanding*. Intuitions – Kant's word for this raw data, organized in time and space – have to be further interpreted by the understanding for them to mean anything to us.

So, the sensibility begins the process of turning raw sense data into something we can know, by arranging it in space and time. However, the real heavy lifting is done by the understanding, during which the mind sorts, organizes, combines and judges. To do this the mind uses what Kant calls *categories*, different conceptual entities that the mind employs to make sense of the incoming sensory data.

The idea that things in the world "out there" could be analysed by means of categories was first used by Aristotle (well, it had to be, really, didn't it...). The original Greek term, *kategoria*, meant an accusation or a charge that could be levelled against someone in a court of law. Aristotle used the term to mean something like a predicate – a thing you could say, or a question you could ask, about something.

Aristotle has ten categories, which he thinks exhaust all the possibilities for describing an object. There is *substance*, i.e. what kind of thing it is, a man or a dog, say, or a tree. Then *quantity* – how many of them are there? Then *quality* – this is a little vaguer but means what qualities it has, such as colour, texture, smell, etc. Then *relation* – the way things relate to each other, so, Monty, you're smellier than me, and I'm taller than you. Then, *place* – we're here on this blanket. Then *time* – it's today! Then *posture* – I'm sitting here, and you're lying on my chest. Then *state* – another slightly trickier one, by which Aristotle means that you're in a condition of having had something done to you – the examples Aristotle gives are having your shoes or your armour on. So, Monty has on his little cute coat… Then *action* – what is the thing up to? We are thinking and talking. And last, *passion*, which is the passive version of acting – having things done to you, being kicked, or shouted at.'

That was a little boring.

'Sorry. I get that, but it's kind of important. We now know everything that Aristotle thought you could say about something! If I analysed you using the categories, there would be literally nothing left to say about you. You've been fully categorized!'

Yippee!

'The key thing to remember is that these things, for Aristotle, are the properties of the subject – they are qualities that belong to the objective reality of whatever the thing is we're talking about. But Kant flips this round 180 degrees. All the ways of categorizing a thing are moved from the world to the mind. In place of Aristotle's ten, Kant has twelve categories, arranged into four subgroups, which he calls *moments*. These moments are Quantity, Quality, Relation and Modality. We don't want to get too bogged down in Kant's categories, but roughly the group under Quantity deals with how many of a thing there are; Quality is to do with a thing being present or not, or limited in some way; Relation is about how things in the world are related to each other, for example by cause and effect; and Modality is about how an object might exist, for example does it actually exist, does it possibly exist or does it necessarily exist. On perceiving anything in the world, the mind instantly imposes the categories on it in an act Kant calls *synthesis*, and this synthesis, this sudden grasping of a thing in relation to the categories, is what understanding, or knowing, truly means.

It's all a bit, er, confusing. In fact, that was pretty well just noise. Can you put it into dog language?

'I'll try. So, for the moment that he calls Quantity, Kant has noticed that I could say, for example, Monty barks, or some dogs bark, or all dogs bark. These are all the possible ways to think about number or Quantity – one, some or all. So, we have the categories Unity, Plurality and Totality, under the moment of Quantity. In the moment of Quality, the possible categories are Reality (Monty's here), Negation (Monty isn't here) and Limitation (Monty's here until we leave).'

I'm still not really… Those pills the vet gave me… they can make it hard to concentrate.

I stroked his nose.

'When I look at you, my mind automatically does all that work, applying all the different categories – insofar as they are relevant – to you, and my understanding of the thing in the world called Monty is the sum of all those subconscious acts. Better?'

I think so. Sorta. Maybe. No, not really.

'The thing to cling to is that idea that my mind is actively engaged in creating the thing that I understand as you. It does it by imposing certain forms on the crazy mad flurry of sense impressions I pick up. First it imposes time and space, and then it fixes you into the various categories. And the space and time and the categories are all in my head, rather than in the world.'

Hang on, does this relate back to the a priori synthetic thingamabob?

'Yes! The categories and so on are a priori, and yet they are also true knowledge, reaching beyond themselves to conquer new cognitive land – in fact, they are the preconditions of me having any knowledge at all. Furthermore, these categories are a basic part of being rational, so any human being will possess them. This means that the world as grasped by the human mind will be a common one, one shared between us, and mutually comprehensible. We're not locked into private worlds, like Leibniz's monads.'

Well, that's a relief. Can you tickle my… aaaaahhhhh yes, that's the spot.

'What we've left out, so far, is the world behind the appearances. I said Kant never denied that something is out there, initiating the chain of events that concludes in me seeing and understanding the thing called Monty. Locke had posited that there are primary and secondary qualities, and he thought that the primary qualities really belonged to the thing, and were, in a sense, what the thing *is*. Berkeley (and Leibniz) thought there is no thing out there, just the idea in your head—'

Don't tell me, Kant takes some perfect middle path – what did Aristotle call it, the golden mean?

'Not quite. Kant calls the thing in itself the *noumenon*. And it is among the most mysterious entities in all philosophy, this *something*, out there, about which we can know literally nothing. Other than that it exists. It has no shape, no weight, no texture. All of those qualities are generated by our mind's active powers of creation. So, yes, there is a presence there, but Kant says that human knowledge and reason is ultimately limited, and it never reaches the noumenon. The categories only work on what is empirically available – and the noumenon, standing behind the empirical, is unreachable. The same, by the way, applies to God.'

Oh, another atheist?

'No one can quite decide about Kant and God. He often talks of God, and of the necessity of believing in him, as a way of grounding morality, but he also says we can never know that God exists. He takes God out of the field of rational or scientific proof, and leaves him entirely in the world of faith.'

Do you basically think that that's it, then, that Kant is right, and that most of what we perceive and understand in the world is imposed on it by the mind?

'Broadly, yeah.'

So that's it, then, we've done epistemology.

'Not quite. Can you cope with a bit more?'

As long as you keep tickling me just there, yep, I can cope.

'Epistemology didn't stop with Kant, but I think that from then on, all epistemology was a matter of wrestling with Kant. And he usually wins. But there's one more theory I'd like to quickly mention, and then I'll tell you what I really think.

Pragmatism is one of the very few new philosophies invented since the Greeks. There's nothing quite like it in the Ancient world. It's associated with a handful of mainly American thinkers, active in the second half of the nineteenth century and first half of the twentieth, including Charles Sanders Peirce, William James and John Dewey. The pragmatists entirely broke away from the idea that there is a truth to be discovered, either empirically out there in the "real" world, or derived by pure rationality inside my head. For the pragmatists, knowledge wasn't a matter of some correspondence between what I think and what the truth is. The truth is simply whatever works best in a given situation. It's essentially an evolutionary hypothesis: we are animals attempting to survive and reproduce in a world that is full of challenges. Some beliefs that we hold will help us to prosper. Those that don't help us will be weeded out, like sickly organisms. This is all that truth can ever mean.

Let's say that I am a mammoth-hunter fifty thousand years ago. I know that at certain times of the year, a herd of mammoths wander down a particular valley. I believe that this is because the spirits of my forefathers drove the mammoths down the valley, on their way to celebrating a feast held in their honour at this time of year. Because I know when the ancestors will be arriving, I know to be ready with my spear. The effect of my belief is that I get a good feed of roast mammoth.

For the pragmatist, my belief in the ancestors is "true". They would not say that the ancestors are really driving the mammoths – that isn't what truth means. Truth is never about what's really there – there is no "really" – it's about what gets me through the day.

Or, I have to catch a bus. I believe the bus is always late on Tuesdays, so I delay my walk to the bus stop. I miss the bus. My belief about the bus was wrong, but only because I missed it. Does believing in God make you happy, and improve the quality of your life? If so, then God is "true".

Pragmatism solved many of the traditional problems of metaphysics and epistemology. It solves them by saying that they are irrelevant. We no longer need to enquire into the ultimate nature of reality, or theorize about the mind's categories or concepts. All that matters is: did I catch the bus? If I caught the bus, then my beliefs about it were true in the only sense that true can ever mean anything.

I've a bit of a soft spot for pragmatism, and my own view borrows a little from pragmatist thinking. However, the philosopher Bertrand Russell (1872–1970) gave pragmatism such a thorough beating that it has never recovered. Russell says that if a belief is "true" only if its effects are good, then we need to know (a) what is good, and (b) what are the effects of the belief. Without discovering these things, we can't ever know what is true. But rather than making life simpler, this process makes it much more difficult. He gives the example of trying to find out if it's true that Christopher Columbus discovered America in 1492. Rather than going to some authority, checking the internet or reading up on the history, the pragmatist has to somehow ascertain the effects of this belief. Will believing Columbus crossed the Atlantic in 1492 be more beneficial to me than believing he crossed it in 1493?

A pragmatist would point out that there are circumstances when giving the answer 1492 would give you a definite benefit, for example if you were sitting an exam. Then it would become "true". But what if on passing the exam, I was in such a good mood that I walked into the road without properly checking for traffic, and was run down by a bus (possibly the same one I had missed earlier on)? Would it now be false that Columbus sailed the Atlantic in 1492 because "knowing" it had killed me?

If I believe that something is true only if it has good consequences, then my belief in this, i.e. pragmatism, must in turn
have good consequences if it is to be true. And my belief that
my belief in the good consequences of pragmatism must also
have good consequences if it is to be true. And this belief in
the belief of the good consequences of the belief in the good
consequences of the belief in good consequences must also
be—'

ENOUGH!

'OK, you get it. The argument goes on forever. The problem
is that truth has been defined solely in relation to my subjective
experiences, with nothing to tether it to anything outside them.
How do we know that Father Christmas exists? Because he
makes more people happy than he makes sad.'

But you were saying there was still something in it ...

'Time for my take on truth and knowledge. You won't be sur-
prised that it's got something to do with that concept of
fuzziness. I think that much of the trouble we get into when
talking about knowledge is because we're confusing different
types of discourse, which each have their own criteria for
knowledge, some demanding a high degree of certainty and
some not. So what we have to do is look closely at each know-
ledge-requiring situation, and decide what counts as true or not
in those circumstances. In effect this is saying that "true" means
nothing unless you specify the conditions.

Imagine that I'm waiting at the bus stop. The bus is due at
11.55. The man next to me in the queue is a little worried about
having missed the bus. He sees that I'm wearing a watch, and
asks me if I know what time it is. I could give several answers. I
might say, "Hold on a sec, and I'll check." I actually know someone at CERN (the European Organization for Nuclear

Research) and they have the most accurate clock in the world, and so I phone them up, reach the switchboard, get put on hold, and finally, as the man boards the bus, I say, "It's 11.54 a.m. and 17.21345621 seconds!"'

Annoying.

'Or I could say, "No."'

Huh? Has your watch stopped?

'No, it's working. But no clock, not even the sort of atomic clock used in scientific labs, keeps exactly the right time. My wristwatch might be reasonably accurate, but it'll be off by several seconds. The CERN clock might be out by a nanosecond or two. So, no, I don't know *exactly* what time it is.'

Don't expect me to protect you if he hits you with his umbrella.

'Or when the man asks me, I say, "It's about twelve noon." But that's also no use, because it's so vague he might or might not have missed his bus. In this situation there's a right answer, and it's not the most accurate ("I don't know") and not the most specific ("11.54 a.m. and 17.21345621 seconds"), and certainly not the vaguest ("about twelve noon"), but the one with the right degree of accuracy ("It's just coming up to five-to").'

This view, that truth is, in some ways, dependent on context, is a little akin to pragmatism, in that truth is tied to usefulness. But it also acknowledges that there is a real time, which isn't real because it makes me happy, but because of certain objective facts about the world.

There are other situations in which the fuzziness is more palpable, where truth is genuinely hard to get at. Often this is because of the nature of language. Language probably evolved as a pragmatic tool for achieving certain things – enabling our ancestors to better co-ordinate hunts, helping to secure the social bonds between individuals; possibly assisting individuals to gain an upper hand over others in the competition for mates and food. But language soon started to be used for other purposes.

It clearly has some ability to convey realities about the world ("Tiger! Run for it!"), but there are times when it is a crude and inadequate tool. You might be asked how you feel about something. That involves turning strange biological and psychological processes into words, which, even if you are extraordinarily eloquent and determined to be truthful, might be impossible.'

Feelings are always a bit tricky. But usually people manage to get their meaning across, don't they? Walkies, din-dins. It's not rocket science.

'It may not be rocket science, but language is a trickier, stranger, more elusive thing than you think. We tend to think of language in a simplistic way, words having a straightforward, unproblematic relationship to objects out there in the world. The word "bus" is just like a finger, pointing at that big red thing with four wheels, full of passengers. Language amounts, in this view, to a sort of picture of the world, and the more closely the picture resembles the world, like a hyper-real computer-generated portrait, the closer we get to truth.

Ludwig Wittgenstein (1889–1951), who we met way back, developed a more sophisticated version of this in the *Tractatus Logico-Philosophicus* (1921). The *Tractatus* is a little like Spinoza's *Ethics*, in that it consists of numbered paragraphs, arranged into sections in a quasi-mathematical way. Each section begins with a bold assertion that, like Spinoza's propositions and Euclid's axioms, is assumed to be self-evident. Each proposition is then illustrated and expanded on in numbered sub-paragraphs. So, it begins:

1. The world is all that is the case.
1.1. The world is the totality of facts, not of things.

Reality consists of a series of facts, or states of affairs. The job of language is straightforwardly to picture these facts. Imagine a car accident. You have to describe what happened. You are given small scale models of the cars involved, and the roads and buildings.'

And a bus?

'And a bus. Each model stands for a thing in the world. You accurately recreate the accident, using the models, carefully placing the toy car and bus in just the right place. The "truth" of the model depends on how closely it corresponded to the facts in the world, as they occurred.

Now substitute words and statements for the models. That's how language works to picture the world. Rather than using the models, I might say *The car that was driving south on Cannon Hill crashed into the bus that was driving north*. Each phrase in the sentence corresponds to a fact in the world. There's a suggestion that perhaps language had an even more literally pictorial origin. In the sentence *The car is to the left of the bus*, the word "car" is physically to the left of the word "bus". And, of course the earliest written forms of language used pictograms to represent objects.

However, there are many things you can't talk about if you see language as having a pictographic relationship with the "facts" in the world. Wittgenstein acknowledges this in the famous last words of the *Tractatus* – it's one of the few lines that every philosopher knows off by heart: "Whereof one cannot speak, thereof one must be silent."

Those things of which one cannot speak are not unimportant – to either Wittgenstein or us. He means religion, ethics, beauty, the meaning of existence. These are all, for Wittgenstein, things that language can never reach, as they are not matters of fact to which words and propositions can be allocated. Wittgenstein believed he had set a limit to what could be said. Within that limit, anything that could be said could be clearly understood. Beyond it was only meaningless waffle – by which Wittgenstein meant most talk about art, philosophy and religion.'

And is this true? Is this what language is, a list of facts about stuff in the world?

'It's an alluring idea, in some ways, that language is simply a matter of linking a proposition to a fact "out there". Truth and lies become readily detectable. Ordinary language suddenly starts to function like mathematics, where there is never any ambiguity about the meaning of a symbol. What the Wittgenstein of the *Tractatus* offers is a cure for fuzziness. If language really was as he projected, then everything that could be said could be said with absolute, mathematical clarity. The price is that much of what we might want to say couldn't be said at all.

Wittgenstein really thought that philosophy had come to an end with his book.'

I'm guessing he was wrong…

'Yep, he was wrong. There are many problems with this view of language, even if we ignore the aching chasm of what it necessarily leaves out. The picture theory might appear to work for nouns, verbs, adverbs and adjectives – *the red bus drove quickly* makes sense as a picture of something that happened. But what about words like "and", "or", "but" and "why"? What are they pictures of?

Eventually Wittgenstein came to see that his early view of language was inadequate. It embodied a reductively atomic view of the world and of language: experience is divided up into tiny, independent units, which are mapped onto a single word or phrase. This oversimplifies both the world, which is made not of isolated units of being, but of complex interconnected networks, and language, where words are woven together, and meaning emerges from their interplay.

Wittgenstein's later philosophy, put forward in *Philosophical Investigations* (published posthumously in 1953), looks in detail at some of the many ways we use language. The ability of language to generate meaning comes not from the word and the object in the world being skewered on the same kebab, but by subtle patterns of use, and complex rules, embedded in the texture of our lives.

However, although this later view of language is much richer, more fecund and, I think, truer, Wittgenstein proposed it before certain developments in linguistics changed completely how we view the relationship between the world, our thoughts and language.

Drat, just when I was getting the hang of things.

'Traditionally, linguistics had studied how words change over time, and the meaning of a word was thought to be wrapped up in this historically evolving relationship between the word and the thing it represented. This *etymological* view is often fascinating in its own right. So, for example, in one of his lectures on metaphor, the Argentinian writer Jorge Luis Borges points out how the English word "threat" comes from the Anglo-Saxon *ðreatt*, meaning crowd. It's quite easy to see how the modern meaning evolved from the earlier one, crowds being places of danger.

But the Swiss linguist Ferdinand de Saussure (1857–1913) took a very different approach to analysing how language works. He thought that rather than tracing how the meanings of words change over time (which is called *diachronic* linguistics), we have to analyse language as it functions now, as a signifying system (*synchronic* linguistics).

Knowing that threat comes from *ðreatt* is fascinating, and perhaps illuminating about Anglo-Saxon society, but it tells us nothing about how the word is used now. If I warn you about the threat of a snake in the grass, you need to know that there's a danger, not a crowd.'

I could take a snake. It's basically just a sausage with a tongue, from what I can see.

'The basic unit of structuralist linguistics is the sign. A sign is made up of two components, the material part, which could be marks on paper or the sounds of spoken language, and the mental part, the idea to which the physical part refers. The material part is called the signifier, and the mental component is the signified. The two are united in the sign. The word DOG is a sign made up of the letters D-O-G, and the idea of a dog. You hit a red traffic light. The red is the signifier, the signified is STOP; the two together are the sign. You woof. The woof is the signifier, the signified is—'

Give me a sausage?

'I give you a sausage. The sausage is the signifier, the signified is "I love you".'

That's sweet. And this sausage is where, exactly… ?

'Just an illustration, for now. Signs never work alone, but function together in a language, their meaning always defined by their relation to other signs. Red only means stop in relation to green (go) and amber (wait).

The relationship between the signifier and the signified is usually arbitrary – the English word "dog" and the French word *chien* both refer to the same idea; and as long as we all agreed, we could use any sound or written squiggle to stand for dog.

This arbitrary link between the signifier and signified means that over time meanings have a tendency to slip and change in unpredictable ways, adding an element of instability to the system of meaning.

The study of signs is called semiology, and remains a fruitful and fascinating way of investigating human culture. I really like a way of looking at signs developed by the pragmatist Charles Sanders Peirce (1839–1914). Peirce described three types of sign, the *Icon*, the *Index* and the *Sign* proper, defined by the different relationships between the signifier and the signified. With an icon, the relationship is one of resemblance between the two – a photograph of you, Monty, is an icon. As would be a portrait of a face, or a drawing of a tree, or an onomatopoeic word like "bang" or "crash". With an index, the connection is less clear-cut, but there is still a physical relationship: a blush would be an index of embarrassment, or a black cloud an index that a storm is coming. Third is the sign proper, in which the connection is purely conventional, as in most spoken and written language. It's quite fun to wander around mentally allocating different types of sign to the right category. Soon you start to see everything in the world around you as signifying something: cars as an index of wealth, the subtle differences indicated by the icons on toilet doors—'

Weirdo.

'It takes all sorts. For Wittgenstein, the structure of the world dictates the structure of language – states of affairs out there call for a word or phrase to describe them. In structuralist linguistics, this relationship is reversed, or at least greatly complicated. Language shapes how we see and understand the world. Just as the signifiers – the terms we use for ideas – are arbitrary, the way language chops the world up is also arbitrary, or, rather, something that varies subjectively with cultures, rather than being an objective fact.

There's a playful example of this in an essay by Borges called "The Analytical Language of John Wilkins" (1952). Borges describes "a certain Chinese Encyclopaedia", *Celestial Emporium of Benevolent Knowledge*, in which it is written that animals are divided into various fanciful categories, such as "those that belong to the Emperor", "embalmed ones", "those that tremble as if they were mad", "those that have just broken a flower vase" and "those that from a long way off look like flies".

I like that. Tickles me.

'The point is that rather than using our system of animal classification based on morphological resemblance and shared evolutionary history, here the criteria for categorization are to do with use, or whimsy.

The most famous example of this idea that language is responsible for how we see the world, not merely a reflection of it, was the view put forward by the anthropologist Franz Boas, and later popularized as part of the Sapir–Whorf hypothesis, that the Inuit had fifty words for snow. Because they had the fine-grained language, they were able to "see" different types of snow that would be indistinguishable to us. This view became a little discredited, but the latest research suggests that Boas may have actually underestimated the Inuit's ability to discriminate. For example, in the Inuit dialect spoken in Canada's Nunavik region there are at least fifty-three words for snow, including *matsaaruti*, for wet snow that can be used to ice a sleigh's runners, and *pukak*, for the sort of powdery snow that looks like salt.

Even such apparently objective things as the colour spectrum are chopped up in different ways. The number of basic colour terms employed in different cultures varies from two to eleven, with those societies with few colour terms being unable to *see* the colours for which they have no names. Similarly, remote tribal groups in the Amazon, and other parts of the world, have never needed to develop number systems that go beyond four (or some other relatively small number). Confronted with assemblages of objects greater than four – including their own children – they resort to "many". Without the language for enumerating, they simply cannot make their minds grasp bigger numbers.

Feminists have argued persuasively that male power and cultural control has ensured that maleness is inscribed in our language, forcing us to see women as inferior, reinforcing negative stereotypes of women and buttressing their subservient position. Racist language serves a similar function in othering and demeaning different racial groups.'

This is all moderately interesting, but I've sort of forgotten what it is we're trying to do here.

'Oh, sorry. I'm trying to show that in these ways language becomes not a simple tool for knowing, but a way in which what is known is controlled and shaped.

Structuralism was an important movement in European thought for much of the twentieth century, influencing everything from anthropology to film studies. The central idea was that all meaningful human behaviour can only be understood as taking part within a structure, which functions in some ways like a language, with a grammar and vocabulary, and in which each individual element only comes to mean something in relation to the others.

Although structuralism allows for some play and slippage of meanings, there is a fundamental stability, which Saussure and the other structuralists thought gave a scientific, objective value to their theories. This confidence was shattered by Jacques

Derrida (1930–2004), who brilliantly undermined the scientific confidence of structuralism. Derrida argued that underlying structuralist linguistics – indeed underlying almost all theories that try to pin down an objective idea of truth, going right back to Plato – is a certain notion about the relationship between truth and language. The truth is a simple, unitary thing inside me. The purpose of language is to convey that simple unitary truth to another person, passing it on, like one person lighting a candle from another's flame. The most reliable and direct method of transmitting the truth is by speech. Speech guarantees the authenticity of the truth, because the speaker is *present*. Truth and presence are closely allied. When I speak my truth to you, I can control it, and ensure that your understanding of it accords with my own. Once speech becomes written language, then it escapes that close control.

Plato bewails this move from speech to writing in the *Phaedrus*, and the same idea – that speech is truth and writing is lies – crops up again and again in the history of philosophy, right down to Saussure, who looked to speech and presence as the best way of preventing that dangerous slippage between the signifier and the signified.

Derrida regards this notion of communication as a myth. In its place he has a view of language in which truth, rather than being a flame inside each mind, kindled and passed on, becomes an elusive property of language itself. In its simplest form, this view of language emphasizes that words always point to other words. Definitions rely on words, which must in turn be defined in words, ensuring that meaning remains always "in-house". Language is an endless chain, and we never reach the end, never reach that final truth inside someone's head, and outside language.

He illustrates this with the Greek word *pharmakon*, used in the *Phaedrus*. The word means poison. Plato describes writing as being a *pharmakon*. However, *pharmakon* can also mean cure. In this sense it's a little like our word "drug" – which can mean a medicine like penicillin, or a recreational substance like heroin. Whatever Plato might intend, as soon as language starts to work, the meanings are uncontrollable. It is impossible not to keep both meanings alive, even if Plato wanted to kill the *pharmakon*-as-cure definition.

Insofar as all attempts to understand the world are linguistic (and it's hard to think how they would not be), we will never have a final answer to the *What do we know?* question. Truth will always squirm out of our grip, like a greased piglet—'

Wait, we've come all this way, only for you to tell me that the sceptics were right, and we can't know anything?

'No, not quite. I think that Derrida is right, in that a final answer will never be found to any question framed in normal language. That's one of the ways in which normal language is different to the language of mathematics. But a "final answer" doesn't mean *no* answer and, going back to our discussion about bus timetables, it doesn't mean that we can't have a *satisfactory* answer to the bus question, just because the meaning of "bus" and "time" will be slightly different for every passenger.'

So what do we know?

'I think that there's a sort of rough consensus. Kant's assumption that there is a real noumenal world out there isn't really challenged much. Apart from mystics and religious thinkers, there aren't many idealists left who think the external world is a phantom. And it genuinely seems as though we're getting closer to seeing or at least understanding it, that elusive noumenon. Quantum physics gives us an insight into the ultimate nature of reality that would have delighted Kant. But the noumenon's strangeness and otherness will mean that it remains always just outside the grip of knowledge.

What remains, the phenomenal world of objects with colours and weight and smells and tastes, is shaped by the extraordinary creative human mind. We can "know it" as long as we define "know" appropriately, applying the right standard of specificity in each case, and keeping ourselves aware that the very nature of language means that, in everything other than mathematical knowledge, the truth is like the light in the fridge: you "know" it goes off when you shut the door, but knowing isn't knowing...

So that's epistemology. There are sceptics who think we can't know anything. There are rationalists who think that we can know everything, but that everything is the universe inside my head. There are empiricists who think our senses give us solid evidence on which to form reliable theories about the world beyond our minds. And then there are those who follow Kant, in thinking that knowledge is an active product of the human mind, which reaches out to carve the raw material of the universe into understandable chunks.

But there is one particular area where knowing fuzzily seems quite inadequate. An area where precise knowledge is surely generated: knowledge that isn't just *analytic*, like mathematics, but *synthetic*, making bold claims about the nature of reality that can be confirmed as objectively true.'

Great. But maybe another day. All I can think about is that sausage...

'OK. Tomorrow we discuss the philosophy of science.'

Ants, Spiders and the Philosophy of Science

On this walk, Monty and I look at one specialized branch of epistemology: the philosophy
of science. We discuss the theory of induction, put
forward by Francis Bacon, and so on to modern theories of science, proposed by Popper, Kuhn, Lakatos
and Feyerabend.

The next day brought one of those fierce, bright winter mornings. Vapour trails stood out clear in the blue sky. This part of
London is relatively elevated, and ours is the top flat in the
block, so the view from the kitchen was all sky. When I was a
kid we used to lie back in the long grass of summer and watch
the trails, the way young people now watch the telly or their
phone screens. I don't think we ever read any significance into
the vapour trails (though now, of course, I see them as an
index ...): we just found an aesthetic delight in the play of white
and blue. Did we even connect the lines with the aeroplanes
that painted them? Perhaps we were still in that primitive,

pre-scientific age, when we ascribed anything sublime to the actions of gods and monsters. I remembered trying to find the exact point at which the vapour disappeared into the blue, straining and yearning my way into the sky. But, of course, this was another example of the sorites paradox, if only I'd known it back then.

A good day for a philosophy of science walk, I thought.

I called to Monty, expecting him to come bounding into the hallway, lead in mouth. But there was nothing. I searched through the rooms, and finally found him lying half-hidden behind the curtains. He gave me a mournful look.

Tired. And my dodgy hip's playing up.

'But we both need some fresh air…'

Do you still have that bag?

'Bag?'

You know, from when I was a pup, and my legs weren't up to walking all the way up the hill on the school run.

The bag was a green canvas army-surplus thing. Monty fitted snugly inside it, with his head sticking out. I guess it looked pretty cute.

'I thought you hated that bag.'

I did. But that was then. We learn, we grow. There's that café where we used to hang out… Warm in there.

I used to try to write in a chain café with good Wi-Fi on Hampstead High Street. But I more just sort of sat there in a stupor after the turmoil of a morning spent getting two kids off to school. Half the time I'd still have my pyjamas on under my jeans and moth-eaten jumper.

I found the bag on the shelf in the coat cupboard where we put things we think we'll never use again, but don't yet want to throw away, and Monty stepped right into it. I tucked his blanket around him, and we began the walk up to Hampstead Village.

'Yesterday we talked about knowledge. Today we're talking about a particular kind of knowledge, one given a special status in our culture. Scientific knowledge.'

The good stuff!

'That's how it's often perceived. Science is usually taken to be a machine for producing certainty, a special, pure kind of truth. It is not *someone's* truth, the truth from a particular standpoint, truth with an angle: it is The Truth. And because it's pure, all you have to do is stick a white lab coat on someone and you can use her to sell you scientific toilet cleaner or toothpaste.'

You're about to do a job on it, aren't you?

'Well, I'm going to question some common misconceptions about scientific knowledge. But as for science in general, I love it! Science has shown us the glory and grandeur of our world, from the smallest particles to the immensity of the universe. It has provided the best answers to the fundamental questions of what we are and why (or how) we are here. But as for being a simple, impartial way of discovering the objective truth, well, that remains to be proven. So what I'm going to do is to talk you through how philosophers have tried to capture what science does, and turn that into a series of prescriptions about what science *should* do.

Let's begin with a slight caricature of the way people think science works. I admit that this is based on watching dozens of old British and American black-and-white films, but I suspect something like it fills the mind of most people when they think of science, despite the efforts of media popularizers to make science seem like fun. A group of men (nearly always) in white coats are working in a lab. They spend their time looking into microscopes, or fiddling with some baffling piece of equipment. They are carefully gathering data, writing down their findings in notebooks or inputting them into spreadsheets. Eventually, a look of surprise, which turns into a look of awe, blending again into exultation, comes over one of the men, our main guy, who has broken his health in the long search for Truth. It's here, the eureka moment!

Next, the scientists busy themselves trying to replicate the dramatic discovery. To their delight and relief, after extensive testing, the finding is confirmed. And after that, the boffins hand the discovery on to the practical men, who will use it to produce a new kind of medicine, or bomb.

This view of science, conceived of as the careful gathering and arranging of data that then coalesces in the mind of the scientist into a theory, was first formulated by Francis Bacon (1561–1626).

Bacon was active at the beginning of a period that was to see breathtaking advances in the physical and biological sciences, but his intellectual world was still formed by the Scholastic tradition, which satisfied itself with endlessly working through the details of Aristotle's philosophy and physics. Bacon reacted violently against this tradition. He compared the Aristotelians to spiders, spinning intricate webs from silk produced entirely within themselves. He also criticized the alternative, under-theorized, mindless gathering of information, which he said was like an ant, merely collecting random grains of sand. We should aim, rather, to be like the bee, both collecting the raw material from the flowers of the garden and the field, and then digesting and transforming it into the honey of true knowledge.'

Bacon, honey, this is making me hungry.

Ants, Spiders and the Philosophy of Science

'You can snack when we get to the café. Bacon is usually regarded as the father of induction, but his position is actually a step on from the most basic inductivist position. The "ant" approach of unsophisticated accumulation is often called induction by simple enumeration. The ant-scientist collects facts, and once enough data has been amassed, a theory emerges inevitably from it, like cream separating from the milk. Bacon was certainly a big fact man – he decried the Scholastic obsession with logic and mathematics, and thought that science must be built on empirical data. He was, however, aware of the shortcomings of simple enumeration, and attempted to overcome them.

Bacon begins, as does the simple enumerator, by amassing facts. The scientist makes many observations, noting them down methodically. But rather than remaining as an undifferentiated mass, the facts are assigned to one of three tables: the Table of Essence and Presence, the Table of Absence in Proximity and the Table of Degrees. Bacon only gives one example of how this is done, but I think it conveys well enough his method. He was interested in the cause of heat, and so he made observations of many instances of heat occurring in natural and man-made situations, ranging from fire to horse manure. These were put into the Table of Essence and Presence. Then there were instances where heat was entirely absent. These were noted in the Table of Absence in Proximity. The third table arranged those instances in which heat was present in varying degrees. Contemplation of these tables then helps the scientist to edge towards a theory of the true cause, or 'form', of heat. The third table, which showed varying degrees of the phenomenon being investigated – for example, the increasing heat of an anvil being struck by a hammer – was the best guide to the underlying cause.

Study of the tables would allow the scientist to transmute the mass of observations into more general propositions, which in turn could be arranged to reveal yet greater generalizations, until the ultimate goal of a law of nature was achieved. So, instances of heat could be grouped into those generated by fire, those generated by friction, those generated by biological processes and so on. Bacon used this method to demonstrate that heat is ultimately caused by the rapid and irregular motion of the smallest parts of which a substance was composed.

Although the arrangement into tables seems a more sophisticated way to organize the facts, it still isn't clear how it overcomes the problem of how a theory emerges from the data. In both cases – simple enumeration and Baconian induction – we have on one side some information, and on the other a general theory, with nothing explaining how to move logically from one to the other. It is simply assumed that, once you have the relevant facts, sorted into the correct categories, the "right" theory can be constructed from them.'

Er, wait a minute. Can we rewind? Didn't what's his name, er, Hume, prove that induction doesn't exist? I'm thinking of that turkey...

'Good dog, Monty! What Hume did was to show that there is no *logic* of induction. Many instances of a phenomenon A being followed by phenomenon B cannot prove that B will always follow A. But Hume never disputes that we do, in fact, use induction. Rather, we have to see its truths not as necessary, but as contingent: one day the turkey will have its head chopped off, and one day the sun might not rise.

Another problem with almost all varieties of induction is that they involve a somewhat naïve view of what counts as a fact. It is simply assumed that empirical data is entirely trustworthy, that the gathering process is objective and uncon-taminated by external factors. We have already seen, on our previous walks, that empirical data is never simple. The obser-vations that count as the raw material of induction are already threaded through with theoretical considerations, like gristle in a bad steak. When gathering data, scientists never simply ran-domly collect facts. They look in a particular place, in a particular way, and both where and how they look, and what counts as data, are influenced by what the scientist already knows.

For example, the planet Neptune was discovered only when astronomers in the early nineteenth century noticed irregular-ities in the orbit of Uranus, which they correctly predicted had to be caused by another planet. The precise nature of the perturbations—'

Perturbations? Really?

'Fair enough, *wobbles* in the orbit of Uranus suggested which part of the sky to observe, and the eighth planet was discovered. Here, Newton's existing theory of planetary motion was the context both for "seeing" that Uranus was behaving in an irreg-ular manner, and for defining the area of the night sky in which to look. So the theory here came before the observations, both directing them and giving them a meaning they wouldn't other-wise have had. In fact, Neptune had been observed two hundred years before, by Galileo, but he had mistaken it for a star, as he lacked the theoretical apparatus for correctly interpreting his observation.

Galileo himself is often put forward as the perfect inductiv-ist, gradually acquiring experimental and observational data that he would use to conceive and support his theories on mechanics and cosmology. Yet Galileo brought to his observations a fully developed theory of what would count as knowledge. He describes his method in *The Assayer* (1623), rejecting the Aristotelian and Scholastic approach, which reverenced tradition and religion, and replacing it with one in which the secrets of the universe would be revealed by mathematics and geometry. Nature is "written in mathematical language, and the symbols are triangles, circles and other geometrical figures, without whose help it is impossible to comprehend a single word of it; without which one wanders in vain through a dark labyrinth".

But isn't that kind of right? Science is all about the numbers, isn't it?

'Of course, but the point is that Galileo argues that without the prior knowledge of geometrical figures, the world of phenomena is a tale told by an idiot, full of sound and fury, signifying nothing. And if he has escaped from Aristotle, it is into the arms of Plato and Pythagoras. And that Platonism is even more overt in Johannes Kepler (1571–1630). Kepler, who eventually refined the Copernican system, replacing circular orbits with ellipses, was convinced that the key to the universe was the five regular polyhedra, the cube, the tetrahedron, the octahedron, the icosahedron and the dodecahedron, which he thought determined both the number of planets and the relationship of their orbits. Exactly like Plato, he was convinced that God had created the universe in accordance with a geometrical master plan, and spent his whole life trying to wrestle the perceived phenomena into the (in fact quite erroneous) pattern.

To point out the fact that the observations made by Galileo and Kepler were immersed in theory from their inception isn't necessarily to invalidate them, or to undermine the theories on which they're based. But it does show that "pure" data is a myth, and it highlights that observations are not always quite as reliable as the inductivist might hope.'

An example?

'In Bacon's time medicine was dominated by the theory of the humours. According to this, good health, both mental and physical, was dependent on the balance of blood, phlegm, yellow bile and black bile in the body. An excess of black bile, which was thought to be secreted by the spleen, would lead to the symptoms of what we would call depression, and they called melancholia – gloomy and morbid thoughts, along with pain and stiffness, indigestion, constipation, and the general signs of low-level metabolic poisoning.'

Sounds like you…

'I'll ignore that. Bacon himself often refers to the humours in his writings. The doctors of the time made many observations of black bile, along with the other humours. But there was one problem. Black bile doesn't exist. Unlike blood, phlegm and yellow bile, there's simply no such thing as black bile.'

But you said that the doctors saw it…

'They saw dark-coloured liquids in the body for sure. But it was blood, or the products of digestion. The point is that those many observations that the doctors made, which in turn fed back into the theory, confirming black bile as present in cases of melancholia, were entirely honest and entirely bogus.

It's not clear if any actual scientists ever employed Bacon's tables to help them devise any useful theories, but the basic structure of science that Bacon describes, of careful observation resulting in a mass of data that would reveal the underlying laws, became the dominant way that science was thought to operate. And, just to clarify, there are three parts to the process. The first is the gathering of data. This will reveal regularities. These regularities will be postulated as laws. This is the inductive part of the system. These laws can then be applied to the world to make predictions. This is the deductive part of the system. I see a thousand white swans. This leads me to formulate the hypothesis that all swans are white. Using this hypothesis, I can predict that the next swan I see will be white. Each swan I see confirms my original hypothesis, reinforcing its status as a law.

The method of induction I've outlined was simply assumed to be the way scientists worked, and was at the heart of the incredible advances made by natural science in the course of the seventeenth and eighteenth centuries – the centuries of Galileo, Kepler and Newton, when the fundamental work in physics and cosmology was done that framed how humanity thought about its place in the universe, until the second revolution brought about by Einstein and the theory of relativity.

So, induction continued as the standard model for scientific practice, albeit with its foundations a little less logically secure than we might hope. The method was further refined by J.S. Mill in the nineteenth century (the utilitarian guy, if you remember). Mill wanted to insulate induction as best he could from the doubts of Hume, and his system is generally felt to be the ultimate evolution of the inductive method. Mill defined five ways by which an observed fact could be linked to its causes – causation being seen as the defining characteristic of scientific explanation.

His first method was to look at a range of data, and see if any factor was present in every case. If so, we can assume that that is the cause. This is called the Method of Agreement. Louis Pasteur found that every bottle of sour wine he analysed contained an abundance of bacteria, which led him to conclude that the bacteria had caused the souring.

Second is the Method of Difference, which is simply the reverse of the coin – is there a missing factor in all the subjects you study? You find a thousand shark carcasses floating in the ocean. You note that each one has had its dorsal fin cut off. You conclude that the cause is shark fin soup—'

Really?

'Really. Third, we have the Joint Method of Agreement and Difference, which is, as you'd expect, a combination of the first two. It differs from the Method of Agreement in that you gather a number of positive and negative cases, and try to find, through a process of elimination, a factor that is always present when the consequence is present, but is never present when the consequence is absent. I investigate a group of subjects, half suffering from scurvy, half healthy. I look for factors present in those not afflicted, and absent from the diseased. I see that the ill guinea pigs have eaten no fruit. I posit this as the cause of scurvy.

Fourth is the Method of Concomitant Variation, which looks for situations where the varying level of one factor is linked to a varying level in the effect. Putting your foot on the accelerator pedal would be a case of that. Or, returning to medicine, increases in sugar consumption lead to exactly correlated increases in dental decay and obesity.'

You never forget the cheesecake, do you?

'Finally, the Method of Residues comes into play when you're fairly advanced in your study of a phenomenon. Let's say you're looking at the effects of eating too much cheesecake. Cheesecake basically consists of sugar, fat and dietary fibre. We've noticed that there are three main effects: your teeth drop out, you get fat and you suffer from wind.'

This is getting quite personal.

'We know from prior inductive and deductive operations that the sugar causes the tooth decay, and the fat causes the obesity. The Method of Residues then presents the dietary fibre as the cause of the wind.'

Charming.

'That was pretty well the state of play in the philosophy of science at the start of the twentieth century. Things were refined a little further by the logical positivists, who mainly worked in Vienna in the 1920s, and so are referred to as the Vienna Circle. The logical positivists looked to transform philosophy and the social sciences, and to fine-tune "hard" science. Their view begins with a philosophy of language, summed up in the slogan *the meaning of a sentence consists in its method of verification.'*

Eh?

'It's designed as a demarcation principle.'

A what?

'A way of sifting the good from the bad. On one side you have sentences that can be verified, i.e. we can find evidence that supports them, and by evidence the logical positivists meant empirical observations.'

And on the other side?

'We have most of philosophy! Any statement that cannot be proved by direct observation, that cannot be *verified*, is, according to the logical positivists, meaningless.'

This reminds me of…

'Wittgenstein! Exactly. He was closely associated with the Vienna Circle in his early years. Logical positivism, as a philosophy of science, is really only a clear restatement of induction. The role of science is to find patterns in experience that can be generalized as rules – or laws – which are then used to make predictions. It says that a theory can only be verified by repeated instances, and never entirely proved. But that verification is sufficient for science to proceed. So, yep, this is pure induction, and so is vulnerable to some of the earlier criticisms of induction. In particular, the logical positivist claimed that each proposition – whether of science or language – had to be tested individually. However, we have seen that the observation statements of science are always already infused with theory. Another way to say this is that any theory of testing has to be holistic. Understanding any single fact involves understanding the whole network of ideas in which it is embedded.'

Maybe another one of your examples…

'When, in the early 1860s, the extraordinary beautiful bird-like fossils of Archaeopteryx began to emerge from limestone quarries in southern Germany, there was no unanimous view among the first German collectors and scientists to see them about what they were or what they signified. There was a vague understanding that fossils represented long-dead animals, some of which had become extinct, so already there was a theoretical matrix around them: they were understood to be ancient, and to represent forms not now living. There was a vigorous debate from the middle of the eighteenth century about what the extinct forms represented, and how they could be fitted into the biblical account of creation. The French zoologist Georges Cuvier (1769–1832) had argued that there had been several creation episodes, followed by catastrophes (including Noah's flood), and that extinct forms were the remains of animals destroyed in these disasters. Cuvier explicitly rejected the idea that one animal could change into another, and his view, before Darwin, was dominant.

The publication of Darwin's *On The Origin of Species* in 1859 transformed the debate, without quite settling it. One major problem for Darwin was the scarcity of the intermediary forms that his theory had predicted must exist. So those first collectors and scientists had to see through a confused muddle of ideas, some pre-evolutionary, some Darwinian, some religious, some merely technical. Some of the scientists looking at the strange feathered creature, captured with such detail in the slabs of limestone, regarded the fossils as belonging to a bird; some to a reptile. Others thought they were fakes.

However, to Darwin and his supporters, the fossils were gold dust. The best of the specimens was purchased by the British Museum, and soon became one of the strongest pieces of supporting evidence for the new theory. And from a Darwinian perspective, the meaning of the fossil was perfectly clear: birds had evolved from reptiles. At some stage in this process we would expect to see an animal with some bird-like and some reptilian features. Archaeopteryx had wings and feathers. It also had teeth and a reptilian tail. *Voilà!*

Although the "true" meaning of Archaeopteryx was only clear when interpreted from the Darwinian standpoint, the fossils had never been the sort of raw, isolated data that the logical positivists envisaged. They were embedded in theory the moment they were disembedded from the quarry.'

Are you absolutely sure disembedded is a word?

'Oh, look who's woken up. And just in time for a muffin.'

We'd reached the café. As I'd hoped, it was almost empty – the school-run gang had been cappuccinoed and gone, and the lunch crowd weren't in yet. There were a couple of paranoid-looking guys hunched over laptops, headphones cancelling out the world. Back in the day I always used to get a filter coffee – always the cheapest option, and bitter enough to deter you from swigging it too swiftly. But I felt like something frothier, and ordered a latte from the smiling barista. We found a quiet spot at the back of the café.

'Want to come out of the bag?'

Be silly to stay in here.

'OK, where were we?'

Disembedded…

'Oh, yeah. So, we're at the point where some form of induction seems like the only game in town, even though Hume has exposed the logical gap between seeing a million white swans and the statement *All swans are white*. It's just assumed that that's how science works, despite the niggle. That was all about to change.

The challenge came from Karl Popper (1902–94), one of the Vienna Circle's own alumni, and it's a challenge from which induction has never really recovered. In his main work on the philosophy of science, *The Logic of Scientific Discovery* (1934), Popper took Hume's logical point about induction seriously. Induction really can't establish a scientific law. Repetition doesn't lead to certainty. Moreover, Popper's investigations into the history of science showed that the great scientists have never used induction as a method for coming up with hypotheses. The idea of the objective, open-minded scientist carefully gathering facts that then blossom into a theory is not just logically flawed, but a fantasy, a figment of the imagination. None of the great scientific discoveries of Copernicus and Kepler and Newton and Einstein were arrived at through inductivist processes. Those tables of Bacon, the five methods of Mill, all were useless *and* unused.'

OK, you've got my attention. So what was going on?

'All in good time. Popper's first insight was the purely logical point that although multiple observations of a phenomenon

cannot prove a hypothesis, a single counterexample can disprove it.'

*Seems a bit negative. How can we get anywhere if you can only
disprove stuff? If I want to know where my chew toy is, what use is it
to disprove my hypothesis that it's in my basket? I still don't have my
chew toy.*

'This takes us to the positive part of Popper's philosophy of
science. Rather than that vision of dedicated, slightly dull scientists combing carefully through data, he posits a more dramatic,
even heroic view of the scientist. Scientists don't creep towards
a new theory, they leap! And these leaps, the great ideas that
transform science, come more or less out of the blue, and fly in
the face of existing patterns of knowledge. We can't know,
Popper says, how the scientific genius comes up with a new
theory. It could come in a dream, such as August Kekulé's fire-
side reverie, in which he imagined a snake seizing its own tail,
and so cracked the ring-like molecular structure of benzene in
1865. Or it might come from non-scientific sources, such as
Darwin's reading of Thomas Malthus, which inspired the idea
for the struggle for existence, and the survival of the fittest.

Whatever their origins, new scientific theories must, for
Popper, have certain qualities. They should be bold: the more
revolutionary the better. There is no place here for the incre-
mental fiddling and faffing of induction. They should explain
everything the theory they replace explains, plus more. And
they should be risky, in the sense that they should make lots of
predictions.

I hate to keep going back to those clichéd swans, but that first
black one disproves the hypothesis that all swans are white.
Actually, I really hate that example. As if for years a group of
zoologists were debating whether or not swans were white, and

quietly amassing what they thought was enough evidence to bring to the Royal Society... Here's a better one. Under the Ptolemaic system, the Earth was at the centre of the universe, and all the other astrological bodies circled around it. It was an OK theory. It explained much of what we observe – the heavens rotating around us, the sun rising and falling. Then Copernicus came along and proposed a sun-centred cosmology, but for the first few decades, the two systems seemed roughly equal in what they could explain, without either able to make a killer blow, partly because of the level of technology – astronomical observations were still made with the naked eye. Then, in 1610, Galileo built himself a telescope, based on an idea that had come from Holland, and pointed it at Jupiter. There he made observations that strongly indicated that Jupiter had moons. For the first time, it was proved that not everything orbited around the Earth, and the Ptolemaic system was toast.'

And that proves Copernicus was right?

'No! The possibility of moons orbiting other planets was certainly a prediction that Copernicus might have made. But for now all you could say was that the theory had not been falsified.

For Popper it was very important that once a hypothesis had been falsified, it had to be thrown out. What you couldn't do was to come up with some explanation to account for an apparent falsification. He termed these explanations *ad hoc hypotheses*. He took particular exception to ad hoc hypotheses that were themselves unfalsifiable.

A good example would be the way that the old Ptolemaic system had some problems, which even Ancient astronomers had noticed. The most glaring of these was that, at times, the planets, rather than moving in a smooth and regular fashion roughly from east to west across the sky, seemed to stop, and then move 'backwards', from west to east – the so-called retrograde motion. We now know that this was simply caused by the fact that as all the planets are circling the sun in different orbits, the Earth will periodically overtake those planets that are further out, making it appear that they are travelling backwards, just as a car we overtake appears, relative to us, to be moving backwards. You see the problem: if all the planets are moving around the Earth, how can some of them go backwards?'

Don't look at me.

'Rhetorical question. The answer they came up with was that some planets, as they orbit the Earth, also indulge in a frisky pirouette – they move in a little circle of their own, known as an epicycle. So you have the big circle of the planet's orbit around the Earth, and the smaller circle of the planet's orbit around … well, nothing, really. This is what creates the impression that the planet is travelling backwards for a time – it's just a period in the smaller circle when it is orbiting in the opposite direction to the planet on its greater orbit around us.

The epicycles adequately explain what we can see, but all they're doing is shoring up a ruined edifice. Using the scientific equipment and knowledge at the time, it was impossible to show that the epicycle theory was wrong, and so it was an *unfalsifiable ad hoc hypothesis.*

The perfect example for Popper of a scientific hypothesis was Einstein's theory of special relativity. This explained everything that Newton's theory of gravity explained, as well as much more. Although Newton's theory had stood up remarkably well to two hundred years of testing, there were some small anomalies, such as a tiny irregularity in the orbit of Mercury, that it couldn't explain. Einstein's special relativity could account for it.

But special relativity still needed a bold prediction that would test it. Einstein had predicted that the gravitational effects of huge masses – such as our sun – ought to cause light rays from distant stars to bend by a specific amount. The only way to test this was during a full eclipse, as otherwise the starlight could not be observed. In 1919 just such an eclipse took place. Einstein bet the farm on the outcome. Measurements showed that light had been bent by precisely the degree he predicted.'

Yay! So special relativity was proved!

'How many times do I have to tell you, NO! According to Popper, you can never prove any theory to be true. All theories have either been falsified, or will one day be falsified. His idea is that theories are like foundations driven into the ground. They can go so far, far enough, indeed, to support the building, for a while. But they never hit bedrock.'

So, if Popper thought you could never have absolutely certain knowledge, was he one of the Sceptics?

'Emphatically not. He was a realist. There's a solid world of matter and scientific laws out there, and the scientists can explore it. He thought that the new, revolutionary theories were a genuine improvement on what they replaced, and that the advances in science were not illusory, but real. Our knowledge of the world was improving. And, crucially, he thought that his idea of falsification meant that science could be rationally critiqued. He believed that you needed constant criticism to stop science becoming conservative and entrenched.'

You're keen on him, aren't you?

'You always make it sound as if I fancy them.'

Tony and Karl, sitting in a tree...

'Oh, grow up. But I am, actually, yes. Popper's fallen out of fashion a bit, but I love the clarity of thought and expression in his writing, and falsifiability really does seem like a useful concept, not just in science, but in everyday life. If you have an idea, it's always good to ask if there is any evidence that could possibly refute it. If not, then perhaps your idea is too woolly to do any actual work. Popper himself thought that falsificationism was most useful as a principle of demarcation, distinguishing science from pseudoscience.'

Pseudoscience?

'Pseudoscience for Popper is any system of thought or discipline that makes a claim to providing knowledge, but the propositions of which cannot ever be falsified. This might be because they are so vague that they fit a vast array of possible facts. Your horoscope, for example, might say, "This week you will encounter problems at work, which you can overcome with a flexible approach." Or it might be that your theory explains too much, once again making refutation impossible. There is no psychological condition that Freudian analysts cannot trace back to some childhood experience. Do you have a mental problem? Yes. Did you have a bad experience as a child? Again, yes. If you say that you did not, we can dig down until we find something. Each new example confirms the theory in the minds of its practitioners, and nothing will ever appear to refute it. Thus by explaining everything it predicts nothing.

A final example of pseudoscience that Popper gives is Marxism. This is a little different in that Popper agrees that Marxism began as a science, making real and testable predictions. Marx predicted that proletarian revolutions were possible only in advanced industrial economies, such as (at the time) were found only in Western Europe and the United States. In fact, the revolutions that came were in the "backward" states, Russia and China. At this point, to remain within the Popperian definition of science, the Marxists should have abandoned their theory. Instead, they erected a buttressing of unfalsifiable ad hoc hypotheses to account for the failure of revolutions in the West, thereby condemning themselves to the realm of pseudoscience.

Another interesting case is Darwinism.'

Hang on, Darwinism…? But Darwinism's scientific, right? Don't tell me I didn't really evolve from an ape. Er, I mean wolf…

'Here we can see falsificationism at its most useful. There's a certain formulation that makes the central Darwinian concept – the survival of the fittest – immune to falsification. So, the fittest creatures survive. Sounds great. Appears like a perfectly good hypothesis. You have a load of animals, and the fittest ones live, while the losers get eaten. But how do you define "fittest"? The danger is that you point to those animals that have survived and say, well obviously, those are the fittest! How do you know they're the fittest? Because they survived. Why did they survive? Because they're the fittest! So, you've made your theory circular and untestable.

To avoid this, Popper would have the evolutionary scientist make a definite prediction that could be tested. For example, the evolutionist might posit that peacocks grew their flamboyant tails to attract females, giving them an advantage over those with smaller tails. You could then predict that in a given population, the peacocks with the biggest tails would have more offspring. That's a testable hypothesis.'

So, the upshot is Popper wins…?

'Certainly many scientists like his take on what they do. His model of the scientist is heroic and appealing. And his theory is clear and easy to understand. However, it's fallen out of favour among philosophers of science.'

Oh, why?

'One problem is that many fruitful scientific theories have been apparently falsified quite early in their existence. For example, Copernicus' theory struggled to account for some observable phenomena. It was rather poor at predicting the positions of the planets, and also required epicycles to account for retrogression – both problems caused by the fact that Copernicus thought the planets moved in perfect circles, rather than ellipses.

The biggest challenge it faced was that, if the Earth moved around the sun, then the relative positions of the stars should change from our perspective – the phenomenon of parallax. Yet the stars do not show this effect. This was a straightforward falsification, and should, with a strict application of Popper's criteria, have resulted in the Copernican system being rejected. Which would have been a shame, as without Copernicus, there would have been no Kepler, and without Kepler, no Newton, and without Newton, no modern science.'

Big claim.

'Actually, too big. How could it be refuted? I'm withdrawing that last sentence on the grounds it's unfalsifiable. But the point remains that a strict application of Popper's falsificationism would have spelled the end for Copernicus. It's like suggesting that as soon as a relationship hits a rocky patch, you finish it, and start searching again on Tinder. Sometimes you have to tough it out…'

Monty gave me one of his consoling licks.

'Many other sciences have had similar rocky periods, which they were later to overcome, either through small adaptations, or because technology came to their aid. Both rescued the Copernican system. Kepler's modification helped it to fit the observed reality better, and superior technology revealed the small degree of parallax that really exists – small because the stars turned out to be much further away than anyone at the time guessed.

The other problem with Popper's theory is that it makes science into a very individualistic activity. Great men and women, whose thought processes cannot be rationally explained and who act largely in isolation, have brilliant flashes of genius, giving birth to new and original hypotheses. Only once they have been concocted does the scientific community come into play, in the more mundane task of testing the hypothesis.

This solitary, heroic idea of science was challenged by Thomas Kuhn (1922–96) in *The Structure of Scientific Revolutions* (1962) – perhaps the most famous and influential of all works on the philosophy and history of science. In place of the solitary scientific genius, Kuhn posits a completely different way of "doing" science, in which communities of scientists work on a common set of problems, using shared assumptions and techniques. These shared assumptions and common goals are referred to by Kuhn as a *paradigm*. Scientists working within a paradigm will have interiorized a block of ideas about what counts as relevant information, about how that information can be gathered, analysed and arranged, and the mechanisms it should go through to be authenticated.'

Can you give some examples of these paradigms?

'Sure. The Scholastic tradition would be one, in which Aristotle's views on the nature of the material world and the

Ptolemaic system of cosmology were assumed. Then there's the Copernican/Keplerian cosmology that replaced it. Newtonian physics, Darwinian evolutionary theory and quantum mechanics are more examples. Each of these paradigms enjoyed extended periods when almost all the researchers in the field agreed on almost all the basic facts. Everyone agreed both on the puzzles to be solved and on the way to go about solving them. Often the researchers in paradigms were employed by large institutions, universities and laboratories, with their own enclosed culture. There were career structures to be followed, with rewards both material and symbolic.

This is what Kuhn calls *normal science*. Most of the history of scientific thought is taken up with these periods of stability, in which the paradigms performed their solid work of methodically extending human knowledge in their various fields.

However, there will come a time when problems start to accumulate in the paradigm. Those puzzles refuse to be solved. There will be anomalies, things that the existing theories can't explain. These anomalies will be particularly troubling if they involve the key concepts at the core of the paradigm: moons around Jupiter, strange reptile-bird fossils, incomprehensible wobbles in the orbit of Mercury, etc. Paradigms then, if these problems cannot be resolved or explained away, enter a period of crisis. Eventually the paradigm will fall and be replaced by a new paradigm – this is the famous *paradigm shift*.

What's interesting about these paradigm shifts is that the new and old paradigms will be what Kuhn calls *incommensurable*. The new paradigm will not simply disagree about some detail, or readily resolved factual difference, but will involve a completely opposed world view, in which there is so little overlap that it is impossible to rationally compare the two paradigms.

The idea of evolution by natural selection is incommensurable with the idea of all living creatures being created (or designed) by a benevolent God. The Ptolemaic and Copernican systems; Newtonian physics and general relativity; general relativity and quantum mechanics: each involves a shift so radical that no real conversation between them is possible.

A startling consequence of the incommensurability of paradigms is that the change from one paradigm to another is, in some ways, irrational. The research of those working within a paradigm, as it involves shared criteria for progress, can be rationally assessed. However, with the shift to a new, incompatible paradigm, there is no common ground for judgement. It's like being asked to describe the taste of a pineapple using numbers.'

But if you can't rationally decide between paradigms, why change?

'Kuhn says that often the actual personnel don't change their minds. The diehards die off, and the young bloods step in. So it's partly a generational thing. The extent to which Kuhn himself regarded his theory as relativistic, and science as irrational, has been much debated. The fact that anomalies appear in a paradigm, and that these are the ultimate cause of revolutions, suggest that science is engaged with the real world, as does the way normal science tackles problems. Yet Kuhn often speaks about *religious conversions* and *gestalt switches* (a *gestalt switch* occurs when the subject shifts suddenly from seeing an image one way to seeing it another – such as the familiar duck-rabbit, or the figure that can be seen as either two faces or a vase), which makes it all appear to be irrational.

One way to square the circle is that it's possible to interpret Kuhn as saying that the individual scientists who change from one paradigm to another do so for irrational reasons, but it may well be – and usually is – the case that the new paradigm will, in fact, be objectively better, in that it explains more and has fewer anomalies than the one it replaces.

Almost as soon as it was published, Kuhn's theory itself brought about a paradigm shift in how science was seen. The very term *paradigm shift* entered the language, applied not just to science, but in almost any area where there was a fundamental change of direction. Indeed, the Kuhnian approach seems to fit very well with how knowledge develops in many areas, from the arts to the social sciences. And, being published in the 1960s, the relativism and apparent radicalism of the theory lent it a certain countercultural kudos. It appeared to knock science a little off its elitist pedestal. Scientific knowledge stopped being a special, privileged form of understanding and became just another "language", another way of talking.

Popper and Kuhn (or, even more so, Popperians and Kuhnians) engaged in a vigorous, indeed cantankerous debate. For Popper, both the irrationality of the paradigm shift model and the mundanity of Kuhn's idea of *normal science* were abhorrent. Kuhn saw the normal science periods as being good: this was when solid work was done. And it was right that those working within the paradigm should defend it. The conception of science for Kuhn is therefore not the sexily countercultural force it was first taken to be, but innately conservative. Kuhn was himself a solid member of the establishment, living and working in the most prestigious American academic institutions, Harvard, Berkeley and MIT, and defending the whole apparatus of the American scientific-military-industrial complex. Popper was far more of a maverick. Falsification in his mind was a brilliant weapon to use against the establishment.'

So who won the argument?

'I think it was honours even in terms of the ideas. Kuhn's portrait of both normal and revolutionary science captures much truth about the way science works; but the logical truth and creative potential of falsificationism have huge merit.'

If only they could be somehow combined…

'You know me too well! That is exactly what happened in the work of Imre Lakatos (1922–74), a Hungarian philosopher working with Popper at the London School of Economics. Lakatos rather brilliantly combined Kuhn and Popper. Rather than paradigms, Lakatos argued that within each scientific discipline there will be a number of competing *research programmes*. Each research programme has a *hard core* of ideas that are fundamental to the programme, and a *protective belt* of less essential concepts and theories that can be criticized without doing mortal hurt to the core. The programme as a whole will attempt to defend itself from criticism, much in the manner of Kuhn's conservative paradigms, but also uses Popperian methodologies in its work. Lakatos says that successful research programmes should be *progressive*, meaning that they expand to explain more features of the world, but each new claim is rigorously tested, and rejected if falsified.

Perhaps the biggest difference between research programmes and Kuhnian paradigms is that for Kuhn there can only ever be one dominant paradigm in any age. For Lakatos, there can be, and should be, competing research programmes. This competition will reveal some programmes to be progressive, and some degenerating. The clearest example of this was the competition between the Copernican and Ptolemaic systems. Several attempts were made in the late sixteenth century to shore up the old programme, such as Tycho Brahe's theory that although the other planets orbit around the sun, the sun still orbits around the Earth. But the programme was degenerating, while the Copernican system, retaining its core of a heliocentric solar system, carried on being progressive, despite major changes to its protective belt.

But even degenerating research programmes can recover, so, Lakatos advises, you shouldn't jump ship too soon. But when is too soon? How can you rationally decide when a research programme has degenerated to the point of no return? Lakatos doesn't tell us.

This uncertainty about when a research programme should be jettisoned is one of the perceived weaknesses of Lakatos's theory. He had tried – in some ways succeeded – to combine the sociological approach of Kuhn with the objectivism and realism of Popper. But his critics saw the lack of a clear way of declaring the death of a research programme as fatal. I still think he got pretty close to establishing both what science does and what it should do.'

Hmmm… So, if I've been paying attention, induction is a sham, falsificationism has been falsified, Kuhn's paradigms have been shifted and Lakatos's research programmes have degenerated. What does that leave?

'I've saved the best till last. Paul Feyerabend (1924–94) made a career out of demolishing the claims of philosophers to understand the scientific method, and of science itself to comprehend and control the world. Feyerabend began as a Popperian, but soon came to see the limits of what falsificationism can do – in particular he was worried about that danger of prematurely throwing out a workable theory because of apparent refutations. But he was also violently opposed to the conservatism of the Kuhnian paradigms.

Feyerabend's answer was that any single attempt to capture the way science operates was doomed to failure. His slogan was *anything goes*. Scientists adopt a huge variety of working methods. Some count swans. Some have inspired ideas, which they test to destruction. Some scientists work in research programmes, following the party line. Some brood and plot in lonely garrets. Some confine themselves to reading the numbers, whereas others pull in ideas from the wider culture. As soon as you say that science works only through induction, or by falsificationism, or any other -ism, you will leave outside the definition activities that should count as science and include activities that shouldn't.

One example (not used by Feyerabend) is string theory. String theory is the latest attempt to answer that question posed all those walks ago by the pre-Socratic philosophers—'

What's the white stuff in bird poo?

'Hah, sort of. I was thinking more generally of *What's the world made of?* String theory is the ultimate Theory of Everything – it aims to supply an account of the four fundamental forces in the universe: gravity, electromagnetism and the weak and strong nuclear forces. It's an elegant and aesthetically pleasing theory. According to it, each of the fundamental particles responsible for the four forces are really tiny loops of oscillating string, and the way the string oscillates dictates what sort of particle it is.'

Sounds great.

'It is. The only problem with string theory is that there is absolutely no experimental evidence for it. Nobody can see a superstring. Nobody can detect them in any way. And it's not at all clear if there will *ever* be a way to detect them, or confirm their existence. So, any inductivist would dismiss the theory, as it isn't the result of repeated observations and experiments, and any falsificationist would throw it right out because it produces no testable prediction. Indeed, it seems to have more in common with one of those old metaphysical theories than the world of science. Parmenides and Empedocles could have come up with it.'

So the point being that many of the philosophers of science you've been talking about would reject what you think is a good theory?

'Exactly. So what if string theory is unfalsifiable? It explains things that are otherwise mysterious, and it might in the future yield spectacular results. For Feyerabend, if you try to be too narrowly rational, then out goes the baby with the bathwater.

As well as his methodological anarchism, Feyerabend was also the first of our philosophers to warn against the dangers of science. Scientists were prone, he thought, to making expansive claims to rationality and universality that they couldn't sustain. The argument that the scientific method is superior to other modes of knowledge is undermined by the fact that he had shown that there is no single scientific method. He doesn't argue that science is entirely bogus, but he does think that it is the duty of every citizen to be sceptical about its claims and vigilant to the desire of scientists to monitor, control and dominate.'

Cripes. Do you agree with that?

'Absolutely. I think that to the best of our powers we should subject scientific claims to scrutiny. "Science" is used every day to try to sell us things, to convince us to spend our own or our government's money on products or research programmes. NASA knows that the best way to boost its funding is by getting the public excited about the possibility of finding life on Mars, and so its scientists make sure that the media is regularly drip-fed stories that work with that narrative. In fact, whenever you hear a science story on the news, you can be sure that it is not because of the intrinsic merits of the research, but because an active public relations department has been busy. Big pharmaceutical companies have been caught out many times manipulating data to distort the truth.'

Remind me, are you being a Sceptic or a Cynic?

'So you *were* listening back then … Both. The Cynic distrusts power; the Sceptic distrusts knowledge. Another of my intellectual heroes, the French post-structuralist Michel Foucault, says that wherever you see power you must resist it, because power is always unequal and always abused. And I think we should open up the Sceptics' toolbox to test claims to knowledge, as best we can. But the end result of this is not to reject all power and knowledge, but to keep power and knowledge honest. But what I don't think is that there is no such thing as truth. Science should be scrutinized, but that scrutiny should use the tools of science. And it's always worth asking the questions: who paid for this research? Who benefits from it? What is being hidden? And what is being over-sold?'

Monty looked at me and rolled his eyes. He isn't really a political animal.

'Sorry, I got a bit carried away there. Talking of carrying, we should go home. Want to go back in the bag, or are you up to the walk, do you think?'

Might be. A short one.

I looked around the café. It was filling up again. There was an elegant poodle and an equally elegant poodle owner at a table near the door. We both did our best not to limp or stumble as we left. A little way down the street Monty gave me a mournful look and I popped him back in the bag.

Schopenhauer's Bubble and the Meaning of Life

On this walk, I take Monty to the vet. We discuss the proofs for the existence of God, and the meaning of life. And death.

There followed a very difficult few days for the McGowan family. All the options were discussed. Some tears were shed. Not in front of Monty, but I suppose he knew.

The day came and I carried him out in his bag. I looked up from the street and saw Rebecca and Rosie standing together, looking down from the French windows. I waved, but Rosie just put her head on her mother's shoulder.

Where are we going?

'The long way round. We're early.'

It's that place, isn't it?

I stroked Monty's nose.

Everything we've talked about on these walks…

'Yeah?'

Well, it's all been very interesting. I think I understand more about what sort of stuff there is in the world, and what counts as knowing about it. And I suppose I've got a better idea of what it means to be a good dog. Or person. But the thing is, and don't take this the wrong way, but I thought there'd be more of the Big Stuff.

'You're talking about the Meaning of Life kind of thing?'

Yeah, I guess.

'We talked a little about what you call the Big Stuff on our ethics walk. Aristotle's idea of happiness meaning leading the life most suitable to a rational animal, a life of contemplation, lived in accordance with the virtues… Or Kant's conception of moral goodness, using your reason to discover the rules that any rational being must obey. Or even the utilitarian life, spent striving always to achieve the greatest happiness for the greatest number. All of these have a nobility. And certainly, any of them will enable you to lead a more ethical life than either just following your whims and fancies, or not troubling yourself at all about right and wrong.'

I can see that. And if the question was what should I do, or how should I act, then fair enough, the ethics stuff helps. But I'm asking a different question. Not what should I do, but what does it mean?

I dipped my head to his head, and breathed in the smell of his fur. My wife had washed him, and he was smelling much better than usual. He curled his tongue up to lick my face.

'You know what the early Wittgenstein would say to that, don't you?'

Whereof one cannot speak, thereof one must be silent.

'He certainly put this sort of question into the *thereof one must be silent* box. And I think on this one he's right. The question *What does life mean?* is a category mistake.'

Just this once, can we skip the jargon?

287

'Sorry. I think the word "meaning" only has a meaning in relation to propositions. The bus is coming. I like cheesecake. The square on the hypotenuse is equal to the sum of the squares of the other two sides. These are all propositions, and they have a meaning. Meaning is a language thing. But a flower, a bumble-bee, a little scruffy dog, a big scruffy man, these things don't have a meaning. They have value, and value is more important than meaning.'

What about God? Most of your philosophers had something to say about him, or it, or her.

'I've tiptoed around God a bit in our talks. Partly because I'm with Kant: I just don't think philosophy helps us much. True, philosophers spent a lot of time and ingenuity trying to prove God exists, but no one has yet come up with a proof strong enough to convert an atheist to a believer.'

What are these proofs?

'There have been dozens, over the centuries, but I think they boil down to three basic types: *cosmological proofs, arguments from design* and the *ontological argument*. We've only got time for the quick and dirty versions…

The cosmological proofs take a few different forms. One is the idea that everything has a cause, and so there must be a first cause that isn't itself caused, or else you have an infinite chain. Sometimes it's put in the language of a first mover – everything that is moved is moved by something else, and you need a first mover to get the ball rolling. It's also sometimes expressed as the idea that everything in our universe is contingent – it could exist, or it might not. It exists, so it must exist for a reason, and that reason is God. One of the most straightforward formulations is set out as a simple syllogism: *Whatever begins to exist has a cause; the universe began to exist; therefore the universe had a cause.*'

And what's wrong with these?

'As you recall, Kant and Hume had both questioned the idea of a cause. Or Hume questioned it, and Kant made it a quality of the human intellect, rather than something out there that could be regarded as God. No cause: no God. Others have argued there's simply nothing illogical about the idea of an infinite causal chain, without a first mover. Others have said that the proof doesn't really prove anything: it begins by saying everything must have a cause, and ends by positing a thing without a cause, so it's self-contradictory. As for a first mover, how can a thing that does not move impart motion? Another objection is that even if you did prove some sort of first cause, what makes us think it has any of the other qualities we ascribe to God – omniscience, omnipotence, love?

I think it's ultimately futile to wonder about this one. Science has given us the Big Bang, a moment of creation. Before the Big Bang we have no idea what was going on. Was there another universe that had expanded and contracted down to a point, and then burst back to life? Or was there nothing? I think all we can do is hand it over to the scientists and then try our hardest to understand and criticize what they come up with.

Next, we have the argument from design. This basically says that there are elements of our world that are so perfectly constructed that they cannot be the result of chance – any more than a watch could be built by chance – but must have been designed by the Divine Watchmaker. There's nothing wrong, philosophically, with this argument. Unfortunately, as it's the only argument for the existence of God that has any claim to being scientific, it has to come up against reality. Its proponents argue that something as wondrous as the eye, which relies on several different complex elements working in harmony, could not have resulted from chance, any more than a tornado blowing through a junkyard could make a Boeing 747. Then along came Darwin, and evolution was shown to be a process that was quite capable of creating an eye – indeed the eye has been "invented" many times over in the Earth's history. And there are still many eyes in the animal world at the different stages of development – from eyes that can do nothing more than distinguish light from dark, to the eagle's eye that can see a flea move on your back from a kilometre away.'

She de-fleaed me this morning. I don't know why she bothered.

'It makes her happy. And you do smell nice… Where were we… oh, yes, the argument from design. All you need is time, and random variation, and then natural selection will make your watch, I mean eye. Coming at it from the other side, the more we investigate the natural world, the more we find things are far from perfect. I don't even mean from an anthropological view: the superabundance of things like fleas and mosquitos and bedbugs and viruses that make life unpleasant. We've said that evolution is able to work wonders, but it had to work those wonders with the materials at hand. The palaeontologist Stephen Jay Gould was very good at finding examples of this "making do" aspect of evolution. My favourite is the panda's thumb. Pandas eat bamboo. What you really want with bamboo is an opposable digit – a thumb – to help you manipulate it. God would have given the panda a decent thumb. Perhaps just moved its first claw around a bit, job done. But the actual panda has a different and, frankly, rather botched solution. One of the bones in its wrist has grown out, and achieved a limited degree of flexibility and articulation. It kind of works, in a just-about-getting-by sort of way, because the panda couldn't just summon up the perfect mutation. It had to wait till one day a panda was born with a slightly projecting wrist bone, which was a little help with the old bamboo, which gave it a slight survival advantage over the other totally thumbless pandas, and so it had a few more babies, each with the same rubbish little proto-thumb. And each generation threw up random variations, and every now and then that would include a slightly improved thumb.'

So the argument from design hits the dust.

'Yeah, it's not needed for the fancy stuff, and there are better explanations for all the botching and making-do that we can see in the natural world. Plus, well, you know, Ebola ...

So finally we have the ontological argument, and I've got to say that I'm oddly fond of this one.'

It's that word ontological, isn't it?

'What's not to love?'

Hit me, then.

'I'm going to give you a definition of "God". God is the thing greater than which nothing can be conceived. Got that?'

I think so. He's the Greatest.

'Now I want you to imagine two Gods. They are exactly the same in greatness, except that one exists, and one doesn't.'

Huh?

'You just need the idea of two Gods, both great, but one's real and one's made up.'

OK ...

'Now which of them is greater?'

I think I see where this is going. Obviously, I'm supposed to say that of those two Gods, the one that exists must be greater.

'Therefore God must exist! We've accepted that God is the greatest thing you can conceive of, and seen that a God that exists must be greater than one that doesn't, therefore God must exist.'

You're kidding me, right?

'This is more or less the version first put forward by the Scholastic philosopher St Anselm (1033–1109). There are a few slightly different versions of it, but they all have this in common, that existence is part of the idea of God, in the way that "the angles add up to 180 degrees" is part of the idea of a triangle.'

This is the nuttiest thing you've told me. You're going to put it out of its misery, aren't you?

'It's been weirdly resilient. No one is really happy with it, but it won't lie down. What I like about it is the way it's a purely conceptual proof. It doesn't touch on anything in the world at all, relying on nothing more than some harmless-sounding definitions, and your acceptance of them. But there have been a couple of ways of attacking it. Kant had one. He said that the proof relies on "existence" being simply one of the predicates that you can attach to a subject – God is all-powerful, omniscient and he exists. So you might say that a sofa is blue and comfy and that it exists, and that blue, comfy and existence are all predicates of the sofa. But Kant says that existence simply isn't a predicate. A predicate must add an extra something to your knowledge of the subject. But existence, or being, simply tells you that the thing exists in reality. I can't quite decide about this, though most philosophers agree with Kant. To me it seems that if I was being told about a character who I assumed to be fictional, and then I was told, "no, she really exists", I'd think that existence was a predicate. Perhaps a better attack is one that makes the ontological argument sound silly. Is it possible to imagine a dog more perfect than which none could be conceived?'

A-hem...

'You're a lovely boy, but not quite perfect. It's impossible to be absolutely perfect in reality. There's always some tiny flaw, like stealing cheesecake... Anyway, I want you to imagine that perfect dog, the one more perfect than which none could be conceived. Done that?'

I'm trying.

'Now, if that dog doesn't exist, it's not the most perfect one of which you could conceive. Because one that existed would be more perfect. We can conceive of the perfect one that exists, therefore it exists! We've proved the existence of the perfect dog.'

But there is no perfect dog.

'Precisely.'

We walked along for a few more minutes in silence. I still had some time to kill, so we were winding a little aimlessly through the backstreets. But each one took us closer to our destination.

You're trying to take my mind off things, aren't you? All that God stuff, I mean.

'Maybe. But we're not there yet, are we, in finding the meaning.'

You said meaning was for words, not lives. The category mistake.

'Perhaps I was being a bit pedantic.'

You think?

'A couple of things come to mind. There's a novel, *Of Human Bondage*, by Somerset Maugham.'

Good title.

'It is, and it's one perfect for our walks – he took it from Spinoza's *Ethics*. It's Spinoza's term for the way humans are enslaved by their passions. Maugham's fallen out of fashion, now, but it's still a fine book. In it, there's a point when the hero, Philip Carey, an aspiring artist, is in Paris. A friend gives him an old Persian rug, telling him that it contains the meaning of life. He carries it around with him through the years, never really knowing what the friend, or the carpet, meant. He never quite achieves his aims in life, never quite finds happiness. His love affairs are unsatisfactory at best, tragic at worst. He settles for a career that he never really wanted. Finally, understanding dawns, and he sees what the friend meant by the gift of the rug. The meaning of life is the pattern we weave.'

Huh?

'The pattern doesn't point to anything beyond itself. It isn't a sign, or an index or an icon, it's just a play of geometric shapes and colours. Those shapes and colours might be complex and intricate, or might be simple and direct. But we weave it for the joy of weaving, and at the end we find that we've created something beautiful, in the life lived, in the warp and the weft.'

I like that. You said a couple?

'Most of the philosophers we've been discussing were OK as people, and some, like Spinoza, lived quietly exemplary lives. Leibniz was a toady, but not a bad man. Nietzsche's bark was worse than his bite. Heraclitus sounds like a jerk but, who knows, down in the tavern he may have been a riot, and no one deserves his ending... But Arthur Schopenhauer (1788–1860) really was a shit. Mean, miserable, arrogant. He lived only for his own pleasure and comfort. Typical Schopenhauer story: in 1821 he was enraged by an old woman making a racket outside his apartment, so he threw her down the stairs. She was seriously injured and unable to work, and the courts forced Schopenhauer to pay her a small pension for the rest of her life. When she finally died, some twenty years later, Schopenhauer celebrated with a grim little Latin pun, *"Obit anus, abit onus"* (the old woman dies, the debt departs).'

Nice man.

'Schopenhauer's philosophy was as grim as his personality. We are driven, he said, by a blind force that compels us to strive towards goals that can never be fully satisfied. Our bodies are nothing but the material manifestations of this drive: our teeth and bowels the embodiment of our hunger, our fists the material form of our rage. The only thing that can bring us relief from this tireless striving is art. When we listen to music, or gaze at a painting, the will is quieted, and we are temporarily sheltered from the storm.'

This isn't cheering me up much, you know, if that was what you were trying to do...

'Oh, sorry, yes, I only mentioned Schopenhauer because, despite the pessimism, he's one of the few philosophers with a nice turn of phrase. Towards the end of his main work, *The World as Will and Representation* (1818), he writes that despite the anguish and torment of life, we carry on. It's like a soap bubble, which we blow out as long and as large as we can, even though we know it must burst. I think for Schopenhauer, the bubble was just a symbol for evanescence, something that is destined to perish soon, but the metaphor has slipped out of his control. Is anything more perfect than a soap bubble, anything that so combines unity, variety and harmony, as great art is supposed to do? Each soap bubble is perfect, yet each one entirely unique. And do they not delight us? Who does not smile as the bubble grows, and sigh a little when it pops? So maybe that's it. We want those who behold—'

Behold?

'... OK, *see* us, we want them to smile and then to sigh.'

Tone?

'Yeah?'

The bubble thing, not really doing it for me.

'One last try, then. As I said, I don't believe it makes sense to talk about our lives having a meaning. We have a value, which is measured, I think, in how much we're loved, and how far we've earned that love. And you, little dog, have been greatly loved, and that love has been earned by the love you've given us.'

If dogs could blush, I'd blush.

'But there's another thing. Remember the *telos*, the purpose that Aristotle thinks is the final cause?'

I switched off a little for Aristotle, but, yeah, vaguely.

'The great thing about being human, er, I mean rational, is that we can choose our purpose, decide why we're here, and what we should make of our lives. It's quite close to the existentialist view, put forward by Jean Paul Sartre in *Being and Nothingness* (1943). For an object like a chair or a hammer, Sartre tells us, the *idea* of the object comes before the *existence* of the object. His way of putting it is that essence precedes existence. But for us, we rational creatures, humans, and clever little dogs, existence precedes essence. We have both the ability and the duty to decide what sort of a thing we are.

Sartre's position was a direct response to Spinoza's determinism. For Spinoza, if you remember, the universe is an irresistible determining force, and the best we can hope for is to understand it and acquiesce. The way to escape our human bondage, for Spinoza, is to comprehend the nature of our chains. Or, to give it a more sympathetic interpretation, it is to see that we are surfers on a wave, and that the best way to live is to go with the wave, becoming one with its majestic, impersonal, indifferent drive. But Sartre says that the human thing is not to ride the wave, but to choose to stand amid the breakers, to breast them, and then walk out, even unto the maelstrom.'

Unto, really?

'Oh, sorry. This meaning of life thing can wreak havoc with your prose. But I think there's something there. We should decide on our purpose, and because we are, as Aristotle said, a social animal, it should be a purpose that we can justify and defend, one that should aim to make the world a little better, or, heck, a lot better. There are the small jobs we can do well, making those we love safe and happy, or not unsafe and not unhappy, if that is the limit of our abilities. And then there are the big jobs, at which we'll fail; but then, we can try again, and—'

Fail better.

'You said it, buddy.'

And then Monty saw where we were, and he struggled, weakly, in his special bag. I comforted him as best I could, and we entered the vets.

I spoke to the young woman at reception, and she asked me to sit. I took Monty out of his bag, and he sat quietly on my knee, trembling a little. The lights were harsh, and so I put my hand over his face, and spoke some words, and felt his eyes close under my palm.

There was an old man with a threadbare cat in a basket, and a father and a daughter and a something in a shoebox with holes punched in it. I smiled at the girl, and she swung her legs and smiled back. I didn't think her hamster or whatever it was would be in too much trouble.

And then it was our turn.

The vet was a small, dark woman called Vesna, from some-where in the Balkans.

'Can I stay?' I asked.

'Is best to not,' she answered. 'Come back after, when is done.'

I went and sat on the Green, where I'd taken him for so many quick walks, on days too miserable to go further afield, or when I was too busy. There's a quaint, old-fashioned fire station just over the road, and the crews were out washing the trucks. The kids used to love the station when they were small, and as a treat I'd take them down to say hello to the firefighters, who'd sometimes let them sit in the cab, the big yellow helmets on their little heads. And I thought about the years passing, and Monty joining our family and, having stupidly come out without a hanky, I wiped my streaming eyes and nose on my cuffs.

OK, That Wasn't Really the Last Walk, This Is

The hours passed and I returned to the vets.

'Is he ready?'

'Which…?'

'Monty, the Maltese.'

The young woman with kind eyes on reception nodded and smiled gently. I went into the back.

The walls were lined with cages. I saw a stunned-looking guinea pig and wondered if it belonged to the girl. Monty was lying on his side on the table.

'Can I take him?'

And then Monty, hearing my voice, beat his tail weakly, and looked around at me.

Ten minutes later I was carrying him home.

You didn't really let people think I was, you know, a goner, did you?

'Maybe. I can't help what people think.'

You're a bad man. You should take responsibility for your acts.

'I don't think you know how traumatic this was for me. Have you any idea how much that operation cost?'

It's only money. You should be more philosophical.

'I'm not being entirely serious. The vet told me that it was a major operation. And, especially at your age—'

Hey!

'I'm just telling you what she told me. At your age there's always a chance you just wouldn't wake up. That's why we had to think so hard about it. But she said it went well. You'll be scampering and capering in no time. But first you rest up. Let the scars heal. We'll have plenty of time to talk.'

I can hardly wait.

And then we were home, and a mighty fuss was made over Monty.

Further Reading

General Introductions to Philosophy

There are three broad historical surveys I'd recommend. The most readable, but also the most flawed, is Bertrand Russell's *History of Western Philosophy* (first published in 1945; latest edition London: Routledge, 2001). Russell writes with great clarity and wit, and is careful to include much relevant detail about the general cultural background. He is also a philosopher of, if not quite the first rank, then certainly solidly the second. The main problem with Russell is that he has his prejudices, and so is harsher on the continental rationalists than on the Anglo-American empirical and analytic traditions. Frederick Copleston's multi-volume *History of Philosophy* (1946–75; latest edition London: Bloomsbury, 2001) is a magnificent undertaking, fluent, engrossing and comprehensive. Copleston is particularly good on the Scholastic tradition, as you'd expect from a Jesuit, but he is scrupulously fair-minded, and sympathetic to all. *A New History of Western Philosophy* by Anthony Kenny (Oxford: Oxford University Press, 2012) is the most up-to-date but not obviously superior to Russell and Copleston. Perhaps even more accessible than any of these is *The Great Philosophers* by Bryan Magee (Oxford: Oxford University Press, 1987), which consists of Magee's interviews with other eminent philosophers about the major thinkers in the Western philosophical tradition. For a swifter taster of the problems of philosophy, *Think* by Simon Blackburn (Oxford: Oxford University Press, 2001) is witty, playful and opinionated. I also recommend pretty much everything by Nigel Warburton, but in particular, *Philosophy: The Basics* (London: Routledge, 2012) and *Philosophy: The Classics* (London: Routledge, 2001). If Warburton has a fault, it is that his clarity can sometimes make difficult philosophers and ideas appear deceptively easy to grasp... However, he will both satisfy your desire to know something of philosophy, and inspire you to read more deeply.

One of the best starting points for anyone coming to philosophy is the series of podcasts and related books by Peter Adamson, *A History of Philosophy Without Any Gaps* (https://historyofphilosophy.net). At present (early 2019), Adamson has covered all of Ancient, medieval and Arabic philosophy, with every significant thinker being addressed in an amusing and user-friendly way. He is also good at including thinkers from non-Western traditions.

Walks 1–3: Ethics
My thinking on ethical issues has been greatly influenced by Alasdair MacIntyre. I recommend his rather idiosyncratic *A Short History of Ethics: A History of Moral Philosophy from the Homeric Age to the Twentieth Century* (London: Routledge, 2002), but more particularly his *After Virtue* (London: Bloomsbury, 2013), a brilliant book that analyses our current ethical woes, and plots a route out of them. It is one of the greatest modern works of moral philosophy.

Plato's dialogues are readily and freely available online. I recommend seeking out the nineteenth-century translations by

Benjamin Jowett. For individual dialogues, the Penguin and Oxford World's Classics editions all have good modern translations and excellent introductions. The same goes for Aristotle, though I'd particularly recommend the *Nicomachean Ethics* in the translation by Jonathan Barnes, which has superb notes (London: Penguin, 2004).

The major works on utilitarianism by Mill and Bentham, along with much useful background, can be found in *Utilitarianism and Other Essays*, ed. Alan Ryan (London: Penguin Books, 1987). Peter Singer's *Practical Ethics* (3rd edition, Cambridge: Cambridge University Press, 2011) is a very readable, but also controversial look at ethics from a rigorously utilitarian view. *Ethics: A Very Short Introduction* (Oxford: Oxford University Press, 2003) is, as it says on the tin, a short and snappy introduction to the subject, wittily and pithily written by the excellent Simon Blackburn.

Mary Midgley's works are all very accessible, beautifully written and trenchantly argued. I particularly recommend *Beast and Man: The Roots of Human Nature* (London: Routledge, 2002) and *Wickedness: A Philosophical Essay* (London: Routledge, 2001).

If you can get hold of it, the best introduction to Kant's moral thought is his *Lectures on Ethics* (London: Hackett, 1980). His most important works on the subject, *The Groundwork of the Metaphysics of Morals*, *The Critique of Practical Reason* and *The Metaphysics of Morals*, can all be found in *Practical Philosophy* (Cambridge: Cambridge University Press, 1997), part of the excellent Cambridge Edition of the Works of Immanuel Kant. However, for the beginner, I can only recommend that you tackle *The Groundwork*, which sets out the categorical imperative with, for Kant, reasonable clarity. *The Critique of Practical*

Reason won't make much sense unless you've studied Kant's metaphysics. *The Cambridge Companion to Kant*, ed. Paul Guyer (Cambridge: Cambridge University Press, 1992), has some excellent introductory essays on the full range of Kant's philosophy, including his ethics.

Walk 4: Other Minds and Free Will
For a fascinating, sideways look at the problem of other minds, read Peter Godfrey-Smith's delightful *Other Minds: The Octopus and the Evolution of Intelligent Life* (London: William Collins, 2017). If you're in the mood for a classic, try Gilbert Ryle's *The Concept of Mind* (London: Penguin, 1990). For the discussion of free will, *The Philosophy of Free Will: Essential Readings from the Contemporary Debates*, ed. Paul Russell and Oisin Deery (Oxford: Oxford University Press, 2013), contains all you need to get you up and running. In particular, you should read two essays in the collection by an unusual father-and-son philosophical tag-team: 'Freedom and Resentment' by Peter F. Strawson, and 'The Impossibility of Ultimate Moral Responsibility' by Galen Strawson. For anyone wanting to know more about the strange world of quantum physics, I can't speak highly enough of Chad Orzel's extremely entertaining *How to Teach Quantum Physics to Your Dog* (London: Oneworld, 2010).

Walk 5: Logic
Aristotle sets out the theory of the syllogism in the *Prior Analytics*. It's very dense, but there's an excellent introduction and notes in the edition translated by Robin Smith (London: Hackett, 1989). *An Introduction to Philosophical Logic* by A.C. Grayling is a good, if at times demanding, place to start if you feel your fancy being tickled by logic (Oxford: Wiley-Blackwell, 1997).

Walks 6–7: Metaphysics

Pre-Socratic metaphysics is very well covered in *Early Greek Philosophy*, trans. Jonathan Barnes (London: Penguin, 1987). For Plato's theory of Forms, I suggest beginning with the edition of the *Phaedo* translated with an introduction and notes by David Gallop (Oxford: Oxford University Press, 1996). Although not really for beginners, the relevant chapters in *The Cambridge Companion to Plato* (Cambridge: Cambridge University Press, 2012) are also excellent. If you want to trace the story of the problem of universals through the convolutions of Scholastic philosophy, the best guides are the second volume, *Medieval Philosophy*, in the latest edition of Copleston, and Peter Adamson's podcast https://historyofphilosophy.net/problem-universals.

Walks 8–9: Epistemology

The best edition of Plato's *Theaetetus* is that translated by Robin Waterfield (London: Penguin, 2004). For the Sceptics (as well as the Stoics and Epicureans), I find *Hellenistic Philosophy: Stoics, Epicureans, Sceptics* by A.A. Long (London: Bloomsbury, 2013) to be the most assured, helpful and thorough overview. My favourite book on the rationalists and empiricists is *Learning from Six Philosophers: Descartes, Spinoza, Leibniz, Locke, Berkeley, Hume* by Jonathan Bennett (Oxford: Oxford University Press, 2003). It can be a little dry, but it's hugely authoritative. The major texts by all of these thinkers are widely available, including free e-book editions. Descartes is the most readable of the rationalists. Try *Meditations on First Philosophy* and *Discourse on the Method*. If you have the time, Locke, Hume and Berkeley are all readable, but equally, their ideas are readily summarized, without much being lost. Hume's *An Enquiry Concerning Human*

Understanding is snappier than the *Treatise of Human Nature*, while covering the same ground.

It's very hard to recommend Kant's masterpiece, *Critique of Pure Reason*, to anyone starting out on philosophy. However, if you want to have a crack, I'd suggest the Cambridge edition, which has a modern translation, a lengthy introduction and good notes, which you will most assuredly need. I'd be inclined to begin with something like *Kant* by Roger Scruton (Oxford: Oxford University Press, 1982), and see how you get on.

Wittgenstein is a tricky one. The *Tractatus Logico-Philosophicus* (London: Routledge, 2001) can be read in a couple of hours, and some of it will seem clear and comprehensible, other parts quite baffling. *Philosophical Investigations* (Oxford: Wiley-Blackwell, 2009) is similar, in that many of the sections are readily understandable, but grasping the overall meaning and purpose can be more challenging. The best introductions are two biographies. *Wittgenstein: A Life: Young Ludwig (1889–1921)* (London: Penguin, 1990) by Brian McGuinness is brilliant on the relationship between the world in which he was brought up and the writing of the *Tractatus*. However, it only covers the first half of his life. Ray Monk's *Ludwig Wittgenstein: The Duty of Genius* (London: Vintage, 1991) completes the picture. *Wittgenstein by David Pears* (London: Fontana, 1985) is a short but dense introduction.

For the background to pragmatism, I'd recommend Louis Menand's *The Metaphysical Club: A Story of Ideas in America* (London: Flamingo, 2011), a very entertaining history, focusing on the personalities; and perhaps a selection from William James, an endearing and beguiling thinker: *Pragmatism and Other Writings* (London: Penguin, 2000).

Structuralism and Since: From Levi-Strauss to Derrida by John Sturrock (Oxford: Oxford University Press, 1979) is an aged but still useful guide to the intellectual revolution launched by Saussure's linguistics.

Walk 11: Philosophy of Science
I'm only going to recommend one introductory text to the philosophy of science: *What Is This Thing Called Science?* by Alan Chalmers (Milton Keynes: Open University Press, 2013). It's a classic, beautifully written and exhaustive. However, if you want to delve deeper, all of Popper's works are clear and vividly written, so feel free to try *The Logic of Scientific Discovery* (London: Routledge, 2002). Kuhn's *The Structure of Scientific Revolutions* (Chicago: University of Chicago Press, 2012) is also perfectly accessible for the non-specialist. A personal favourite is *Against Method* by Paul Feyerabend (London: Verso, 2010).

The Last Walk: The Meaning of Life
As for the meaning of life, well, you could try Terry Eagleton's brisk, brief and entertaining *The Meaning of Life: A Very Short Introduction* (Oxford: Oxford University Press, 2008). On our ethics walks, I was harsh on Nietzsche, but it is undoubtedly the case that reading him will make you ponder deeply on what it means to be human. *Beyond Good and Evil* and *The Gay Science* are profound and often beautiful works, but probably the best place to start is *The Twilight of the Idols*, which in a hundred or so pages gives a good overview and summary of Nietzsche's philosophy. The Penguin edition, translated by R.J. Hollingdale, pairs it with *The Anti-Christ*, Nietzsche's most sustained attack on the ethics of Christianity (Harmondsworth: Penguin, 1968).

Acknowledgements

My thanks to all at Oneworld, but especially Sam Carter for his input throughout the enterprise. And I owe much to Tamsin Shelton, who saved me from innumerable blunders. I've chewed many of the ideas in this book with Andy Stanton, who can't open his mouth without something brilliant spilling out. And nothing would have happened without Charlie Campbell's firm hand on the tiller.

Reaching further back in time, I'd like to thank Professors John Harris and Stuart Sim, who guided me through various stages of my life in academia.

And, finally, a brilliant educator, Mrs Margaret Freeman, who set the ball rolling four decades ago.

Index

Index

Harrison, John 61–2
Harvey, William 11
Heraclitus 9, 98, 99, 163, 294
   and logos 131
   and motion 181
Hipparchia 8
Hitler, Adolf 32, 90
Hobbes, Thomas 49, 212
Homer 6, 20–1
Hume, David 42, 43, 213, 218,
   221–8
   and causation 289
   and induction 260
   and intersubjectivity 87–8
   and Kant 231, 233
Hutcheson, Francis 46
Hypatia 163

James, William 240
Jesus Christ 69, 85, 131

Kant, Immanuel 39, 63–5, 86,
   89, 103–4
   and categories 236–9, 253–4
   and causation 289
   and epistemology 181
   and God 292
   and imperatives 71–2, 76–7,
   85, 91, 111
   and knowledge 9–10, 230–3
   and lying 77–8
   and maxims 73–4, 75–6,
   78–80
   and reason 70–1, 72–3
   and space and time 233–5

   and utilitarianism 83
Kekulé, August 270
Kepler, Johannes 262–3, 264,
   269, 276, 277
Knox, Robert 219–20
Kuhn, Thomas 277–81, 282

La Mettrie, Julien Offray de 64
Lakatos, Imre 281–2
Leibniz, Gottfried Wilhelm 140,
   144, 204–10, 220, 238, 294
   and Kant 231
Leucippus 145
Leviathan (Hobbes) 212
Locke, John 197, 212–19, 222,
   228, 233, 238
Logic of Scientific Discovery, The
   (Popper) 269

Malebranche, Nicolas 12, 199
Malthus, Thomas 270
Mandeville, Bernard 49–50
Marx, Karl 103, 274–5
Maugham, Somerset 293–4
Maxwell, James 113, 114
Meno (Plato) 156
Mill, John Stuart 81, 82, 85, 93,
   104
   and causation 264–6, 269
Montaigne 192
Moore, G.E. 47–9
Mussolini, Benito 32

Nero, Emperor 55
Newton, Sir Isaac 105, 106, 140,

313

About the Author

Anthony McGowan has a BA, MPhil and PhD in philosophy, and has lectured widely on philosophy and creative writing. An award-winning writer for children and young adults, his novels include *The Donut Diaries*, *The Knife that Killed Me* and *Rook*, which was shortlisted for the Carnegie Medal. He lives in north London, with his wife, two children and a dog.

Also by Anthony McGowan

'The funniest book [of the year]' *Observer*

'You'll laugh and feel mild pity' Matt Haig

What is a writer's life really like?

A man at odds with the universe, Anthony McGowan
stumbles from one improbable fiasco to the next. On the
mean streets of West Hampstead he reflects upon all that is
at the heart of life itself – socks with holes, underwhelming
packed lunches, broken washing machines, Kierkegaard, liver
salts, British Library eccentricities and disapproving ladies
on trains. In this chronicle of one man's daily failures and
disappointments, McGowan can't help but speak his mind
– with cringeworthy and hilarious results.